BUILDING MATERIALS FROM SOLID WASTES

BUILDING MATERIALS FROM SOLID WASTES

Edited by O.S. Renfroe

NOYES DATA CORPORATION
Park Ridge, New Jersey, U.S.A.
1979

Copyright © 1979 by Noyes Data Corporation
No part of this book may be reproduced in any form
without permission in writing from the Publisher.
Library of Congress Catalog Card Number: 79-16988
ISBN: 0-8155-0771-2
Printed in the United States

Published in the United States of America by
Noyes Data Corporation
Noyes Building, Park Ridge, New Jersey 07656

Library of Congress Cataloging in Publication Data

Main entry under title:

Building materials from solid wastes.

(Pollution technology review ; no. 61)
Includes bibliographies and index.
1. Building materials. 2. Waste products.
I. Renfroe, O. S. II. Series.
TA403.6.B83   624'.1   79-16988
ISBN 0-8155-0771-2

Foreword

The United States is a major producer of industrial, mining and municipal wastes. Because of current emphasis on coal utilization and the development of alternate sources of energy, the rate of waste generation is expected to increase further. Traditional methods of solid waste disposal, such as landfill, stockpiling and incineration could be expensive and detrimental to the quality of our environment. Recycling is one possible solution, and in recent years a considerable interest in developing waste-derived, marketable products such as energy, chemicals, and animal feeds has become evident.

While billions of tons of waste materials are generated annually in the United States alone, only relatively small amounts have been utilized heretofore by the construction industry. This book describes the advances being made in obtaining viable building materials from mining, industrial, agricultural and municipal wastes. In several instances construction materials obtained from wastes have been at least the technological equivalent of new materials produced from previously unworked, natural resources.

This book is directed toward the utilization of solid wastes for building materials. Particularly products with application for residential and commercial buildings are of interest here. Other construction uses, e.g., for highways and embankments are mentioned, but are not extensively explored. The use of coal ash and fly ash in nonbuilding applications is the subject of another recent NDC volume.

The first chapter is an overview of U.S. waste sources with emphasis on the particular waste materials which have construction potential. This is followed by two chapters reporting a feasibility study in regard to waste-derived building composites. Specific applications including the use of fly ash and slag in blended cements, waste glass as a raw material for lightweight aggregates and a large section devoted to the building product possibilities of coal mining refuse are described in the last three chapters.

Cost figures provided are those given in the report cited, the date of which is always given. When the dates of the cost figures themselves are given, we have included them.

The large expanded table of contents is organized so it can serve as a subject index. It provides easy access to the information contained in this book which is based on various studies produced by and for diverse governmental agencies under grants and contracts. These primary sources are listed at the end of the volume under the heading Sources Utilized. The titles of additional publications pertaining to topics in this book are found in the text.

Contents and Subject Index

Sources of Waste Materials
for Use in Construction

The information in this chapter is based on *Survey of Uses of Waste Materials in Construction in the United States,* NBS Report IR 77-1244 prepared by J.R. Clifton, P.W. Brown, and G. Frohnsdorff of the National Bureau of Standards.

INTRODUCTION

Solid Wastes in the United States

The United States is both a major consumer of natural resources and a major producer of mining, industrial, agricultural and municipal waste materials. For example, it has been predicted that, within the next 100 years, the United States will consume over 6.8×10^9 tons (amounts are given in metric tons throughout this chapter) of iron ore, 1×10^9 tons of phosphate rock and 1.5×10^9 tons of aluminum ore, resulting in a massive generation of mining waste (1).

U.S. production of mining waste and coal refuse exceeds 360,000 tons daily, which is being added to some 23×10^9 tons already accumulated. The generation of large amounts of municipal refuse, building rubble, sulfate wastes, fly ashes, industrial processing and other wastes is also contributing to massive disposal problems. Disposal of wastes is posing increasingly difficult problems because of rapidly growing concern for the quality of the environment and enactment of legislation to ensure its protection.

Many waste materials can be used directly as, or be converted into, viable construction materials, thereby conserving natural resources and energy, and mitigating the harmful effects of the wastes on the environment. Because of the large quantities of materials used in construction, such applications could consume significant amounts of the wastes.

Developments in the Use of Wastes in Construction

With the exception of the program established some 60 years ago by the Bureau of Mines (2), the United States government gave little emphasis to research and development on the use of waste materials in construction until the late 1960s. Consequently, only a small fraction of the construction materials used in the United States is derived from waste materials. During the past decade, however, significant programs which should facilitate the increased use of waste materials in construction have been established by federal and state governmental agencies.

For example, the feasibility of using waste materials as sources of aggregate is being explored in projects sponsored by the Federal Highway Administration; the Federal Energy Administration and the Energy Research and Development Administration are supporting work relating to the conservation of energy by substituting waste materials for more energy-intensive materials; the Environmental Protection Agency is supporting demonstrations of uses of waste materials as an approach to improve the nation's environment; and the Bureau of Mines is continuing its program on developing uses for mineral wastes. In addition, the recently passed Resource Conservation Act of 1976 (3) is intended to stimulate the increased use of waste materials.

The business sector of the United States is also promoting the recycling of solid waste. For example, the National Center for Resource Recovery is a nonprofit organization founded by leaders of major United States industry and labor organizations to advance the technology of resource recovery from solid wastes. Its present emphasis is on resource recovery from municipal refuse.

Other important activities in the United States which are stimulating interest in the use of waste materials include the Mineral Waste Utilization Symposia, the Ash Utilization Symposia, and the work of Committee E-38 on Resource Recovery of the American Society for Testing and Materials (ASTM). Within the committee, subcommittee E38.06 was specifically established to cover "Materials of Construction from Other Recovered Materials."

Scope

This chapter covers the sources, amounts and disposal of major mining, industrial and municipal wastes available in the 48 conterminous states of the United States along with their present and potential uses as construction materials. Agricultural wastes are not included because only in a few cases has their use as viable construction materials been seriously considered. One of the few examples is research with the conversion of certain types of agricultural waste into construction materials. It has recently been shown (4) that hydraulic acid-resisting cements can be produced using the ash of rice hulls. Similar cements probably could be produced using residues from the straw from wheat, barley, oats and rye. Furthermore, much of the agricultural waste rapidly re-enters the biological cycle which facilitates its disposal.

Wastes from mining, industrial and municipal sources are treated separately and in that order. This is the order of decreasing amount of usable wastes available from each major classification (Table 1.1). Wastes from mineral, metallic ore and coal mining operations are covered first.

Industrial wastes follow and include a variety of important wastes which have found few markets; by-products from coal combustion, which are examples of wastes for which there are growing markets; and slags, by-products which are already extensively used as aggregates in construction but for which there may be higher value uses.

Municipal wastes, including municipal refuse, incinerator residue, glass, demolition waste and sewage sludge, are covered next. Wastes which may be generated in substantial amounts by emerging technologies related to energy production and environmental protection are then discussed. Obstacles to and incentives for the increased use of waste materials in construction conclude the chapter.

Table 1.1: Amounts of Mining, Industrial and Municipal Wastes

Type of Waste	Annual Amounts* $(10^6$ tons)
Mining	2,270
Industrial	180
Municipal	180**

*Estimates based on amounts given in this survey.
**Includes some 135×10^6 tons of municipal refuse of which about 36×10^6 tons might be suitable for use in construction.

Source: NBSIR 77-1244

MINING WASTES

Mining wastes, considered collectively, form the greatest part of the solid waste material generated in the United States with over 2.2×10^9 tons being generated annually. A distinction is usually made between mineral mining wastes and coal refuse. Mineral mining wastes are usually described as being either waste rock or mill tailings. Waste rock is the coarse material that is excavated to expose the ore during mine development.

Mill tailings are the residues obtained from the separation of minerals from their ores. Wastes from the sizing and cleaning of coal, from either underground mining or from strip mining operations, are defined as coal refuse. Coal refuse may contain mine rock, carbonaceous shale, pyrites, and other debris from mining operations. Dredge spoils are also covered in this section because their mineralogical compositions and physical states are like those of mining wastes.

This section is concerned with the sources, amounts, disposal, and present and potential uses of wastes resulting from mining operations. Much of this information has been provided by the members of ASTM Subcommittee E38.06.

Inventory and Sources

Estimates of the amounts of waste rock, mill tailings, and coal refuse produced annually by major mining industries in the United States are listed in Table 1.2. This table includes estimates of the amounts of the mill tailings and phosphate processing wastes which have accumulated over the years.

The copper industry accounts for nearly one half of the mining waste generated annually. Other operations which produce large amounts of waste include the mining of iron ore and taconite, coal, uranium, phosphate, gold, gypsum, lead, and zinc.

Areas of the United States in which large quantities of waste rock and mill tailings are located as shown in Figure 1.1. These include the large copper producing states (Arizona, Utah, Montana, Michigan, and Tennessee); the Mesabi Range taconite mines (northeastern Minnesota); the major iron ore mining areas (Minnesota, Michigan, Missouri, Pennsylvania, California, and Wyoming); and several lead-zinc regions (Idaho, Tennessee, and Wisconsin). There are also large accumulations of dredge tailings from past gold mining in the Mother Lode district (northern California) and of chat (coarse tailings) from past mining of lead-zinc ores in the Tri-State mining district (Missouri, Kansas, and Oklahoma) (5).

The largest accumulations of coal refuse are located (Figure 1.2) in the eastern states of Pennsylvania, West Virginia, Tennessee, and Kentucky. Other significant accumulations are in Illinois, Ohio, and Wyoming. There are more than 3×10^9 tons of coal refuse in Pennsylvania and Kentucky alone. The amount of coal refuse produced annually will certainly increase because of the greater emphasis being placed in the United States on coal utilization. It is estimated that while 560×10^6 tons of coal was produced in 1975, approximately 900×10^6 tons will be produced in the year 2000 mainly in western states (6).

Most of this western coal will probably be burned in the uncleaned state directly from the mine resulting in a smaller ratio of coal refuse to coal production than is currently obtained (6). Nevertheless, there is no doubt that stockpiles of coal refuse will continue to grow for many years.

Dredge spoil is available along the major navigable waterways in the United States, such as the Mississippi and Columbia rivers and from coastal sites.

Table 1.2: Amounts and Possible Uses of Major Mining Wastes

Mining Industry	Waste Rock Annual Quantity* (10^6 tons)	Mill Tailings Annual Quantity (10^6 tons)	Estimated Accumulated Mill Tailings (10^6 tons)	Possible Uses of Tailings in Construction	References
Copper	624	234	7,700	Brick, embankments, mineral filler in bituminous mixtures	(5)(19)
Dredge spoil	270–360	–	Uncertain	Landfill	–
Taconite	100	109	3,600	Concrete aggregate, skid-resistant aggregate, building block	(5)(19)
Coal	**	>100***	2,700***	Highway construction, land and minefill	(5)(6)(20)(28)
Phosphate	230	54†	907††	Landfill, dikes for phosphate slimes	(5)
Iron ore	27	27	730	Concrete aggregate	(5)(7)(9)
Gold	15	5	450	Brick, sand and gravel, mineral filler	(5)(12)
Uranium	156	5.8	110	None because of concern with low level radioactivity	(33)
Lead	0.5	8	180	Mineral filler in bituminous mixtures; refractory brick	(5)(8)
Zinc	0.9	7.2	180	Mineral filler in bituminous mixtures; refractory brick	(5)(8)
Quarry	68	–	Uncertain	Aggregate	(5)(19)
Gypsum	14.2	2.7	Uncertain	Brick	(13)
Asbestos	0.6	2	14	Ceramic tile, refractory brick, mineral filler in bituminous mixtures	(5)(13)
Barite	1.9	3.1	24	Road surfacing material	(5)
Fluorspar	0.1	0.4	Uncertain	Aggregate	(5)
Feldspar	0.2	0.8	Uncertain	Manufacture of brick and lightweight building materials	(13)(14)(15)

*Includes overburden in some cases.
**Included in tailings.
***Coal refuse, which includes mine rock, shale, pyrite and other mining debris.
†Includes both phosphate slimes and phosphogypsum.
††Includes estimated 136×10^6 tons of phosphogypsum.

Source: NBSIR 77-1244

Figure 1.1: Locations of Large Accumulations of Waste Rock and Mill Tailings

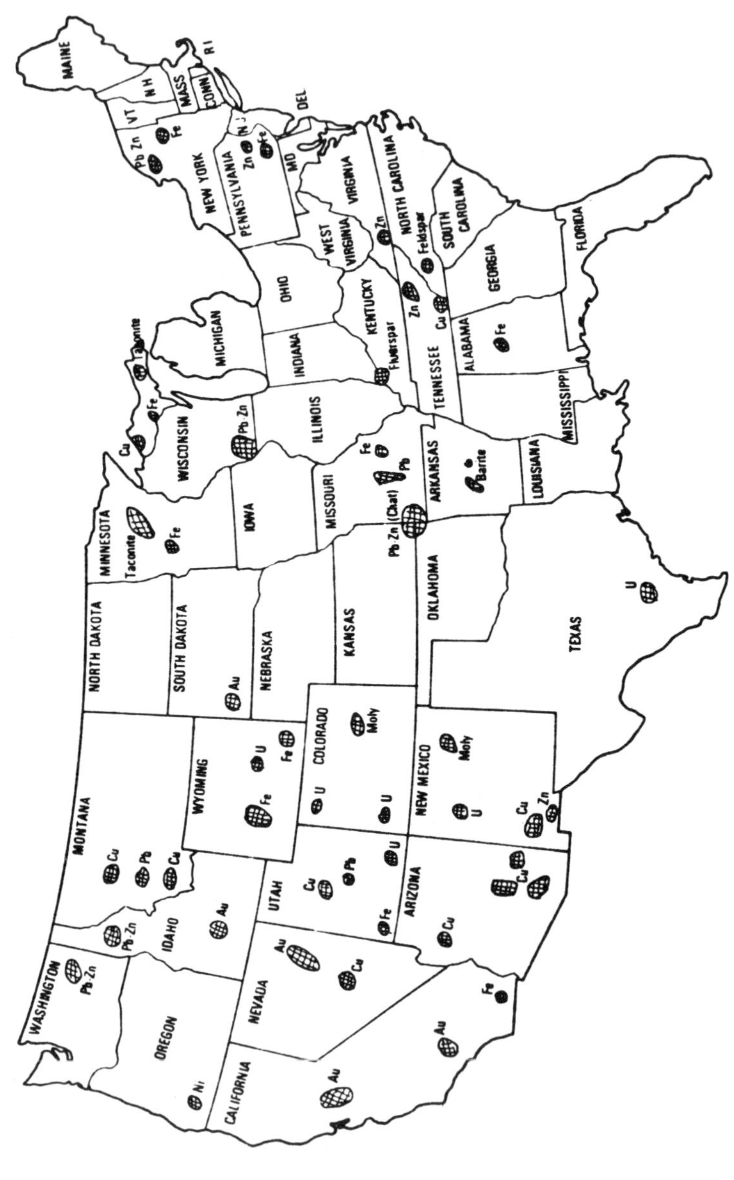

Source: NBSIR 77-1244

Figure 1.2: Locations of Large Accumulations of Coal Refuse

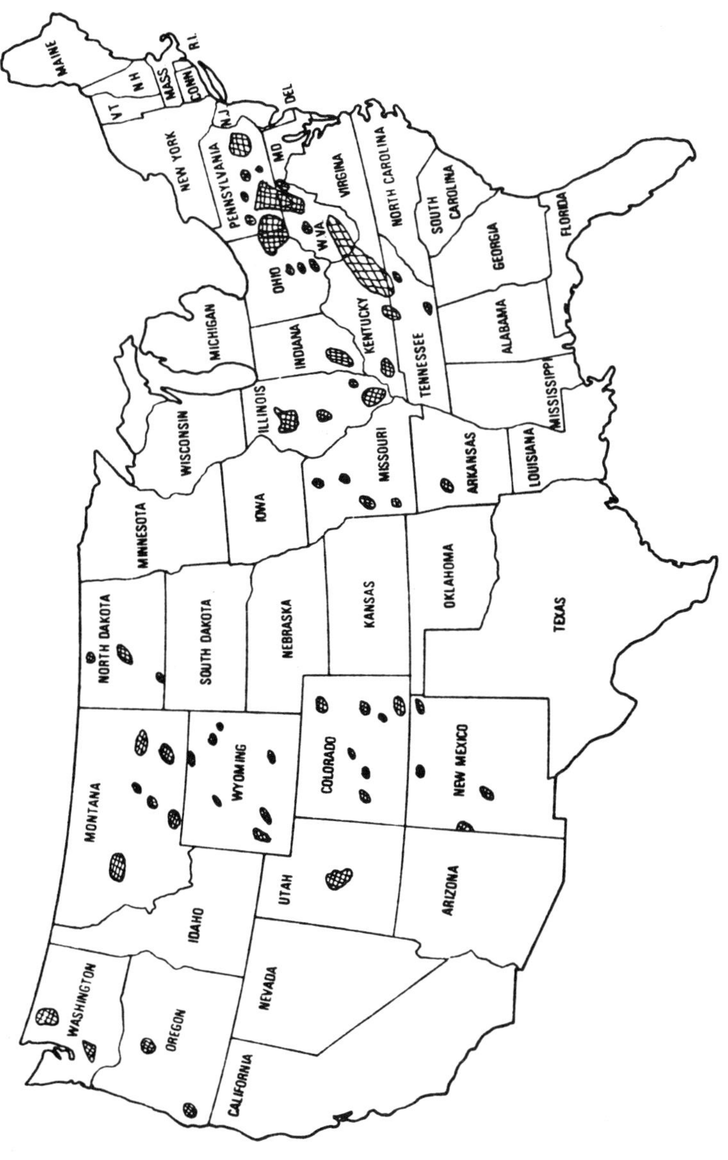

Source: NBSIR 77-1244

Description, Disposal and Uses

Waste Rock: Over 1.1×10^9 tons (Table 1.2) of waste rock are removed each year during mineral mining operations. Most of this waste rock comes from open-pit mines. The composition of waste rock can vary from one mining operation to another. Depending on the geological formation from which the ore is removed, the waste rock may be igneous, metamorphic, or sedimentary. Generally, igneous and metamorphic rocks are harder than sedimentary rocks and are more suitable for uses requiring hard rock, such as aggregate for concrete. However, some well consolidated sedimentary rocks, such as some limestones, are also good aggregate materials (5).

The particle size of waste rock can vary because of variations in geological formations and differences in mining methods. While individual pieces might be larger than 1 meter in diameter, waste rock is usually less than 0.3 meter. Waste rock from any source can generally be reduced to a desired size range by normal crushing and sizing methods.

Waste rock along with overburden is often disposed of in large dumps. For example, over 5,580 hectares in Minnesota are covered with a waste rock overburden from the mining of iron ore (7). Waste rock is sometimes used as backfill in open-pit mining operations and in highway construction. The total use of waste rock in construction appears, however, to be only a small fraction of the amount generated each year. The largest use of waste rock has been in highway construction using rock from iron ore mines (5).

Traprock from an underground mine in Pennsylvania was used to resurface a section of the Pennsylvania Turnpike and in Missouri a similar waste rock is being crushed and marketed as a skid-resistant aggregate. Waste rock from ore mining in Michigan, New York, Wisconsin, and Wyoming has also been used successfully in highway construction as aggregates, subbase material, and for embankments. Waste rock from copper mining has occasionally been crushed and used as a base or subbase material in Arizona and Michigan. Waste rock from gold mining has been used as an aggregate in Colorado and as a highway resurfacing material in South Dakota. Waste rock from lead-zinc mines has been used as an aggregate for bituminous paving in Washington, Wisconsin, and Missouri.

Mill Tailings: The physical and chemical characteristics of mill tailings depend on their source and the method of ore processing. For example, the tailings from lead-zinc mining are often dolomitic (8), while those from taconite, gold, and copper ore mines have high silica contents (9)(10) (Table 1.3).

In operations where the tailings are not a residue produced by size separation, they are usually finely divided having particle sizes in the silt-clay particle size range. The processing of copper, taconite, gold, uranium, lead, and zinc ores all require about the same degree of crushing and fine grinding. Between fifty and ninety percent of the particles from these tailings are smaller than 75 μm. Where size separation is practiced, the coarse fraction of the tailings approximate a well-graded sand, predominantly in the fine to medium sand range. Iron ore tailings are often separated into a fine fraction which is in the silt to coarse particle size range and a coarse fraction which is graded from a fine sand to a gravel (5).

Table 1.3: Oxide Analyses of Some Taconite, Copper, Gold and Lead-Zinc Tailings

Constituent	Taconite Tailings*	Copper Ore Tailings*	Gold Tailings**	Lead-Zinc Tailings*
	. . . . .Percent.			
SiO_2	59	71.1	93	9.8
Fe_2O_3	21	4.9	1.9	1.1
Al_2O_3	2.7	13.2	3.5	0.3
MgO	3.7	2.1	0.41	17.8
CaO	2.7	1.1	1	29.4
Na_2O	–	0.3	0.07	–
K_2O	–	3.3	0.33	–
Loss of ignition	7.4	2.6	0.22	42

*Reference (9)
**Reference (5)

Source: NBSIR 77-1244

Tailings are usually separated from ore minerals by wet processing and are transported as a slurry by pipelines for disposal in tailing ponds. Coarse tailings and waste rock are used for construction of the containment dikes. Much of the slurry water is recirculated or allowed to evaporate resulting in the formation of slimes in the case of iron (7) and copper tailings (9). Tailings are also disposed of through use as mine backfill materials (11). Coarse tailings are often stockpiled (7)(8).

As with waste rock, the amount of mill tailings used annually in construction appears to be only a small fraction of the amount produced. However, there are many examples of the use of mill tailings in highway construction (5). Coarse taconite tailings have been used successfully as skid-resistant aggregate for bituminous overlays of highways in Minnesota. Chat, the coarse by-product from the milling of lead-zinc ores, has been an approved highway construction material for many years in Kansas, Missouri, and Oklahoma.

In Utah, millions of tons of copper tailings have been used in highway embankments and as mineral filler in bituminous mixtures. Gold dredge tailings are routinely used as sand and gravel in northern California and have been used for similar purposes in Colorado. These and other mill tailings have performed well in many highway applications. Other possible uses of mill tailings include the manufacture of ceramic products such as brick (10)(12)–(17) lightweight building block (9)(14)(18), and mineral wool (19). Many mill tailings have excellent engineering properties (11)(20) and are suitable for the construction of small earth dams and as backfill materials (11).

Coal Refuse: Coal refuse from anthracite and bituminous coal mine operations consists of a variety of minerals (Table 1.4) and is usually rich in SiO_2, Al_2O_3, and Fe_2O_3 (21)(22). Anthracite refuse has a high proportion of coarse particles with over 65% being 13 mm or larger in size (21). The refuse from bituminous coal mines in Kentucky is usually separated into coarse and fine fractions through separation by sedimentation (22).

Table 1.4: Oxide and Mineralogical Analyses of Coal Refuse

Oxide	Percent	Mineral	Percent
. . . . Anthracite Refuse*.			
SiO_2	50–57	Kaolinite	70
Al_2O_3	30–37	Illite	1–10
Fe_2O_3	3–10	Gypsum	1–10
TiO_2	1–2	Quartz	1–20
CaO	1–2	Calcite	1–10
MgO	0–1	Pyrite	1–10
$K_2O + Na_2O$	1–3	Rutile	1–10
SO_3	0–1	—	—
. . . . Bituminous Refuse**.			
SiO_2	43–61	Kaolinite	16–72
Al_2O_3	14–20	Illite	16–50
Fe_2O_3	2–31	Quartz	7–32
TiO_2	0.8–2.2	Calcite	0–17
CaO	0.1–10	Pyrite	0.4–12
MgO	0.5–3	Magnesite	0–4
$K_2O + N_2O$	2–5.5	Apatite	0.1–4
SO_3	0–2	—	—

*Anthracite refuse from Pennsylvania, Reference (21).
**Bituminous refuse from Kentucky, Reference (22).

Source: NBSIR 77-1244

In the past, coal refuse has been placed in refuse piles or banks. Coal refuse often contains carbon which can be ignited by spontaneous, accidental, or intentional ignition. If it is ignited, and if sufficient oxygen is available, a bank becomes a self-sustaining source of air pollution. State and federal programs have been established to extinguish existing burning banks of coal refuse. Furthermore, atmospheric or other oxidation of pyrite creates a sulfuric acid effluent which may pollute water resources.

Most states require that coal refuse be placed in cleaned sites free of underground or surface drainage and laid down in layers followed by compaction, contouring, and vegetation. The effectiveness of the legislation and of these disposal methods is still a controversial subject (23)–(25). Coal refuse has also been disposed of by being flushed into underground mines. Over 1.8×10^8 m^3 of coal refuse had been flushed into mines by 1968 (21).

A small amount of coal refuse has been used in the past for construction purposes, primarily for highway applications such as base and subbase material (6), and aggregates for pavement (26)(27), including antiskid material (28). Anthracite coal refuse has been used, on a relatively small scale, to make concrete block, lightweight aggregate, and brick (21). Other small scale uses of coal refuse have been in the manufacture of mineral wool and cement (21). These applications represent only a small tonnage and seem to have only a small potential for growth. Another possible use of coal refuse is as landfill material (6). Coal refuse has been used successfully in England as landfill for a variety of construction purposes (29)(30). In general, coal refuse appears to have many of the engineering properties, handling characteristics, and availability desired for a landfill material (21). (The feasibility of utilizing coal refuse for construction purposes is examined in the last chapter of this book.)

Dredge Spoil: Dredge spoil, the waste from dredging operations, is usually divided into three types of materials for engineering purposes: coarse grained, fine grained, and organic. Fine grained materials are defined as those smaller than 75 μm. It is the fine grained and organic spoils that normally cause dredging problems (5). Over two-thirds of dredge spoil is disposed of in open water and the remainder is disposed of in landfill.

Prospects for Increased Use

Large amounts of mining wastes are produced annually in the United States and it is anticipated that most types of mining wastes will be generated even more rapidly in the next several decades. Only a small fraction of these wastes is currently being used in any application. Probably their largest use is for self-containment purposes. The most promising prospective use of mining wastes appears to be in large engineering projects such as the construction of highways and earth dams, and in land and mine fills. Their application as highway materials, especially as aggregates, continues to receive significant attention (5)(31)(32)(33).

Waste rock, coal refuse, and gold and taconite tailings have often performed better as aggregates and fillers than conventionally used materials. Furthermore, a significant portion of these waste materials is located in regions of the United States which have shortages of high quality aggregates (34)–(37). There appear to be no significant institutional obstacles to the use of these mining wastes as aggregates and current ASTM specifications for aggregates do not preclude the use of mining wastes, with beneficiation if required, provided they meet essential physical requirements. The main factor which determines the use of specific waste materials as aggregates is the economics (36).

As shortages of high quality natural aggregates from traditional sources develop regionally and transportation costs increase, the use of locally available waste materials may become economically attractive (35). Therefore, it is expected that waste rock and coal refuse generated near large construction activities will find increasingly wide use as aggregates in many types of construction.

The prospects for large scale use of mill tailings (with the exception of gold and taconite tailings and coarse tailings) as aggregates and highway construction materials are not encouraging based on present technology and economics (31). A more promising application is their use in the production of ceramic building materials such as brick and lightweight building blocks, and in autoclaved calcium silicate insulation materials. However, even these applications would consume only a small portion of the available mill tailings.

SULFATE WASTES AND WASTES FROM THE PHOSPHATE, ALUMINUM AND CEMENT INDUSTRIES

Major processing waste materials generated in the phosphate fertilizer, aluminum extraction, and cement manufacturing industries, and those which can be classified as waste sulfates are considered in this section. The amounts of these waste materials generated annually in the United States are given in Table 1.5. Only small quantities of these waste materials are used for construction or any other purpose. However, as discussed in this section, many of these materials could be used to produce construction materials.

Phosphate Ore Processing Wastes

Production and Sources of Phosphate Ore: The primary ore for phosphorus fertilizers is phosphate rock, in which the phosphate occurs as apatite, i.e., calcium fluophosphate, $Ca_5F(PO_4)_3$. Phosphate ore is generally composed of roughly equal quantities of sand, clay, and phosphate (37).

Phosphate mining operations consist of stripping off the overburden and transferring the phosphate ore to large sumps or wells where it is converted into a slurry by high pressure jets of water. The slurry is then pumped to the ore processing plants. In the processing operation, the clay particles are removed from the sand and phosphates are pumped to large settling ponds. The sand tailings, which are mostly silica, are used for building dikes around the waste settling ponds and for filling mined areas being reclaimed. The phosphate concentrate is dried and shipped to chemical manufacturing plants.

Phosphate rock is mined in Florida, North Carolina, Tennessee, Idaho, and Montana. Florida produces about 70% (about 23×10^6 tons annually) of all the phosphate rock produced in the United States, with most of it coming from a 32 x 48 kilometer area in the Bone Valley District of central Florida (37).

Characteristics and Disposal of Phosphate Processing Wastes: The major waste materials from the processing of phosphate ores are silica sand and phosphate slimes. Few problems are encountered in the disposal or use of the sand as it can be used without further treatment in concrete and landfill operations, and for

Table 1.5: Amounts and Possible Uses of Some Major Industrial Wastes

Waste Material	Accumulated Quantity (10^6 tons)	Annual Production (10^6 tons)	Possible Uses for Construction Purposes	References
Phosphate processing waste				
Sand	NA*	9–13	Landfill, pond dikes, concrete	(37)
Phosphate slime	1,800**	9–13	Lightweight aggregate	(37)–(40)
Sulfate wastes				
Phosphogypsum	136	5	Plasterboard, floor and roof filler, admixture in concrete	(15)
Fluorogypsum	NA	0.1	Plasterboard	(42)
Gas scrubber waste	>5***	5***	Combined with fly ash and lime to form highway construction and landfill materials	(44)(47) (48)
Mud residues from aluminum extraction	90	5	Ceramic foam, cement, light-weight aggregate	(49)–(53)
Cement kiln dust	NA	5†	Incorporation in blended cements, substitute for lime and limestone	(54)(57) (58)(59)

*Not available.

**Contains about 75% water.

***Contains calcium sulfite.

†Altogether about 17 x 10^6 tons are collected, with 12 x 10^6 tons being fed back into the process and the remainder discarded.

Source: NBSIR 77-1244

the construction of dikes. The most significant problem of the phosphate mining industry is the handling, disposal and reclamation of the slimes. Phosphate slimes constitute over one-half of the plant wastes. Between 9×10^6 and 13×10^6 tons of phosphate slimes are produced each year and their production is increasing at about 4% per year.

Phosphate slimes consist of colloidal clay particles with 75% of the particles being under 3 microns and 50% under 0.3 microns. The slimes are rich in SiO_2, Al_2O_3, CaO, and P_2O_5 (Table 1.6).

Phosphate slimes are pumped to large ponds where the clay gradually settles. As much of the supernatant water is reused as possible. Many of the slime ponds are large being up to 3 km long and 3 km wide, and surrounded by walls and dikes up to 13 meters in height. It has been estimated that nearly 2×10^9 tons of phosphate slime, containing about 1.4×10^9 tons of water, are stored in these ponds. The colloidal clay particles settle very slowly and after about 25 years the slimes have a solids content of between 20 and 30% and the consistency of grease (38).

Table 1.6: Oxide and Mineralogical Compositions of Phosphate Slimes*

	Percent
Oxide composition	
P_2O_5	9–17
SiO_2	31–46
Fe_2O_3	3–7
Al_2O_3	6–18
CaO	14–23
MgO	1–2
Loss on ignition	9–16
Mineralogical composition	
Calcium fluophosphate	20–25
Quartz	30–35
Montmorillonite	20–25
Attapulgite	5–10
Wavellite	4–6
Feldspar	2–3
Heavy minerals	2–3
Dolomite	1–2

*Taken from Reference (37).

Source: NBSIR 77-1244

Prospective Uses of Phosphate Slimes: Major problems encountered in the use of phosphate slimes are their slow settling rates, their low percentages of solids, and the extreme fineness of the mineral constituents.

Slimes have been stabilized and used as landfill materials by being mixed with sand tailings from phosphate rock processing plants. The sand tailings capture the slimes and a paste with about 90% solids content is produced when the mixture is passed through a narrow channel at high velocity. This paste is then allowed to settle in long, narrow, mined-out channels which are subsequently backfilled in land reclamation projects (39). This method can consume only 35% of the slimes generated at a processing plant because of the resultant ratio of slime to tailing in the landfill material (37).

Other uses of phosphate slimes depend on thermally drying the slimes to high solid levels. Cross-flow fluid dryers have been found to be efficient in drying slimes to a 95 to 99% solids content (40).

The most promising application of dried slimes to date has been in the production of lightweight aggregates. Dried phosphate slime is pelletized and heated to between $1050°$ to $1100°C$ in a rotary kiln, producing an aggregate with a bulk density between 320 and 480 kg/m^3. These aggregates meet the requirements of ASTM Specification C330, Lightweight Aggregates for Structural Concrete (41). Furthermore, they appear to have better load-bearing characteristics than some conventional lightweight aggregates such as perlite and vermiculite (40). Brick and sewer pipe have been manufactured from phosphate slime but neither product was of high quality (40).

Sulfate Wastes

Calcium sulfate is generated as a by-product or waste material in a variety of processes, the major one being the manufacture of phosphoric acid. Scrubbing of combustion gases from coal burning power plants is also expected to produce large quantities.

Phosphogypsum: During the conversion of phosphate rock to chemical fertilizers and other products, the rock is treated with sulfuric acid to form phosphoric acid and gypsum:

$$Ca_5F(PO_4)_3 + 5H_2SO_4 + 10H_2O \rightleftharpoons 3H_3PO_4 + 5CaSO_4 \cdot 2H_2O + HF$$

The phosphoric acid is then often used to produce fertilizers such as triple superphosphates and mono- and diammonium phosphates (37). The by-product gypsum is pumped into diked areas where it settles out and the supernatant water is reused. The dike walls are often constructed with dewatered gypsum. Because the gypsum contains a significant amount of phosphoric acid it is called phosphogypsum. Phosphogypsum is also disposed of by being placed in exhausted phosphate mined areas. Approximately 5×10^6 tons of phosphogypsum are produced annually in the United States (5), primarily in areas where phosphate ore is mined. Accumulated amounts have been estimated to be 136×10^6 tons (5).

At present, gypsum recovered from phosphogypsum has little commercial value because of its impurity (42) and also because adequate alternative sources of gypsum are generally available (43). Nevertheless, the feasibility of producing plasterboard and filler materials for floor and roof systems from the recovered gypsum is being investigated (15)(42). The recovered gypsum could possibly be used as a set-regulating admixture for portland cement.

Fluorogypsum: Approximately 90×10^3 tons of anhydrite ($CaSO_4$) are produced annually in the production of hydrofluoric acid from fluorspar and sulfuric acid. The anhydrite by-product is a dry material containing 4 to 6% calcium fluoride and smaller amounts of various other salts. The anhydrite by-products are disposed of by dumping on dry land or use as landfill material. They have little commercial value at present. A possible use is production of an impure plasterboard.

Gas Scrubber Waste: Gas scrubber waste is the material obtained using the lime or limestone slurry process for removing sulfur dioxide from the stack gases of coal burning power plants. The sulfur dioxide is converted to calcium sulfite and calcium sulfate in the processes used in the United States. The resulting gas scrubber waste is a sludge having solid contents in the range of 19 to 50% (44)(45).

At present about 5×10^6 tons per year of gas scrubber waste are generated in the United States (45). Because of the increasing use of high sulfur coals, the amounts of waste generated will increase rapidly; it has been estimated that 64×10^6 tons of solid scrubber waste will be generated in 1980 (45). Approximately 17 power plants which incorporate scrubber systems are either being planned or are in operation (44)(46). Proposed methods for disposing of most of the scrubber wastes include placing it in ponds and using it in landfill operations (45).

Prospective Uses of Sulfate Wastes: Recent studies have indicated that sulfate wastes from a variety of sources can be mixed with lime and fly ash to form structurally stable construction materials (44)(47). Potential applications of the waste sulfate-lime-fly ash material include use as a structural landfill material (47), and as highway construction material for embankments, subbases and bases for pavements (44)(48). These materials appear to have acceptable mechanical properties but their durability, especially to freezing and thawing appear to be marginal in the present state of their development (44). The proximity of fly ash and waste sulfate sources to each other and to large metropolitan areas (44) could result in sulfate-lime-fly ash material becoming an economically viable construction material if additional development work indicates it has acceptable long-term performance.

Muds from the Processing of Aluminum Ores

The feedstock for the reduction of alumina to aluminum metal is obtained from the processing of bauxite. Bauxite ores are mined in Arkansas or imported from Caribbean area deposits and are processed in domestic plants located in the southern states of Arkansas, Alabama, Louisiana, and Texas.

The major waste materials from the processing of bauxite are "red muds" and, to a lesser amount, "brown muds." Over 5×10^6 tons of solid waste are produced annually from the processing of bauxite and approximately 90×10^6 tons have been accumulated in settling ponds (49). Red muds comprise about 90% of this tonnage. During the processing of bauxite from Arkansas, a "black sand," comprising 8 to 18% by weight of the total waste, is separated from the mud (49).

The red muds are pumped from alumina extracting plants as slurries containing about 20% solids. The slurries are stored in ponds where the solids settle and the supernatant water is reused. The solid contents of slurries gradually approach 50% after years of settling (49).

Properties of Muds: The properties of a red mud depend on the source of the bauxite. The oxide and mineralogical compositions of typical red muds are given in Table 1.7. The chemical compositions of muds derived from the same source of bauxite may vary by 10%. Their mineralogical compositions depend on the ore as well as processing conditions, and they have been described as being clay-like materials similar to noselite in composition (49). The oxide analysis of a typical brown mud shown in Table 1.7 suggests that it is composed largely of dicalcium silicate. The particle size distribution of dried muds also depends on the source of the ore and processing conditions. Red muds consist of fine particles with almost 90% being smaller than 45 μm (50).

Prospective Uses of Muds: Considerable effort has been devoted to finding uses for muds from the processing of bauxite including the recovery of valuable minerals and by-products. Possible direct uses include use as an additive to concrete, as a thermal insulation material and as a highway road bed stabilizer; other possible uses are incorporation in building materials such as portland cement, binders (e.g., for taconite pellets), and bricks (42)(49). Some of these uses have reached the commercial stage but no consistent use has been maintained on a sufficient scale to even consume current output.

The Bureau of Mines has sponsored work to develop new uses for red muds (42) (51). Recently, it has been demonstrated that lightweight structural building materials can be produced from red muds (50). These materials have densities ranging from 480 to 1,120 kg/m^3 with excellent thermal and acoustical insulation properties (49)(50). Another prospective use for red muds is the manufacture of synthetic aggregates. Red mud has been molded into balls and heated in a muffle furnace at 1260° to 1316°C to produce a dense synthetic aggregate (52).

However, the performance of these aggregates either in concrete or in asphalt has not yet been investigated. Granular lightweight aggregates of bulk density 704 kg/m^3 have been prepared in West Germany by firing a 1:1 mixture of red mud and fly ash (53).

Table 1.7: Oxide and Mineralogical Analyses of Some Red Muds and a Brown Mud*

| | | . . . . Oxide Analysis (%). . . . . | | |
| | Domestic | . . .Imported Ores . . . | | Brown |
Oxide	Ore	Source 1	Source 2	Mud
Al_2O_3	26.5	19.1	20.0	6.4
Fe_2O_3	10.7	38.3	49.0	6.1
SiO_2	22.9	9.3	3.4	23.3
CaO	8.1	5.3	6.8	46.6
Na_2O	11.8	6.4	0.5-5.0	4.1
TiO_2	3.3	6.7	4.5	3.0
P_2O_5	–	1.0	0.8	–
SO_3	2.8	–	trace	0.5
Loss on ignition	12.9	11.0	13.1	7.3

Mineralogical Analysis of Red Mud from Jamaican Bauxite

Mineral	Percent
Hematite	75-80
Goethite	5-10
Calcite	5-10
Boehmite	3-5

*Taken from References (49)(50).

Source: NBSIR 77-1244

Cement Kiln Dust

In the manufacture of portland cement clinker in rotary kilns, between 10 to 20% of the weight of the raw material leaves the kiln as dust. Approximately 17×10^6 tons of kiln dust were collected in 1972, of which about 12×10^6 tons were fed back into the process and the remaining 5×10^6 tons were discarded (54). The most common method of discarding the collected dust is to dump it on surface piles or in abandoned quarries.

Cement kiln dust consists primarily of fine particles with more than 90% being smaller than 12 μm (55). The chemical analysis of a kiln dust is given in Table 1.8, which indicates that it has a high alkali content, particularly potassium. Dust fractions which have low alkali contents, usually the coarser fractions, are usually returned to the kiln. However, dusts with high alkali contents often cannot be returned to the kiln because of limitations on the alkali contents of the clinker. For example, according to ASTM C150 (56), cements with 0.6% or less total alkali expressed as Na_2O are classified as low-alkali cements. Low-alkali cements may be necessary when certain alkali-reactive aggregates are incorporated in the concrete. Low-alkali cements are often specified even where higher alkali cements would be adequate. This results in the producers disposing of more kiln dust than would be necessary if the cement users did not overspecify. Problems associated with disposal of high-alkali kiln dust also could be reduced by only using raw materials, especially clays, which have small amounts of alkalis. However, low-alkali materials are usually more expensive than those commonly used.

The substitution of kiln dust for lime and limestone in a variety of applications has been investigated. Possible applications include agricultural uses (57), reclamation of acidic bays and lakes (58), and the treatment of municipal or process waters (59). Kiln dust has been used as a soil stabilizer and as a subbase for secondary roads and parking lots. Bituminous paving materials and asphalt roofing materials have been filled with cement kiln dust in a few applications. However, kiln dust has found little use in construction. Current research may result in its increased use. For example, the feasibilities of incorporating kiln dust in blended cements and of using it in the manufacture of lightweight aggregates are being investigated (54).

Table 1.8: Oxide Composition of a Cement Kiln Dust *

Oxide	Percent
SiO_2	11.1
Al_2O_3	5.5
Fe_2O_3	2.9
CaO	44.0
MgO	2.5
Na_2O	0.9
K_2O	6.0
SO_2	5.6
Loss on ignition	21.5

*Taken from Reference (54).

Source: NBSIR 77-1244

BY-PRODUCTS FROM COAL COMBUSTION

By-products from coal combustion for steam generation are classified as fly ash and, depending on the design of the boiler, as bottom ash or boiler slag. Fly ashes are the small particles carried in combustion gases up the stacks of coal burning units. Their emergence from stacks is largely prevented by electrostatic precipitators or by other collection methods.

In open-grate boilers, the ashes with the largest sizes fall through the grates and are collected in water-filled ash hoppers. This material is called bottom ash. In slag-tap boilers, molten ash is allowed to run down into a water-filled hopper. This material is called boiler slag (60).

Table 1.9: Percentage Compositions of U.S. Coal Ashes

Coal Type	SiO_2	Al_2O_3	Fe_2O_3	CaO	MgO	SO_3	Alkalis (as Na_2O)	Unburned Carbon	Reference
Bituminous (range)	34-52	13-31	6-25	1-12	0.5-3	0-2	0.2	1-12	(61)
Bituminous* (actual)	50	22	15	5.2	1.1	0.7	1.8	4.5	(65)
Bituminous* (actual)	58.6	30.6	6.3	0.9	1.0	NA	0.6	2.7	(65)
Lignite (range)	15-52	8-25	2-19	11-36	2-11	0.7-27	0-7	1-12	(62)
Lignite (actual) (Montana)	37.7	24.7	3.9	24.4	5.8	1.2	0.1	NA	(63)
Lignite (actual) (North Dakota)	36.9	11.9	14.2	27.4	5.5	2.9	0.6	NA	(63)
Lignite (actual) (Minnesota)	20.4	17.5	9.0	22.9	6.5	125	7.0	NA	(63)

*Used in production of ASTM Type IP cement.

**NA denotes no data available.

Source: NBSIR 77-1244

Fly ash, bottom ash, and boiler slag from bituminous coals have a wide range of compositions, but in general they consist primarily of SiO_2, Al_2O_3, and Fe_2O_3, with smaller amounts of CaO, MgO, unburned carbon, and alkali sulfate. Ashes and slags from lignite or subbituminous coal also tend to consist largely of SiO_2, Al_2O_3, and Fe_2O_3; however, CaO and MgO are present in greater amounts than in the corresponding products from bituminous coal. These higher CaO contents generally will result in higher free lime contents. Table 1.9 lists typical ranges of fly ash composition along with a few actual compositions.

Fly ash occurs as small spherical particles whose diameters range from a few micrometers to about 100 micrometers. Bottom ash particles range in size from about 0.08 to 20 mm, have angular shapes, and are very porous. Boiler slags have particle size distributions similar to bottom ashes. They also have angular shapes but are glassy and the larger particles often have porous surfaces (64).

Amounts and Disposal of Combustion Products

The accumulated amounts of fly ash, bottom ash, and boiler slag and the amounts collected in 1975 by the U.S. electric power generating industry are listed in Table 1.10 along with the amounts utilized. Over a two-fold increase in the amount of fly ash collected occurred between 1965 and 1975 and an even greater rate of growth is anticipated in the next decade because of the increased dependence on coal as an energy source. The largest amounts of coal are, of course, burned in high population density areas and this concentration has caused serious disposal problems. However, this also means that ash is available in areas where the largest amount of construction occurs. Figure 1.3 shows, by state, the approximate coal consumption in millions of tons in the U.S. in 1972.

The ash produced comprises 12 to 20% of the weight of coal burned. About 50% of unused ash is sluiced to disposal ponds. The remaining 50% is trucked to disposal areas, mixed with about 20% water, compacted, and used as fill. However, 65 to 80% of power plants have facilities for dry collection and loading of ash which could be used if markets were available (65).

Table 1.10: Amounts and Uses of By-Products from Coal Combustion (65)

	Fly Ash (10^6 tons)	Bottom Ash (10^6 tons)	Boiler Slag (10^6 tons)
Ash collected (1975)	42.3	13.1	4.6
Amounts accumulated	200–300	50–100	25–30
Ash utilized (1975)			
Use in ASTM Type IP cement or as raw material in cement manufacture	0.23	0.07	0.04
Use as a mineral admixture for concrete or concrete products	0.95	–	–
Lightweight aggregate manufacture	0.09	0.04	–

(continued)

Table 1.10: (continued)

	Fly Ash (10^6 tons)	Bottom Ash (10^6 tons)	Boiler Slag (10^6 tons)
Soil stabilization subbase	0.45	0.53	0.07
Filler in asphalt	0.14	–	–
Blast grit and roofing	–	0.42	0.41
Total used	1.86	1.06	0.52
Percent used	4.4	8.1	11.3

Source: NBSIR 77-1244

Use of By-Products

In 1975, less than 10% of the coal by-products were used in construction (Table 1.10). However, it appears that promising markets are being developed in the construction industry as discussed in the following.

Cement Manufacture and Concrete Products: While only a relatively small amount of ash and boiler slag have been used in cement manufacture and in concrete products, much larger amounts could potentially be used. Ash can be introduced into the cement manufacturing process either as a raw material for portland cement clinker manufacture or as a pozzolanic ingredient of a blended cement (66). Bottom ash and boiler slag have also been used as raw materials for cement manufacture. Many fly ashes are also used as mineral admixtures in concrete. When used in blended cements or as an admixture in concretes, fly ash is usually required to comply with ASTM Specifications C595 (67) or C618 (68).

Blended cements produced by intergrinding fly ash with portland cement clinker to comply with the ASTM requirements for Type IP cement (67) must contain between 15 and 40% fly ash by weight. The anticipated increased use of fly ashes by intergrinding will result in several benefits to the cement industry including decreased energy consumption in cement manufacture and increased capacity for a relatively low capital expenditure.

At present, incentives for the use of fly ash in cement are low because of the reduced demand for cement coupled with lack of experience in manufacture and the use of blended cement (69). The limitations on the minimum amount of fly ash permitted in a blended cement under ASTM C595 may also hinder experimentation with different levels of fly ash addition. (A later chapter discusses the utilization of fly ash in blended cements.)

The use of fly ash as a mineral admixture by the ready mixed concrete industry, which uses over 60% of the cement manufactured in the U.S., is rapidly increasing. Fly ash is also finding commercial use in the manufacture of steam-cured concrete products.

Figure 1.3: Coal Consumption by State in 1972 (10^6 tons)

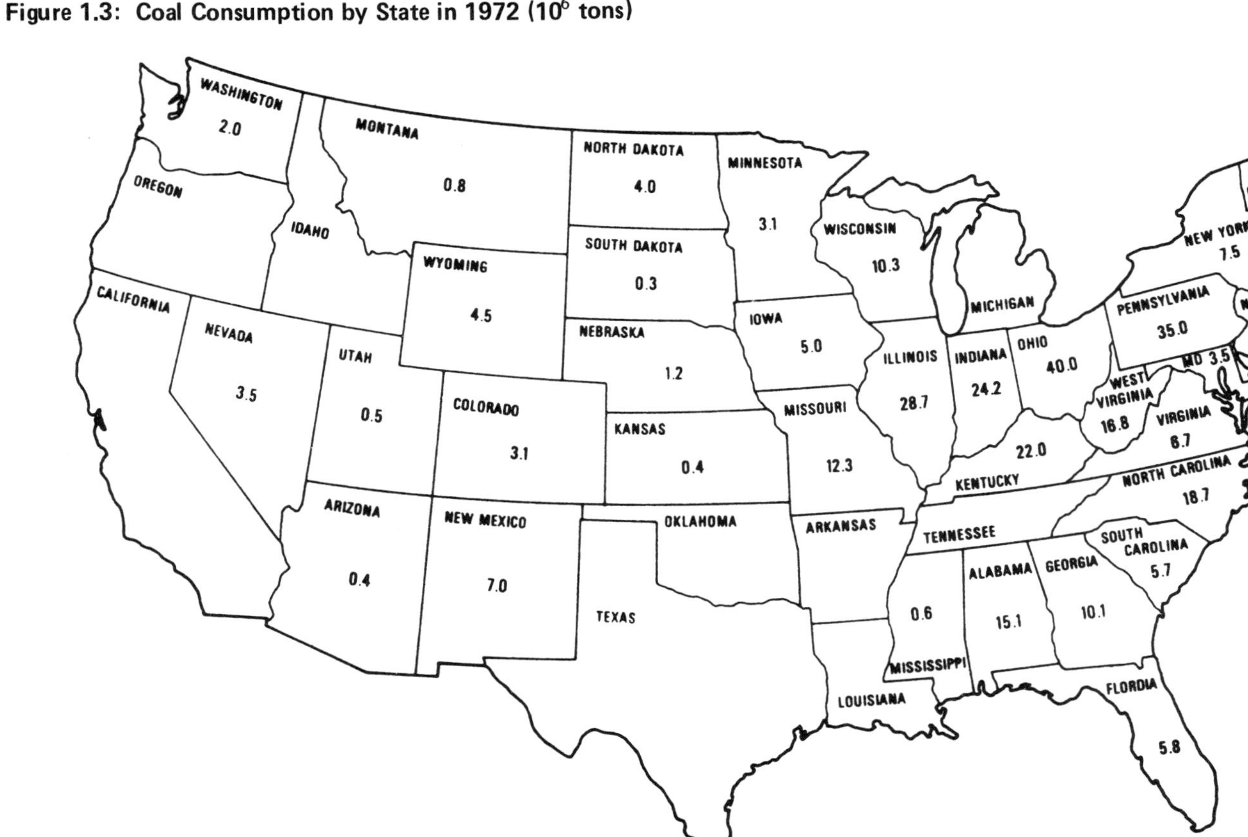

Source: NBSIR 77-1244

Conventional and Lightweight Aggregates: Fly ash may be used in the manufacture of lightweight aggregates. The U.S. lightweight aggregate production in 1970 was 13.3 x 10^6 tons, of which about 10 x 10^6 tons were manufactured (70) and the remainder was natural lightweight aggregates. Lightweight aggregates include expanded clay, shale and slate, along with some slag and sintered fly ash. Sintered fly ash aggregates have good strength to weight ratios and they facilitate the mixing of concretes (70). The extent to which sintered fly ash will supplant expanded clay, slate, and shale is uncertain.

The use of bottom ash as a lightweight aggregate may be preferred because it is available in larger sizes than sintered fly ash and it does not require sintering. The use of bottom ash and boiler slag as conventional aggregate should also increase significantly in view of the aggregate shortages developing in some of the larger metropolitan areas. These products have been used as aggregate base course as well as base course with portland cement for highway construction (71).

Lime-Fly Ash-Aggregate Mixtures: Lime-fly ash-aggregate (LFA) mixtures and lime-fly ash-portland cement-aggregate mixtures have been used successfully in the construction of highway bases and subbases. In 1971, for example, 2 x 10^6 tons of LFA were placed in the U.S. (72). The compressive strengths of LFA range from about 5.2 to 14 MN/m^2 after about 1 year, depending on the mix design, and these materials exhibit adequate durability (73) and good dimensional stability (72). As mentioned earlier, lime and fly ash are also being mixed with sulfate wastes to form construction materials.

Miscellaneous Uses: Fly ash has been used in small quantities in a variety of other materials of construction including asphalt, roofing shingles and brick. However, one midwestern utility has sold over 1.2 x 10^6 tons of fly ash for use as an asphalt filler since 1939 (74). Fly ash is also used in granules for roofing shingles. Several studies (75)(76)(77) have indicated that bricks meeting or exceeding the current ASTM requirements (78) for strength, saturation coefficient, and water absorption can be successfully produced from fly ash. In addition, bricks from fly ash can in some cases be produced more rapidly while requiring less energy than conventional bricks. Although bricks manufactured from fly ash have not been marketed commercially in the U.S., brick manufacture could become a large tonnage market for fly ash (13).

METALLURGICAL AND MINERAL SLAGS

The term slag is generally used to describe the nonmetallic melt which forms during the thermal reduction of metallic ores. This term is also applied to similar materials produced in other processes such as coal combustion or phosphorus production. Slags are usually composed of the same major constituents although their relative proportions vary widely. Generally, slags contain oxides of calcium, silicon, aluminum, iron, and smaller amounts of magnesium oxide. The compositions of slags from a variety of processes are listed in Table 1.11 and the annual amounts produced are listed in Table 1.12.

Table 1.11: Oxide Compositions of Some Slags

Slag	Oxide Composition, wt %						Reference
	SiO_2	Al_2O_3	FeO	CaO	MgO	Other	
Copper reverberatory slag	36	8	46	6	–	–	(79)
Ferromolybdenum slag	37	36	21	1.9	1.0	–	(79)
Tin slag	23	15	12	5	11	27*	(79)
Phosphate slag	44.8	6.2	1.4	41.7	0.8	1.1** 2.8***	(80)
Typical blast furnace slag	34-38	11-15	1.3-4.5	45-47	1.3	–	(81)
Converter slag†							
Open hearth (average of 3 slags)††	25.6	6.7	16	25.1	10.6	3.3†††	(66)
BOF†† (average of 6 slags)	21.7	3.8	14.7	40.3	4.4	3.5†††	(66)
Foundry slag (average of 4 slags)	33.3	18.2	9.8	40.9	3.8	–	(82)

*Heavy metal oxides.
**Alkalis as Na_2O.
***Fluorides.

†Slag produced when pig iron is converted into steel.
††Basic oxygen furnace.
†††MnO.

Source: NBSIR 77-1244

Table 1.12: Annual Production of Slags

Type of Slag*	Annual Production (10^6 tons)	Year	Reference
Blast furnace slag	27.5	1973	(83)
Converter slag	9.7	1973	(83)
Phosphate slag	4.0	1976	(5)
Copper smelting slag	5.2	1965	(84)
Foundry wastes**	20.0	1976	(5)

*Data not available for all types of slags listed in Table 1.11.
**Includes both dust and slag of which approximately 2×10^6 tons are slag.

Source: NBSIR 77-1244

Slag Production

The bulk of the slag generated in the U.S. comes from the production of iron and steel and, therefore, largely consists of blast furnace, converter, and foundry slags. Annual productions of blast furnace and converter slags (converter slag is the molten residue of the conversion of pig iron into steel) are about 27.5×10^6 tons and 9.7×10^6 tons, respectively (83). Foundry slag is produced in smaller amounts. Other types of slag are also produced in small amounts; however, because their production tends to be concentrated within small geographic areas, their use might be attractive in such areas. For example, about 2×10^6 tons of slag from phosphorus production are produced annually at two sites in Idaho (80).

Uses of Slags

While slags are used in a variety of construction materials (Table 1.13), their primary use is as aggregate. In 1973, 21 of the 27.5×10^6 tons of blast furnace slag produced were used as some form of aggregate. Similarly, 7.8 of the 9.7×10^6 tons of converter slag produced were used as aggregate (83). If unsoundness is anticipated because of a high free CaO content, converter slag is stockpiled to allow CaO to hydrate prior to utilization of the slag as aggregate. Other uses for slags produced by the iron and steel industry include railroad ballast, mineral wool production, use in roofing, and raw materials for manufacture of portland and blended cements (the last application is discussed in a later chapter of this book).

Unlike many other industrial by-products, the quantity of slags produced by the iron and steel industry is relatively constant. In addition, virtually all of these materials, with the exception of foundry slags, are used. However, the extensive use of slags as aggregate may not represent their highest value use. Because most slags, if properly quenched, exhibit hydraulic properties, slags could be extensively used as cementitious materials as is done in other industrialized countries.

Table 1.13: Uses of Slags

Type of Slag	Uses in Construction	Amount Used or Produced per Year (10^3 tons)	Reference
Blast furnace (all types)	(total produced)	27,543	(83)
Converter	(total produced)	9,739	(83)
Blast furnace (all types)	Aggregate	20,973	(83)
Blast furnace (air cooled)	Railroad ballast, mineral wool, roofing slag	4,436	(83)
Blast furnace (granulated)	Cement manufacture	232	(83)
Blast furnace (expanded)	Cement manufacture	450	(83)
Converter	Aggregate, railroad ballast	9,204	(83)
Phosphate slag	Aggregate, ceramic tile	NA*	(80)
Zinc smelter slag	Fine aggregate	NA	(5)
Foundry waste	Fine aggregate, pigments	NA	(5)

*NA indicates data not available.

Table 1.14: Amounts of Major Municipal Wastes Generated Annually (15)(87)

Municipal Waste	Estimated Annual Production (10^6 tons)	Prospective Uses in Construction
Municipal refuse	135	Landfill
Incineratory residue	5.0	Aggregate for concrete and asphalt
Glass	11	Glasphalt, ceramic brick, lightweight aggregate
Demolition waste	25	Aggregate for concrete and asphalt
Sewage sludge	7-11	Landfill, embankments
Rubber tires	3-5	Landfill

Source: NBSIR 77-1244

Use in this way should offer advantages in terms of energy conservation, raw materials conservation, cost savings, and possibly in the durability of the concrete produced (85). In addition, air-cooled slags which are low in MgO may be suitable as raw materials for the manufacture of cement. It has been demonstrated that portland cements can be produced by the pyroprocessing of blast furnace and converter slags along with limestone and a small amount of sand (86).

MUNICIPAL WASTES

A wide variety of municipal wastes, which include domestic wastes, are being generated in the U.S. Collectively, they amount to more than 172×10^6 tons annually. The types, amounts, and possible uses of these wastes are given in Table 1.14. Refuse constitutes the most abundant municipal waste and its rate of generation is increasing at an annual rate of 4.5% (87). However, at present, little refuse is used in construction other than as a landfill material.

The National Center for Resource Recovery is investigating other prospective uses of refuse. Incineration of the refuse produces a residue which can be converted into aggregate. Extraction of the glass fraction from the refuse yields another material which has a potential market either as aggregate or as a raw material for the manufacture of building materials. Demolition wastes and sewage sludge also are being considered for use in construction.

Incinerator Refuse

Incineration is becoming an increasingly important method for disposing of municipal refuse in the United States. It facilitates disposal of the refuse because the volume of the residue is usually between 3 and 20% of the initial refuse volume. Furthermore, power plants are being developed which can utilize the combustible portion of the municipal waste as a supplementary fuel source (87).

During 1975, there were 141 incinerators and 1 pyrolysis plant operating in the United States, treating an estimated 15×10^6 tons of refuse and producing approximately 5×10^6 tons of residue (87). Most of these plants are located in metropolitan areas of the northwestern states. Little information about the future availability of incinerator residue has been published; however, current programs should result in its increased availability. Landfill is currently the major disposal method for incinerator residues.

With the exception of unburned combustibles, the compositions of incinerator residues from different sources throughout the United States are relatively uniform regardless of the size of plant and method of incineration. Based on a moisture and combustible free basis, incinerator residues consist of approximately 43 to 55% glass; 23 to 37% ferrous metals; 13 to 16% ash; 1 to 3% ceramics and stone; and 1 to 4% nonferrous metals (87).

A promising application of incinerator residue is as aggregate for both portland cement concrete and asphaltic concrete (88). Pilot plant tests carried out at the Franklin Institute Research Laboratories (Philadelphia, PA) indicated that aggregate could be produced at a cost of $4 to $5 per ton (including capital cost) based on the production of 109 tons of aggregate per day (89).

Aggregate from this pilot plant is being incorporated in a bituminous wearing surface of a test highway pavement (90). The residual aluminum in this type of aggregate may preclude its use in portland cement concrete (89). The feasibility of using incinerator residue as aggregate in asphaltic concrete is also being investigated in Houston, Texas (91) and Baltimore, Maryland (89). The feasibility of using aggregate from incinerator residue in the manufacture of concrete block has recently been demonstrated (88).

Glass

Glass comprises some 6 to 11% by weight of municipal and commercial refuse or at least 11×10^6 tons annually (92). At present, only a small amount of the waste glass in municipal refuse is used as cullet in the manufacture of new glass. Cullet for glass manufacture must be essentially free of nonglass constituents and be color sorted. This requires an advanced separation technology which is being developed (93)(94). Normally, waste glass is not extracted from municipal refuse and the refuse is disposed of in dumps and landfills.

One approach being developed to utilize waste glass is its incorporation as an aggregate in asphaltic mixtures for pavements (92)(95)(96). The composite material is commonly referred to as "glasphalt." Glasphalt appears to give adequate performance in numerous test strips laid in the United States and Canada (93). However, the substitution of glass for conventional aggregates may produce a slightly more abrasive asphaltic pavement surface (92). The prospective use of waste glass as aggregate in portland cement concrete is not encouraging because of the potential for the occurrence of expansive reactions between the cement matrix and the glass (97).

Possibly, replacing part of the portland cement with reactive fly ash could mitigate the expansive effects of these reactions (98). Other uses for waste glass for construction purposes include the manufacture of mineral wool (99)(100); a raw material in the manufacture of ceramic brick (101); and a raw material for the production of lightweight aggregate (an application discussed in a later chapter here) (102)(103).

A wide range of potential markets exists for waste glass. However, waste glass is relatively thinly distributed throughout the United States and is abundant only in large metropolitan areas. These are areas of high levels of construction, and in such areas construction materials produced from waste glass could possibly become economically and technologically competitive with materials produced from virgin resources. Advances are being made in the technology of collection and separation of municipal waste which could facilitate the increased use of waste glass in the production of construction materials.

This has led to the establishment of a section in ASTM Committee E-38 on Resource Recovery for the purpose of developing standard test methods and specifications covering the use of waste glass in the manufacture of brick.

Building and Highway Demolition Waste

The demolition of buildings and highways results in the generation of large amounts of potentially usable materials. Studies have been carried out to determine the types, amounts, and potential uses of demolition materials being produced in the United States. In many cases only crude estimates of the amounts being generated are available and little is known about the extent of their reuse.

Amounts of Demolition Waste: The annual amount of waste material resulting from the demolition of buildings and highways has been estimated to be of the order of 27 x 10^6 tons (104). This figure is a gross estimate extrapolated from demolition rate data and the combination of population and building densities. Estimated amounts of the major demolition materials generated annually and their levels of reuse are given in Table 1.15.

Table 1.15: Estimated Amounts of Materials in New Construction and in Demolition Waste

Material	Used as Construction Material in 1971 (105)	Annual* Demolition Waste	Demolition Waste Reuse (106)
	. . . . (10^6 tons).		(%)
Concrete	315	18	**
Wood products	42	1.3	5
Iron and steel	22	1.7	50
Gypsum products	11	***	***
Clay products	18	1.4	**
Plastics	1.2	**	**
Aluminum	0.9	0.01	13
Copper	0.34	0.07	50
Asphalt	2.3†	***	***

*Based on 25 X 10^6 tons of demolition waste produced annually (104).
**Negligible.
***Information not available.
†Amount used in highway construction during 1973 (107).

Source: NBSIR 77-1244

The amount and type of demolition material available depends on the age of demolished structures. For example, the mean age of demolished buildings in Boston, MA, is approximately 65 years; in Atlanta, GA, 35 years; and in Los Angeles, CA, 45 years. These ages are reflected by the compositions and relative amounts of the various types of demolition wastes available in these cities (104).

Uses and Disposal of Demolition Waste: The level of use of recovered material depends on the specific material and the geographic region. Metals are recycled to a significant extent and, as deposits of rich ore are consumed, metal scrap will become more valuable. The market for used bricks varies substantially across the country, with most of the recovered brick in the New England region being reused, whereas used brick has little value in the midwest region (106). At present, only an insignificant portion of the available concrete, wood, gypsum, asphalt, and plastics from demolished buildings and highways are recycled. Large quantities of these materials are disposed of in landfills.

Concrete clearly constitutes the major fraction of demolition material currently generated in the United States and, based on current levels of use (Table 1.15) (105), it will be the predominant demolition material for at least the next 100 years. This fact, coupled with prospects of future regional aggregate shortages, has stimulated investigations of the feasibility of using crushed concrete rubble as aggregate for new concrete. Buck (108) has concluded that concrete of adequate quality for many applications can be produced using crushed concrete rubble as both the fine and coarse aggregate. This is consistent with the experience gained in Europe after World War II when concrete rubble was used as aggregate in the reconstruction of devastated cities (109). Recently, the American Concrete Paving Association reported (110) the first full scale use, in the United States, of crushed old concrete as the aggregate in new concrete.

As with the recycling of concrete, the technological and economic feasibility of recycling of asphalt pavements has been demonstrated (107)(111). Over 2.3×10^6 tons of asphalt are used in highway construction annually in the United States (107) and the materials from old asphalt pavements are being recycled in demonstration projects. It was estimated that about 500,000 tons of asphalt pavement would be recycled during 1977.

The low level of recycling of demolition materials is attributable to several factors (104)(105)(106) including higher processing cost of the demolition materials compared to virgin materials; low cost of dumping demolition materials; and institutional restrictions. The technology of separating the materials present in rubble needs to be improved.

For example, large amounts of sulfate from gypsum plaster and board could contaminate concrete rubble. If such concrete were used as aggregate for new concrete, the concentration of sulfate ions could be sufficient to produce disruptive reactions with the cement matrix. Another factor which appears to be limiting the recycling of demolition materials is lack of data on amounts and availability of specific types of demolition materials.

Sewage Sludge

Between 7 and 11×10^6 tons (5) of sewage sludge are generated annually by the chemical treatment of municipal sewage. The sludge is usually deposited in settling basins and allowed to thicken. This thickened sludge is usually either

dumped into waterways or incinerated. The incinerator residue is an ash somewhat similar to fly ash. The ash is disposed of in the dry form or as a slurry by
being mixed with plant effluent (5).

Sewage sludge ash can be compacted to a high strength mass which gradually
gains additional strength (112); therefore, it could be used in landfills. Sewage
sludge, itself, has been combined with a mixture of soil, lime, fly ash, and waste
calcium sulfate to produce a material which could be used in highway embankments (113). However, its freeze-thaw resistance was found to be marginal.

WASTE MATERIALS FROM EMERGING TECHNOLOGIES

Increasing demands for energy, coupled with depletion of petroleum reserves are
stimulating the development of new technologies for energy production and for
protection of the environment. The commercialization of these technologies will
probably result in the generation of substantial amounts of processing and mineral wastes. The types and prospective uses of some of these potential waste
materials are discussed in this section.

Oil Shale Residues

Massive deposits of oil-rich sedimentary marlstone are located in Colorado, Utah
and Wyoming, which may contain over $288 \times 10^9 \, m^3$ ($1,800 \times 10^9$ barrels) of ex-
tractable oil (114). The average yield per ton of processed shale is $0.13 \, m^3$ (0.74
barrels) of oil (114).; therefore, over $2,180 \times 10^9$ tons of oil shale residue could
be produced if the deposits were fully developed.

Although progress has been slow in developing these resources, generation of
significant amounts of oil and residue may commence within the next 20 years.
The amount of residue requiring disposal will depend on the oil extraction
method; if the rock is processed above ground, then essentially all the residue
will require disposal; on the other hand, if the oil is extracted in situ only a small
amount of residue will require disposal (115)(116).

Raw oil shale generally consists of dolomite, quartz, clay, calcite, and a number
of minor inorganic constitutents, and the organic substance kerogen (117). Kerogen is readily vaporized and converted to shale oil when the shale is heated to
about $450°C$ which results in the generation of an expanded porous residue. This
residue when mixed with limestone and calcined produces a hydraulic cement,
which may merit further investigation (118). Other potential uses of the residue
are as lightweight aggregate, fines in asphaltic concrete, and as a surface coarse
layer for secondary roads (117).

Slags and Ashes from Coal Gasification and Liquefaction Processes

Substantial amounts of fly ash and coal slag having pozzolanic value may become available in the next two decades if coal gasification proves economically

feasible. By 1985 as much as 180×10^6 tons of coal may be converted into gas annually (119) resulting in an annual production of approximately 18×10^6 tons of ash and slag.

Coal gasification fly ashes should have compositions similar to the fly ashes generated by burning coal from the same source, except that the former should be virtually free of sulfates and unburned carbon. Coal gasification slags should also be similar in composition to the fly ashes except that limestone may be added to the coal to improve the rheological properties of the slags, thereby producing slags which may have intrinsic hydraulic properties (66).

The coal liquefaction process will probably produce slags having pozzolanic or hydraulic properties similar to the slags produced by coal gasification. Although coal liquefaction technology is lagging behind that for coal gasification, it may result in the annual production of as much as 14×10^6 m^3 (90×10^6 barrels) of oil by 1985 (119). This could require the processing of approximately 30×10^6 tons of coal per year with the generation of about 3×10^6 tons of slag.

The slags and fly ashes with pozzolanic properties from the coal conversion processes could be used in the manufacture of cement and concrete products in the same way as fly ash is being utilized. The slags may have sufficient cementitious value to be used as hydraulic cements by themselves or with suitable activators.

Elemental Sulfur

The slight oversupply of sulfur which currently exists in the United States is anticipated to grow rapidly because of the necessity for the removal of sulfur from solid, liquid, and gaseous effluents, and wastes for the protection of the environment. The recovery of sulfur from coal gasification and liquefaction processes could greatly aggravate the oversupply problem (120). The amount of recovered sulfur is rapidly increasing, e.g., it has increased by over 50% between 1969 and 1973, with approximately 2.1×10^6 tons being recovered in 1973 (43).

Elemental sulfur has many potential applications for construction purposes, including sulfur-impregnated concrete (121)(122), sulfur concrete (123)(124), and sulfur-asphaltic mixes for pavements (125). Experimental houses have been constructed using sulfur-concrete blocks (126) and also by surface bonding cinder blocks with a sulfur-fiberglass formation (127).

OBSTACLES TO AND INCENTIVES FOR THE INCREASED USE OF WASTE MATERIALS IN CONSTRUCTION

The direct use, processing or conversion of waste materials into construction materials has the potential of consuming significant amounts of the over 3×10^9 tons of wastes generated annually in the United States. This is because over 1.5×10^9 tons of nonmetallic materials (sand, gravel, crushed stone, gypsum, slag, and cement) and over 140×10^6 tons of steel are consumed annually in construction (33). No reliable estimates of the total amount of wastes used in construction are available, but it appears that only a small amount of the total wastes are used.

Several major barriers must be overcome before any material is widely accepted for use in construction. These include those posed by economic, institutional and technical considerations. An example of an economic barrier to the use of waste materials is the higher costs sometimes charged for their transportation as compared to virgin materials. Apparently, few obvious institutional restrictions have been placed on the use of waste materials; only in the case of recycling demolition wastes have such restrictions been mentioned (104)(105)(106).

Technical requirements for construction materials are usually defined by standards and specifications. The lack of such technical requirements, as well as overly restrictive requirements, can discourage experimentation with the use of waste materials in construction. Building materials standards which are based on performance tests and criteria do not appear to pose any severe restrictions on the use of waste materials. However, specifications based on compositional requirements can be more restrictive. For example, the ASTM specification for blended cements, C595, (67) appears to place unnecessarily narrow restrictions on the amounts of fly ashes and slag materials which can be added to portland cement to form Types IP and IS blended cements, respectively. Recent developments suggest that this specification may be broadened.

Many technical programs have been carried out in the past to develop viable construction materials from wastes. While some of these endeavors have been technical successes, few have resulted in products reaching the commercial stage. Often the building materials from wastes have not been economically competitive with those from virgin materials, or the necessary markets have not existed near the wastes disposal areas.

Forces are emerging in the United States because of changing patterns of supply and demand of materials and energy, economic factors, and heightened concern for the quality of the environment, which are providing new incentives for the increased use of waste materials. Overall the United States has abundant resources, except for petroleum, but material shortages may exist in some areas. For example, Witczak (34) has identified areas in the United States which lack good quality aggregates. Many of these areas have large amounts of waste rock and coarse mill tailings which could be used directly as aggregates. Increasing energy costs coupled with energy conservation policies should increase the recycling of energy-intensive materials such as steel, aluminum, asphalt, and ceramic building materials.

These pressures will also facilitate the substitution of waste materials for energy-intensive materials as, for example, in the addition of fly ashes to portland cement to form Type IP blended cements (81)(85). Regulations established to protect the environment will provide incentives for using wastes in construction because both the complexities and costs of disposing of wastes will be increased.

Land reclamation policies coupled with environmental concerns will provide incentives for using accumulated wastes, especially the wastes stored near highly populated areas or on land containing important minerals.

The various pressures for direct use of wastes as, or for converting them into construction materials will be effective only if the wastes are technically and economically competitive with conventional materials.

As indicated throughout this survey, some of the construction materials produced from virgin resources, and the technology of converting other wastes into usable materials is rapidly advancing. Growth in the use of waste materials in construction, therefore, appears to depend on the development of economic incentives, either formed in the market place or created by governmental policies.

REFERENCES

(1) Hansen, J.B., "Providing a Solution," *Proceedings of the Third Mineral Waste Utilization Symposium,* pp 4-6 (Chicago, 1972).

(2) Kenahan, C.B., Kaplan, R.S., Dunham, J.T., and Linnehan, D.G., "Bureau of Mines Research Programs on Recycling and Disposal of Mineral-, Metal-, and Energy-Based Wastes," U.S. Bureau of Mines Information Circular No. 8595 (Washington, DC 20240, 1973).

(3) Resource Conservation Act of 1976 (Public Law 94-580), Congressional Record—House, H11174, (September 27, 1976).

(4) Mehta, P.K. and Pitt, N., "Energy and Industrial Materials from Crop Residues," *Resource Recovery and Conservation* 2 (No. 1), pp 23-38 (1976).

(5) Miller, R.H. and Collins, R.J., *Waste Materials as Potential Replacements for Highway Aggregates,* National Cooperative Highway Resource Program Report No. 166 (1976); available from the National Academy of Sciences, Washington, DC 20418.

(6) Maneval, D.R., "Utilization of Coal Refuse for Highway Base or Subbase Material," *Proceedings of the Fourth Mineral Waste Utilization Symposium,* pp 222-228 (Chicago, 1974).

(7) Fine, M.M., "Iron Ore Waste Occurrence, Beneficiation and Utilization," *Proceedings of the First Mineral Waste Utilization Symposium,* pp 67-72 (Chicago, 1968).

(8) Heinz, R.W. and Gaynor, G.H., "Potential Utilization of Mine Waste Tailings in the Upper Mississippi Valley Lead-Zinc Mining District," *Proceedings of the Second Mineral Waste Utilization Symposium,* pp 181-193 (Chicago, 1970).

(9) Nakamura, H.H., Aleshin, E., and Schwartz, M.A., "Utilization of Copper, Lead, Zinc and Iron Ore Tailings," *Proceedings of the Second Mineral Waste Utilization Symposium,* pp 139-148 (Chicago, 1970).

(10) Mindess, S. "Production of High Pressure Steam-Cured Calcium Silicate Building Materials from Mining Industry Waste Products," *Proceedings of the First Mineral Waste Utilization Symposium,* pp 153-154 (Chicago, 1968).

(11) Pettibone, H.C., "Engineering Properties and Utilization Examples of Mine Tailings," *Proceedings of the Third Mineral Waste Utilization Symposium,* pp 161-169 (Chicago, 1972).

(12) Mindess, S. and Richards, C.W., "Criteria for Selection of Mineral Wastes for Use in the Manufacture of Calcium Silicate Building Materials," *Proceedings of the Second Mineral Waste Utilization Symposium,* pp 155-165 (Chicago, 1970).

(13) "Building Bricks from the Waste Pile," *Environmental Science and Technology* 6 (6), 502-503 (1972).

(14) Stoops, R.F. and Redeker, I.H., "North Carolina Feldspar Tailings Utilization," *Proceedings of the Second Mineral Waste Utilization Symposium,* pp 177-180 (Chicago, 1970).

(15) Cutler, I.B. and Nicholson, P.S., "Ceramic Products from Mineral Wastes," *Proceedings of the Second Mineral Waste Utilization Symposium,* pp 149-154 (Chicago, 1970).

(16) LaRosa, P.J., Ricciardella, K.A., and McGarvey, R.J., *Carbonate Bonding of Taconite Tailings,* Environmental Protection Technology Series Report No. EPA-670/2-74-001, (Office of Research and Development, U.S. Environmental Protection Agency, Washington, DC 20460, January 1974).

(17) Heinz, R.H. and Geiger, G.H., *Utilization of Mine Waste Tailings in Southwestern Wisconsin,* Grant No. SWD-13, 1974; available from U.S. Bureau of Mines, Washington, DC 20240.

(18) *Utilization of Mining and Milling Wastes,* Illinois Institute of Technology Research Institute Contract No. H0109397, 1971; available from U.S.. Bureau of Mines, Washington, DC 20240.

(19) Collings, R.K., Winer, A.A., Feasby, D.G., and Zoldners, N.G., "Mineral Waste Utilization Studies," *Proceedings of the Fourth Mineral Waste Utilization Symposium,* pp 2-12 (Chicago, 1974).

(20) Pettibone, H.C. and Kealy, C.D., "Engineering Properties of Mine Tailings," *Journal of the Soil Mechanics and Foundation Division (ASCE),* 97 (SM9), pp 1207-1225 (1971).

(21) Spicer, T.S. and Luckie, P.T., "Operation Anthracite Refuse," *Proceedings of the Second Mineral Waste Utilization Symposium,* pp 194-204 (Chicago, 1970).

(22) Rose, J.G., Robl, T.L., and Bland, A.E., "Composition and Properties of Refuse from Kentucky Coal Preparation Plants," *Proceedings of the Fifth Mineral Waste Utilization Symposium* pp 122-131 (Chicago, 1976).

(23) "Digging into Mine Waste," *Environmental Science and Technology* 8 (2), pp 110-111 (1974).

(24) Haas, A., "Switching to Coal is Buying Trouble," *Business and Society Review,* pp 52-57 (Winter 1974-75).

(25) Parker, W.W. and Gray, R.E., "Indicators of Coal Refuse Embankment Stability," *Proceedings of the Fifth Mineral Waste Utilization Symposium,* pp 86-91 (Chicago, 1976).

(26) Luckie, P.T., Peters, J.W., and Spicer, T.S., "Evaluation of Anthracite Refuse as a Highway Construction Material," Pennsylvania State University Experiment Station Report SR-57 (1966).

(27) Bryenton, D.L., and Rose, J.G., "Utilization of Coal Refuse as a Concrete Aggregate (Coal-Crete)," *Proceedings of the Fifth Mineral Waste Utilization Symposium,* pp 108-113 (Chicago, 1976).

(28) Charmbury, H.B. and Maneval, D.R., "The Utilization of Incinerated Anthracite Mine Refuse as Anti-Skid Highway Material," *Proceedings of The Third Mineral Waste Utilization Symposium,* pp 123-128 (Chicago, 1972).

(29) Tanfield, D., "Construction Use for Colliery Spoil," *Contract Journal* (1971).

(30) Glover, H.G., *Coal Mine Refuse Disposal in Great Britain,* Special Report SR-81, Coal Research Station, The Pennsylvania State University (1971).

(31) Miller, R.H. and Collins, R.J., "Waste Materials as Potential Replacements for Highway Aggregates," *Proceedings of the Fourth Mineral Waste Utilization Symposium,* pp 50-61 (Chicago, 1974).

(32) Emery, J.J. and Kim, C.S., "Trends in the Utilization of Waste for Highway Construction," *Proceedings of the Fourth Mineral Waste Utilization Symposium,* pp 22-32 (Chicago, 1974).

(33) *Optimizing the Use of Materials and Energy in Transportation Construction,* Transportation Research Board Special Report No. 166 (National Research Council, Washington, DC, 1976).

(34) Witczak, M.W., Lovell, C.W., and Yoder, E.J., "A Generalized Investigation of the Potential Availability of Aggregate by Regional Geomorphic Units within the Conterminous Forty-Eight States," Highway Research Board No. 343, pp 31-42 (1971).

(35) Collings, R.J., "Waste Products as a Potential Replacement for Aggregates," *Proceedings of the Fourth International Ash Utilization Symposium,* pp 93-113 (St. Louis, 1976).

(36) Fondriest, F.F. and Snyder, M.J., *Synthetic Aggregates for Highway Construction,* National Cooperative Highway Research Program Report No. 8 (National Research Council, Washington, DC, 1964).

(37) Cox, J.L., "Phosphate Wastes," *Proceedings of the First Mineral Waste Utilization Symposium,* pp 50-61 (Chicago, 1968).

(38) Vasan, S., "Utilization of Florida Phosphate Slimes," *Proceedings of the Third Mineral Waste Utilization Symposium,* pp 171-177 (Chicago, 1972).

(39) Timberlake, R.C., "Disposal of Mining Wastes in the Central Florida Phosphate Field," *Proceedings of the Second Mineral Waste Utilization Symposium,* pp 237-240 (Chicago, 1970).

(40) *Utilization of Phosphate Slimes,* Water Pollution Control Research Series, United States Environmental Protection Agency Report No. 14050 EPU 09/71 (1971).

(41) "Standard Specification for Lightweight Aggregates for Structural Concrete," ASTM Designation C330-69 (American Society for Testing and Materials, Philadelphia, Pennsylvania 19103).

(42) Dean, K.C., "Utilization of Mine, Mill and Smelter Wastes," *Proceedings of the First Mineral Waste Utilization Symposium,* pp 138-141 (Chicago, 1968).

(43) Commodity Data Summaries 1974, Appendix 1 to Mining and Minerals Policy, U.S. Bureau of Mines (Washington, DC, 1974).

(44) Smith, L.M. and Larew, H.G., *User's Manual for Sulfate Waste in Road Construction,* Federal Highway Adminsitration Report No. FHWA-RD-76-11 (Washington, DC, 1975).

(45) Evans, R.J., "Potential Solid Waste Generation and Disposal from Lime and Limestone Desulfurization Processes," U.S. Bureau of Mines Information Circular 8633 (Washington, DC, 1974).

(46) Beychok, M.R., "Coping with SO_2," *Chemical Engineering—Deskbook Issue,* pp 79-85 (October 21, 1974).

(47) Minnick, L.J., "Progress in the Conversion of Sulfur Oxide Scrubber Sludges into Environmentally Acceptable Products," *Proceedings of the Fifth Mineral Waste Utilization Symposium,* pp 285-290 (Chicago, 1976).

(48) Smith, L.M. and Larew, H.G., "Technology for Using Waste Sulfates in Road Construction," *Proceedings of the Fourth Fly Ash Utilization Symposium,* pp 114-128 (St. Louis, 1976).

(49) Pincus, A.G., "Wastes from Processing of Aluminum Ores," *Proceedings of the First Mineral Waste Utilization Symposium,* pp 40-49 (Chicago, (1968).

(50) *Utilization of Red Mud Wastes for Lightweight Structural Building Products,* IITRI Project No. G6015—Final Report (1968); available from U.S. Bureau of Mines, Washington, DC 20240.

(51) Fursman, O.C., Mauser, J.E., Butler, M.O., and Stickney, W.A., *Utilization of Red Mud Residues from Alumina Production,* U.S. Bureau of Mines Report of Investigation 7454 (Washington, DC, 1970).

(52) Blank, H.R., "Red Mud from Alumina Plants as a Possible Source of Synthetic Aggregate," *Journal of Testing and Evaluation* 4 (5), pp 355-358 (1976).

(53) Wargalla, G., "Einsatz von Ratschlamm bei Zement-und Blahtonherstellung," *Erzmetall* 26 (1), pp 18-20 (1973).

(54) Davis, T.A. and Hooks, D.B., "Utilization of Waste Kiln Dust from the Cement Industry," *Proceedings of the Fourth Mineral Waste Utilization Symposium,* pp 354-363 (Chicago, 1974).

(55) Greening, N.R., Hinchey, R.J., and Hagao, H., *Elimination of Water Pollution by Recycling Cement Plant Dust,* Portland Cement Association (Skokie, Illinois, 1973).

(56) "Standard Specification for Portland Cement," ASTM Designation C150-74 (American Society of Testing and Materials, Philadelphia, Pennsylvania 19103).

(57) Carroll, D.M., Erickson, C.J., and Whittakers, C.W., "Cement Kiln Flue Dust for Soil Liming," *Agronomy Journal* 56, pp 373-376 (1974).

(58) Trembley, F.J., Mihursky, J.A., and Hertz, E.W., "Use of Cement Plant Stack Dust as a Neutralizing Agent in Acid Water Lakes," *Transactions of Northwest Wildlife Conference,* 1, pp 55-60 (1958).

(59) Farnham, W., "Process of Clarifying Turbid Water using Cottrell Flour and Acidifying Coagulant," U.S. Patent 2,964,466 (1960).

(60) Moulton, L.K., "Bottom Ash and Boiler Slag," pp 148-169, U.S. Bureau of Mines Information Circular 8640 (Washington, DC, 1974).

(61) Barton, W.R., "Raw Materials for Manufacture of Cement," pp 46-51, *Fly Ash Utilization,* U.S. Bureau of Mines Information Circular 8348 (Washton, DC 1967).

(62) Abernathy, R.F., Peterson, J.J., and Gibson, F.N., *Major Ash Constituents in U.S. Coals,* U.S. Bureau of Mines Report of Investigation 7240 (Washington, D.C., 1969).

(63) Manz, O.E., "Lignite Production and Utilization" *Proceedings Fourth International Ash Utilization Symposium,* pp 39-57 (St. Louis, 1976).

(64) Seals, R.K., Moulton, L.K., and Ruth, B.E., "Bottom Ash: An Engineering Material," *Journal of the Soil Mechanics Division, (ASCE)* 98, pp 311-25 (1972).

(65) *Ash At Work* 8 (2), p 6 (1976).

(66) Brown, P.W. and Clifton, J.R., "Energy Conservation Through the Utilization of Mineral Waste Products in Cement Manufacture," *Proceedings of the CANMET Seminar on Energy and Resource Conservation in the Cement and Concrete Industry* (Ottawa, 1976).

(67) "Standard Specification for Blended Hydraulic Cement," ASTM Designation C595-75 (American Society for Testing and Materials, Philadelphia, Pennsylvania 19103).

(68) "Standard Specification for Fly Ash and Raw or Calcined Natural Pozzolans for Use in Portland Cement Concrete," ASTM Designation C618-72 (American Society for Testing and Materials, Philadelphia, Pennsylvania 19103).

(69) Brown, P.W., Clifton, J.R., Berger, R.L., and Frohnsdorff, G., "Limitations to Fly Ash Use in Blended Cement," *Proceedings of the Fourth International Ash Utilization Symposium, pp 518-529* (St. Louis, 1976).

(70) Morris, G.R., "Lightweight Aggregates in the U.S.", pp 201-204, U.S. Bureau of Mines Information Circular 8488 (Washington, DC, 1972).

(71) Blocker, W.V., Morrison, R.E., Morton, W.E. and Babcock, A.W., "Marketing Power Plant Aggregates as Road Base Material," pp 208-233, U.S. Bureau of Mines Information Circular 8640 (Washington, DC, 1974).

(72) Barenberg, E.J., "Utilization of Ash in Stabilized Base Construction," pp 180-196, U.S. Bureau of Mines Information Circular 8640 (Washington, DC, 1974).

(73) Barenberg, E.J., "The Behavior and Performance of International Asphalt Pavements with Lime-Fly Ash-Aggregate Bases," *Proceedings of the Second International Conference on Structural Design of Asphalt Pavements,* pp 619-33 (Ann Arbor, Michigan, 1967).

(74) Ziminer, F.U., "Fly Ash as Bituminous Filler," pp 49-76, U.S. Bureau of Mines Information Circular 8488 (Washington, DC, 1972).

(75) Sieffert, P.L., "Test Firing of Fly Ash Brick on a Short Time Cycle," pp 327-330, U.S. Bureau of Mines Information Circular 8488 (Washington, DC, 1972).

(76) Shafer, H.E., Cockrell, C.F., Humphreys, K.K., and Leonard, J.W., "Status Report on Bricks from Fly Ash," pp 195-203, *Fly Ash Utilization,* U.S. Bureau of Mines Information Circular 8348 (Washington, DC, 1967).

(77) Slonaker, J.F., "Production of Forty Percent Core Area Fly Ash Bricks Using Selected Fly Ashes," *Proceedings of the Fourth International Fly Ash Utilization Symposium,* pp 231-237 (St. Louis, 1976).

(78) "Standard Specification for Building Brick (Solid Masonry Units Made from Clay or Shale)" ASTM Designation C62-66 (American Society for Testing and Materials, Philadelphia, Pennsylvania 19103).

(79) Gomes, J.M., Uchida, K., and M.M. Wong, "Recovery of Metal Values from Industrial Slags By the Use of a 2-Phase Molten Electrolyte System," *Proceedings of the Third Mineral Waste Utilization Symposium,* pp 55-61 (Chicago, 1972).

(80) Valdez, E.G., Dean, K.C., and Warner, L.L., *Utilization of Phosphorus Furnace Slag in Ceramic Wall and Floor Tile,* U.S. Bureau of Mines Report of Investigation 7829 (Washington, DC, 1974).

(81) Brown, P.W., Clifton, J.R., and Frohnsdorff, G., *Energy Conservation Through the Facilitation of Increased Blended Cement Use,* National Bureau of Standards Report NBSIR 76-1008 (1975).

(82) Gutt, W., "Manufacture of Cement from Industrial By-Products," *Chemistry and Industry,* pp 189-97, February 13, 1971.

(83) *Minerals Yearbook 1973,* Volume I, pp 1139-42, U.S. Bureau of Mines (Washington, DC, 1973).

(84) Vogely, W.A., "The Economic Factors of Mineral Waste Utilization," *Proceedings of the First Mineral Waste Utilization Symposium,* pp 7-19 (Chicago, 1968).

(85) Brown, P.W., Clifton, J.R., and Frohnsdorff, G., "The Utilization of Industrial By-Products in Blended Cement," *Proceedings of the Fifth Mineral Waste Utilization Symposium,* pp 278-84 (Chicago, 1976).

(86) Kondo, R. Daimon, M., Goto, S., Nakamura, A., and Kobayashi, T., "Furnace Converter Slags," *Proceedings of the Fifth Mineral Waste Utilization Symposium,* pp 329-40 (Chicago, 1976).

(87) Pindzola, D. and Collins, R.J., *Technology for Use of Incinerator Residue as Highway Material: Identification of Incinerator Practices and Residue Sources,* Federal Highway Administration Report No. FHWA-RD-75-81, 1975; available from National Technical Information Service (NTIS), Springfield, Virginia 22161.

(88) Lauer, K.R. and Leliaert, R.M., "Profitable Utilization of Incinerator Residue from Municipal Refuse," *Proceedings of the Fifth Mineral Waste Utilization Symposium,* pp 215-218 (Chicago, 1976).

(89) Pindzola, D. and Chou, R.C., *Synthetic Aggregate from Incinerator Residue by a Continuous Fusion Process,* Federal Highway Administration Report FHWA-RD-74-23 (Washington, DC, 1974).

(90) Pindzola, D., *Large Scale Continuous Production of Fused Aggregate from Incinerator Residue,* Federal Highway Administration Report No. FHWA-RD-76-115 (Washington, DC, 1976).

(91) Haynes, J. and Ledbetter, W.B., *Incinerator Residue in Bituminous Base Construction,* Federal Highway Administration Report No. FHWA-RD-76-12 (Washington, DC, 1975).

(92) Malisch, W.R., Day, D.E., and Wixson, B.G., *Use of Domestic Waste Glass for Urban Paving,* Environmental Protection Agency Report No. EPA-670/2-73-038, 1973: NTIS PB 222-052.

(93) Abrahams, J.H., "Recycling Container Glass—An Overview," *Proceedings of the Third Mineral Waste Utilization Symposium,* pp 35-44 (Chicago, 1972).

(94) Palumbo, F.J., "Concentrating Glass Cullet Recovered from Unburned Urban Refuse and Incinerator Residues," *Proceedings of the Third Mineral Waste Utilization Symposium,* pp 323-390 (Chicago, 1972).

(95) Malisch, W.P., Day, D.E., and Wilson, B.G., "Use of Domestic Waste Glass as Aggregate in Bituminous Concrete," *Highway Research Record No. 307,* pp 1-10 (1970).

(96) Malisch, W.R., Day, D.E., and Wixson, R.G., "Use of Waste Glass for Urban Paving," *Proceedings of the Second Mineral Waste Utilization Symposium,* pp 369-373 (Chicago, 1970).

(97) Johnston, C.D., "Waste Glass as Coarse Aggregate for Concrete," *Journal of Testing and Evaluation* 2 (5), pp 344-350 (1974).

(98) Phillips, J.C., Cahn, D.S., and Keller, G.W., "Refuse Glass Aggregate in Portland Cement Concrete," *Proceedings of the Third Mineral Waste Utilization Symposium,* pp 385-390 (Chicago, 1972).

(99) Cahoon, H.P. and Cutler, I.B., "Feasibility of Making Insulation Material by Foaming Waste Glass," *Proceedings of the Third Mineral Waste Utilization Symposium,* pp 353-357 (Chicago, 1972).

(100) Goode, A.H., Tyrrell, M.E., and Feld, I.L., "Mineral Wool from High-Glass Fractions of Municipal Incinerator Residues," *Proceedings of the Third Mineral Waste Utilization Symposium,* pp 391-396 (Chicago, 1972).

(101) Tyrrell, M.E., and Feld, I.L., "Structural Products Made from High Silica Fractions of Municipal Incinerator Residues," *Proceedings of the Second Mineral Waste Utilization Symposium,* pp 355-362 (Chicago, 1970).

(102) Shotts, R.O., "Waste Glass as an Ingredient of Lightweight Aggregate," *Proceedings of the Third Mineral Waste Utilization Symposium,* pp 411-422 (Chicago, 1972).

(103) Liles, K.J. and Tyrrel, M.E., *Waste Glass as a Raw Material for Lightweight Aggregate,* U.S. Bureau of Mines Report of Investigation 8104 (1976); available from NTIS (Springfield, VA 22161), No. PB 250-692.

(104) Wilson, D.G., Foley, P., and Wiesman, R., "Demolition Debris: Qualities, Compositions and Possibilities for Recycling," *Proceedings of the Fifth Mineral Waste Utilization Symposium,* pp 8-15 (Chicago, 1976).

(105) Jones, G.V. and Holley, M.J., *Improved Utilization of Construction Materials,* Department of Civil Engineering Research Report R73-34, Massachusetts Institute of Technology 1973; available from NTIS (Springfield, VA 22161), No. PB 224-244.

(106) Wilson, D.G., "The Resource Potential of Demolition Debris in the United States," *Resource Recovery and Conservation* 1, pp 129-140 (1975).

(107) Saylak, D., Gallaway, B.M., and Epps, J.A., "Recycling Old Asphalt Concrete Pavements," *Proceedings of the Fifth Mineral Waste Utilization Symposium,* pp 16-25 (Chicago, 1976).

(108) Buck, A.D., *Recycled Concrete as a Source of Aggregate,* Miscellaneous Paper C-76-2, Concrete Laboratory, U.S. Army Engineer Waterways Experimental Station, Vicksburg, Mississippi (1976).

(109) Graf, O. "Uber Ziegelsplittbeton, Sandsteinbeton, and Trummerschutt-beton," *Die Bauwirtschaft* Nos. 2 to 4 (1948): English translation available from U.S. Army Engineer Waterways Experimental Station (Vicksberg, Mississippi) as Translation No. 73-1.

(110) *Newsletter,* American Concrete Paving Association 11 (No. 10), (October 1975).

(111) Proudy, H., Hodge, J., and Gregory, G., *Recycled Asphalt Concrete,* Federal Highway Administration Implementation Package 75-5 (U.S. Department of Transportation, 1975).

(112) Gray, D.H., "Properties of Compacted Sewage Ash," *Journal of the Soil Mechanics and Foundation Division (ASCE)* 96 (SM2), pp 439-451 (1970).

(113) Kawam, A., Smith, L.M., Ross, J., Larew, H.G., and Rude, L., *Feasibility of Using Sewage Sludge in Highway Embankment Construction,* Federal Highway Administration Report FHWA-RD-75-38; available from NTIS (Springfield, Virginia 22161), No. PB 242-260.

(114) *Modern Energy Technology,* Volume 2, Chapter 57, (Research and Education Association, New York, 1975).

(115) Teller, E., "How Technology Can Solve the Problems," *Worcester Polytechnic Institute Journal,* Worcester, Massachusetts, (August 1974).

(116) Conkle, N., Ellzey, V., and Murthy, K., *Environmental Considerations for Oil Shale Development,* Environmental Protection Agency Report EPA-650/2-74-099 (1974); available from NTIS (Springfield, Virginia 22161), No. PB 241-942.

(117) Gromko, G.I., "A Preliminary Investigation of the Feasibility of Spent Oil Shale as Road Construction Material," *Transportation Research Record No. 549,* pp 47-54 (1975).

(118) Nevens, T.D., Culbertson, W.J., and Hollingshead, R., *Disposal and Uses of Oil Shale Ash,* Bureau of Mines Open File Report 32-74 (1970); available from NTIS (Springfield, Virginia 22161), No. PB 234-208.

(119) *Materials Technology in the Near-Term Energy Program,* National Academy of Sciences (Washington, DC, 1974).

(120) *First Annual Report of the Secretary of the Interior Under the Mining and Mineral Policy Act of 1970,* PL 91-631 (U.S. Government Printing Office, Washington, DC, 1972).

(121) Thaulow, N., "Sulfur Impregnated Concrete, SIC," *Cement and Concrete Research* 4 (2), pp 269-277 (1974).

(122) Platou, J., "Sulphur-Impregnated Concrete," *Sulphur Institute Journal* 11 (1), pp 2-4 (1975).

(123) Crow, L.J. and Bates, R.C., *Strengths of Sulfur-Basalt Concretes,* U.S. Bureau of Mines Report of Investigation No. 7349 (Washington, DC, 1970).

(124) "BuMines Develops Improved Sulphur Concretes," *Sulphur Institute Journal* 12 (1), pp 6-8 (1976).

(125) McBee, W.C., and Sullivan, T.A., "Utilization of Secondary Sulfur in Construction Materials," *Proceedings of the Fifth Mineral Waste Utilization Symposium,* pp 39-51 (Chicago, 1976).

(126) Rybczynski, W., "A Sulphur House at Saddle Lake," *Sulphur Institute Journal* 10 (1), pp 2-5 (1974).

(127) "BuMines Builds a Sulphur House," *Sulphur Institute Journal* 9 (4), pp 2-7 (1973).

Technical and Economic Feasibility

Information in this chapter is based on *A Study of the Feasibility of Utilizing Solid Wastes for Building Materials, Phase I Summary Report,* EPA Report 600/2-78-091, prepared by B.L. Duft, H. Levine, and A. McLeod of the Material Systems Corporation for the U.S. Environmental Protection Agency (Municipal Environmental Research Laboratory, Cincinnati, OH); *A Study of the Feasibility of Utilizing Solid Wastes for Building Materials, Phase II Summary Report,* EPA Report 600/2-78-092, prepared by B.L. Duft, H. Levine, A. McLeod and Y. Tsur of the Material Systems Corporation for the U.S. Environmental Protection Agency (Municipal Environmental Research Laboratory, Cincinnati, OH); and *The Feasibility of Utilizing Solid Wastes for Building Materials, Executive Summary,* EPA Report 600/8-77-006, prepared by G. Jackson and S.A. Ware of the Ebon Research Corporation for the U.S. Environmental Protection Agency (Municipal Environmental Research Laboratory, Cincinnati, OH).

INTRODUCTION

The Material Systems Corporation (MSC) and the Solid and Hazardous Waste Research Laboratory (SHWRL), Environmental Protection Agency have performed a joint study to evaluate the technological and commercial possibilities of waste-derived building composites.

A comprehensive literature search identifying the wastes was followed by experimental evaluation, process development, production studies and qualification of the products to determine the technical and economic feasibility of the concept. A composite material is a product containing a filler, a reinforcement and a matrix. A filler is a small fiber, flake or particle whose purpose is to displace the matrix from areas other than the reinforcement matrix interface and to assist in reinforcement. The reinforcement is a fiber, particle or a sheet whose primary purpose is to transfer load through the composite. Integration of the three elements of the composite material is accomplished by chemical adhesion by the matrix (binder) to the surfaces of the reinforcement and the filler.

This chapter covers selection of waste materials as potential components of construction composites, their development and determination of structural and aesthetic characteristics of the composite products. Production and qualification are discussed in the following chapter.

Reinforcement, filler, and matrix materials are closely related. Under certain conditions, the reinforcement and filler serve the same purpose. Under other conditions, the effectiveness of the reinforcement is directly related to the matrix. This will be evident from the data presented here. Waste economics, processability and availability are included with each appropriate section.

EVALUATION OF MATERIALS

Reinforcements

The reinforcing system in this study can serve a variety of purposes. In an organic matrix it can reinforce the resin and in many cases be the source of the resin and/or both. In an inorganic matrix it can reinforce the matrix, create voids in the matrix (syntactic foam) and/or work as a combination of both. A combination of agricultural waste, industrial waste, commercial waste and nonwaste sources were considered and will be discussed in detail.

Reinforcement Candidates: Fiber Reinforcements — Carbonized lignin: Carbonized lignin is in an extremely preliminary research state. If it would be possible to produce high strength-high modulus graphite fibers, a major market would be available in the high-rise building and even in the aerospace business. However, this development work is too preliminary to be considered for use here.

Bagasse: Bagasse is the pulp remaining from the processed sugar cane. The fibers have good mechanical properties and process well with most resins. The fibers must be processed to insure the removal of all sugar or the resulting material could be attacked by insects. The availability of the material is limited in the U.S. and highly localized. The fibers will support combustion, if exposed.

Wheat Straw (Cereal Straw): Wheat straw is the waste from the cereal harvest. These straws are relatively stiff and fragile. The surfaces have a wax or oil type film which creates difficulty in developing a surface bond. The material is plentiful but would create a collection problem. The potential mechanical properties are good but the fragile characteristics of the straw structure creates processing problems that prevent achievement of the properties. The material will support combustion if exposed to flame and will also be attacked by insects and fungi if not protected.

Bark: Bark is a waste from the lumber industry. It is available in a number of forms. Most of the outer bark materials are of large particles and are poor reinforcements. The inner materials have short discrete fibers and can be used to develop adequate mechanical properties. The fibers will support combustion and if not protected will be attacked by insects and fungi. The material is available in large quantities and is being refined into useable forms. One such product is Silvacon 412. These fibers have excellent geometric ratios and can be used as the primary reinforcement or in combinations with other reinforcements.

Kenaf: Kenaf is known as a cordage crop or a substitute for jute. It is grown in Central America and Southeast Asia. It may grow 8 to 20 feet tall and does produce a highly adaptable fiber for reinforcements. Some efforts have been made to introduce kenaf in this country by the Department of Agriculture. Efforts have been made to acquire samples of kenaf for evaluation. However, there appears to be a world-wide shortage of the fiber, which obviously does not make it a waste product. Like other organic fibers, kenaf will support combustion and can be attacked by insects or fungi if exposed.

Bamboo: Bamboo fibers have demonstrated acceptable mechanical properties. Experiments by the U.S. Army Corps of Engineers show it to be a potential reinforcement for concrete. The cane is difficult to fiberize. This results in large clumps of fiber or pith which makes it difficult to utilize in the usual approach to composite material design. The load paths become concentrated and result in premature failures of the composite. Bamboo, like all organic fibers, will support combustion and will deteriorate by insect and fungus attack if exposed. The fibers in some cases have film surfaces, such as straw, which reduce the interface bond strength. The supply is localized and limited within the United States.

Wood Chips: Wood chips are a waste product of the lumber industry. The chips, although composed of fibers, are not generally fiberized. Fiberizing is also difficult and results in short, large diameter groups of reinforcements creating internal stress problems for composite materials similar to that of bamboo. These materials are being used to produce low strength particle board on an economically acceptable basis. In general, the supply of wood chips have an already defined market and can be described as a recovered waste. The chips are affected by fire, insects and fungi if exposed.

Cotton Waste: Cotton waste is the hulls, leaves, stems and some seeds that remain after the gin process. The material is available in large quantities in the South and Southwest sections of the United States. The waste is a conglomeration of fiber sizes and particles. The mechanical properties are marginal. However, the composite can be designed to accommodate the limitations of the material. The material can be affected by fire, insects, fungi and moisture if exposed. Its availability and the size of the waste problem it generates makes it an interesting candidate for this program.

Glass Roving: Glass roving is a product produced from widely available materials. It is not a waste. However, it is readily available and provides a reinforcement of exceptional properties at an acceptable economical value. As an inorganic it resists fire, insects, fungi and moisture very well. It should be considered a candidate for use with the waste matrices and/or filler where higher performance materials are required.

Sheet Reinforcements — Paper Wastes: Paper wastes provide an excellent source for reinforcement. Although primarily available in sheet form, the material can be fiberized. There are multiple sources for providing paper waste. However, at this time waste paper can be reprocessed into new paper and a variety of other products to such an extent that in some locales a shortage exists. Waste paper provides reinforcement with excellent mechanical and physical properties, sometimes comparable to properties provided by glass roving. The fine size of the fiber promotes compatibility with a matrix.

Particle Reinforcements — Sewage Sludge: Sewage sludge is available from municipal sanitation sources. The reinforcement is primarily particulate in form with a few fibers. Mechanical properties developed by such a reinforcement are low and the process for refining and producing it is yet to be developed. Bricks have been made on an experimental basis from the material. Its use would require a major joint effort program with a large municipality. The economics could be justified only by the cost of waste removal.

Sawdust: Sawdust is a particularized waste from the lumber industry. It is being used on an economically feasible basis for a variety of products ranging from fuel to low strength particle board. When used in a composite a very dense product results. The particle size restricts mechanical properties and the large surface area requires a high matrix content to insure an adequate composite. Sawdust is also flammable. The existing application of this material in other products, and its limitations, makes it a questionable candidate here.

Rice Hulls: Rice hulls are waste from rice harvesting. The ash of the hulls have 94.5% silica content, which results in good mechanical and physical properties. The hulls have some mechanical disadvantage because of their particularized shape. The high silica content of the hull permits fire and environment protection to be accomplished with a minimal effort. Collection of the hulls can be a problem but the supply is immense, particularly in California and the Gulf Coast. Bricks and concrete have been made from rice hulls. A house was constructed of cement-rice hull blocks in Rayne, Louisiana in 1923 and is in excellent condition to date.

Plastic Scrap: Plastic scrap is derived from both municipal and industrial waste. The material can be shredded but is usually available as particles. Although the basic material generally has acceptable mechanical properties, its size and shape create some difficulty in the design of the composite, similar to that of bamboo and wood chips. The primary supply source at this time would be industrial as few municipalities have the facilities for sorting their refuse. This reinforcement would be considered for specialty applications.

Waste Glass: Waste glass is also derived from municipal and industrial waste. The material is crushed, is in particle form and has good mechanical properties. Its shape and size create composite design problems similar to those of plastic scrap. The material has been used experimentally to reinforce bricks and concrete. It can also be recycled into new glass. The economic potentials for the product in other applications in combination with its limitations for composites reduce its appeal for this program.

Miscellaneous — Previous studies conducted by MSC indicate that structural quality building panels can be constructed from polyester resin reinforced with sisal, jute and waste paper.

Ratings of Properties: The materials described above were evaluated for the following properties: tensile strength and modulus; surface-to-volume ratio; length-to-width ratio; absence of aroma; availability; and, compatibility with matrix. The rating system is presented in Table 2.1. Table 2.2 summarizes ratings for each of the reinforcement candidates evaluated. These ratings are based on the literature search. References are listed at the end of this chapter.

Table 2.1: Rating System for Reinforcements

	Points
Mechanical properties	
Tensile strength, psi	
100 and greater	5
50 to 99	4
less than 50	1
Modulus, psi	
2,000,000 and greater	5
1,000,000 to 1,999,999	4
500,000 to 999,999	3
less than 500,000	1
Surface-to-volume ratio	
High	5
Medium	3
Low	1
Length-to-width ratio	
High	5
Medium	4
Low	2

(continued)

Table 2.1: (continued)

	Points
Absence of Aroma	
None	5
Mild	2
Strong	1
Stench	0
Availability	
Available in usable state	10
Usable but in short supply	4
Raw material broadly available, collectable, process known	8
Raw material broadly available, collectable, process to be developed	7
Raw material broadly available, collection problems, process known	6
Raw material broadly available, collection problems, process to be developed	5
Raw material availability localized, collectable, process known	3
Raw material availability localized, collectable, process to be developed	2
Raw material availability localized, collection problems, process known	1
Raw material availability localized, collection problems, process to be developed	0

Source: EPA 600/8-77-006

Table 2.2: Reinforcement Rating

Reinforcement	Tensile Strength	Modulus	Surface/ Volume	Length/ Width	Absence of Aroma	Availa- bility	Score
Carbonized lignin	5	5	5	5	2	0	22
Paper	5	4	5	5	5	4	28
Sewage sludge	1	3	3	2	1	7	17
Sawdust	1	4	1	1	5	10	22
Bagasse	4	3	3	3	2	8	23
Wheat straw	4	3	5	5	2	6	25
Rice hulls	1	4	3	4	5	8	25
Bark	4	4	3	4	5	8	28
Plastic scrap	4	3	5	5	5	6	28
Kenaf	4	3	5	5	2	4	23

(continued)

Table 2.2: (continued)

Reinforcement	Tensile Strength	Modulus	Surface/ Volume	Length/ Width	Absence of Aroma	Availa- bility	Score
Bamboo	1	5	3	4	5	3	21
Wood chips	4	3	1	3	3	8	20
Waste glass	4	5	1	1	5	6	22
Cotton waste	4	4	3	4	5	3	23
Glass roving	5	5	5	5	5	5	30

Source: EPA 600/8-77-006

Materials Selected for Composite Application: Before final selection of materials for screening the possible uses of the composite bricks were examined in relation to properties exhibited by bricks made with specific fillers. The bricks could be used as primary structural materials; bearing and framing materials; secondary structural materials; and floor surface materials.

Primary Structural Materials — These are materials that are used for transferring primary loads, such as tension, compression and shear. Typical applications would be a load bearing wall surface, wall structural core such as a corrugation, roof surfaces, etc. Typical axial stress levels would range from 3,000 to 10,000 pounds per square inch, depending on design. Fiber reinforcements are the primary candidates. Glass roving, although not a waste, is inexpensive, available and can be used with any of the matrix sections. Paper is also an acceptable reinforcement but is currently less available than glass roving. Kenaf, sisal, jute and similar fibers also perform well but are in short supply. The candidates chosen, based on all the above criteria, were glass roving and waste paper.

Bearing and Framing Materials — These materials are used to transfer joint loads and close out openings. Typical applications are sill plates, window and door frames, roof and floor beams. Typical axial and bearing stress levels would range from 100 to 3,000 pounds per square inch, depending on design. For this use of brick, the candidates chosen were rice hulls, bark, plastic scrap, wood chips and cotton waste.

Secondary Structural Materials — These are materials used for nonload bearing wall and ceiling panels. Typical axial stress levels would range from 100 to 1,000 pounds per square inch, depending on the design. The candidates selected for further study in this category were rice hulls, bark, wood chips and waste paper.

Floor Surface Materials — These materials are subjected to bearing and abrasion. The reinforcing candidates selected were waste paper, rice hulls, bark and wood chips.

Table 2.3 summarizes reinforcement candidates selected for application and further screening on the basis of properties, availability and economics.

Table 2.3: Selected Reinforcing Candidates

| | . . . . .Material. . . . . | | | |
Reinforcement	Primary Structural	Bearing and Framing	Secondary Structural	Floor Surface
Glass roving	X	—	—	—
Waste paper	X	—	X	X
Rice hulls	—	X	X	X
Bark	—	X	X	X
Wood chips	—	X	X	X
Plastic scrap	—	X	—	—
Cotton waste	—	X	—	—

Source: EPA 600/2-78-091

Screening for Acceptability and Feasibility: Acceptability and feasibility of products produced from the selected reinforcing materials using both an organic and an inorganic matrix were determined. Acceptability was defined as the production of a material with properties achieving commercial standards. Feasibility of use indicated that it was possible to produce a composite brick with a particular reinforcement candidate and either an organic or inorganic matrix. Table 2.4 summarizes this data. Costs of the materials were determined FOB source and are presented in Table 2.5.

Table 2.4: Summary of Reinforcements

| | . . . . Used with. . . . . | | | |
| | . . .Organic Matrix. . . | | . . Inorganic Matrix . . | |
Reinforcement	Feasible	Acceptable	Feasible	Acceptable
Agricultural waste				
Corn cobs	X	X	—	—
Straw	X	X	X	—
Rice hulls	X	X	X	X
Cotton waste	X	X	X	X
Peanut shells	X	X	—	—
Industrial waste				
Wood bark	X	X	X	X
Sawdust	X	X	—	—
Pine shavings	X	X	—	—
Alder shavings	X	X	—	—
Douglas fir shavings	X	X	—	—
Redwood shavings	X	X	—	—
Ash shavings	X	X	—	—
Plastic scrap	—	—	X	X
Reject styrofoam beads	—	—	X	X

(continued)

Table 2.4: (continued)

Reinforcement	Organic Matrix		Inorganic Matrix	
	Feasible	Acceptable	Feasible	Acceptable
Reject graphite fibers	—	—	X	X
Sisal scrap	—	—	X	X
Fly ash	—	—	X	X
Commercial waste				
Waste paper	X	X	—	—
Paper pulp	—	—	X	X
Computer cards	—	—	X	X
Nonwaste				
Glass fibers	—	—	X	X
Silvacon 412	X	X	X	—

Source: EPA 600/8-77-006

Table 2.5: Typical Costs of Reinforcement FOB Source

Reinforcement	$/lb
Corn cobs	0.0075
Straw	0.0020–0.010*
Rice hulls	0.0020–0.0025
Cotton waste	0.0020–0.010
Peanut shells	0.0075**
Wood bark	0.01
Sawdust	0.01
Pine shavings	0.01
Alder shavings	0.01
Douglas fir shavings	0.01
Redwood shavings	0.01
Ash shavings	0.01
Plastic scrap	***
Reject styrofoam beads	0.25
Glass fibers	0.43
Silvacon 412	0.0465

*The cost would vary with demand. It will not be less than rice hulls or more than wood shavings.

**This is a nominal cost paid by shipboard manufacturer. Cost may vary 10% with supply and demand.

***Unable to establish a cost.

Source: EPA 600/8-77-006

Figure 2.1: Ratings of Reinforcements with Inorganic Matrices

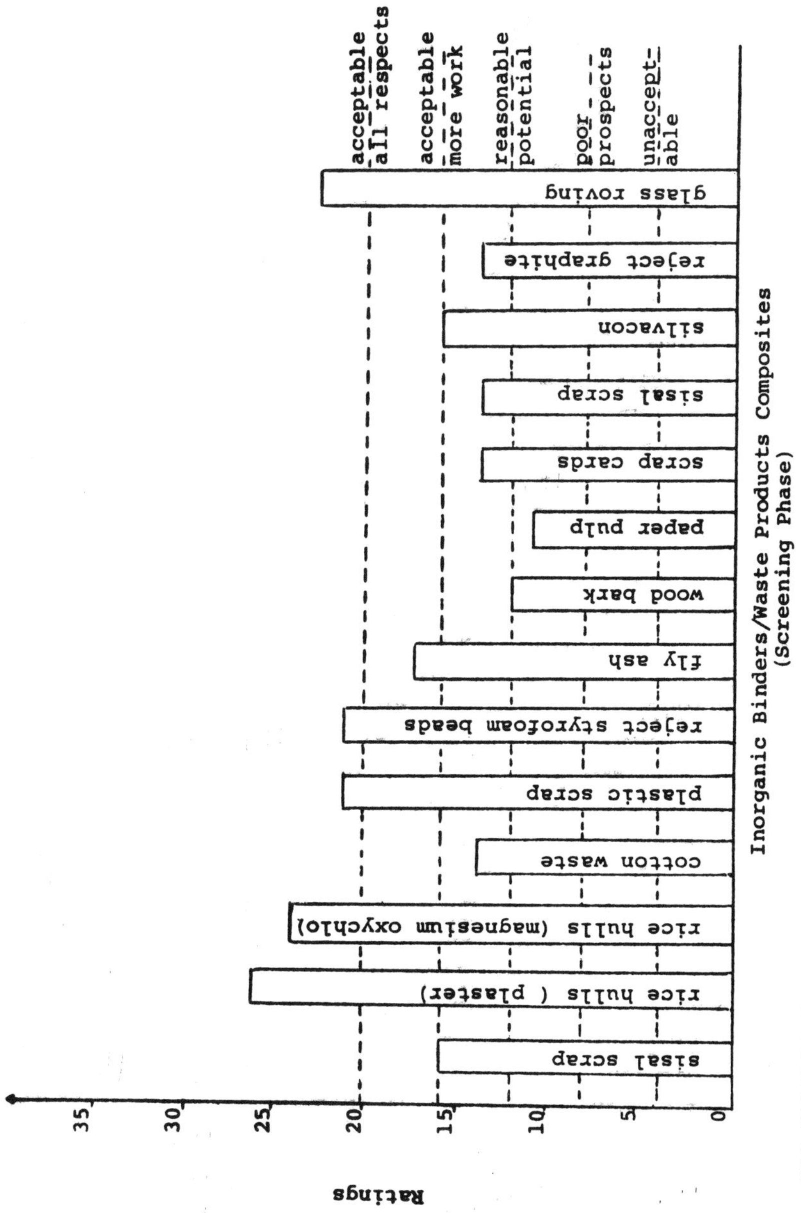

Source: EPA 600/8-77-006

Figure 2.2: Ratings of Reinforcements Use

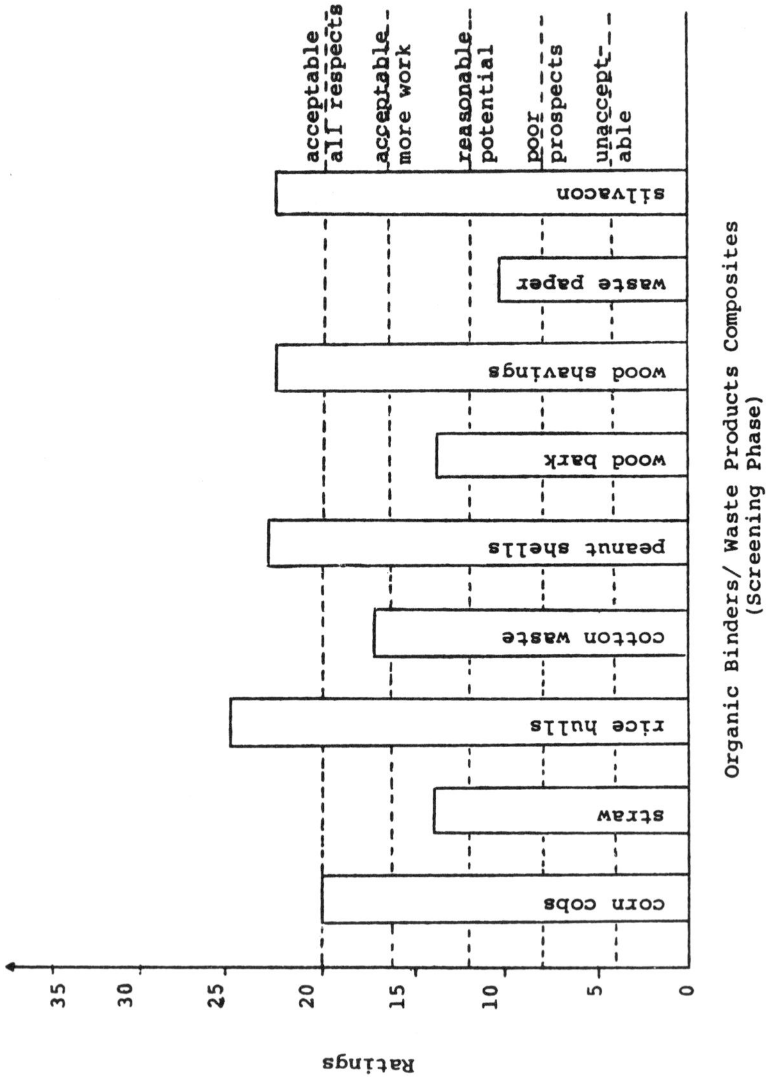

Source: EPA 600/8-77-006

Transportation costs are a function of material density; the lighter the material, the higher the per pound cost. Therefore, it would be desirable to densify the lighter materials by compacting or baling where practical.

A 500-mile transportation radius was selected as this would provide a factory with 785,400 square miles for producing waste sources. This area was considered more than adequate to supply necessary reinforcement material.

Transportation costs for some reinforcement candidates gathered within a 500-mile area are in dollars per pound: 0.0062 to 0.0125 for corn cobs; 0.014 for rice hulls; 0.013 for peanut shells and 0.010 for wood shavings.

The reinforcement candidates were rated according to product potential. Figure 2.1 illustrates the ratings for reinforcements used with inorganic matrices and Figure 2.2 shows the ratings with organic matrices. The ratings were based on availability, ease of drying, nail retention, dimensional stability, ease of processing, flammability and total materials cost and graded from 0 to 4 for each criterion. While a score of 32 represented the maximum points obtainable, the value of 20 points was established as the preferred level of selection. A rating of 16 was considered acceptable and represented average reasonable potential. For an individual criterion, a rating of 2 points represented reasonable potential. Nail retention was used as a criterion for applicability to conventional construction; the other criteria represented requirements for a feasible product.

Reinforcements Selected for Application in Composites: It was concluded that rice hulls, peanut shells, corn cobs, wood shavings and Silvacon would be the best candidates as reinforcements with an organic matrix. Cotton waste should only be considered a possible reinforcement material if the disposal problems are sufficient to counterbalance poor characteristics displayed. Straw must be pretreated to destroy or break up its resistant surface before it can be used as a reinforcer. Waste paper cannot generate furfural and, therefore, by itself was not effective. Even when used in combination with other materials it showed little promise.

Rice hulls are the best reinforcement for an inorganic matrix. Plastic scrap and reject styrofoam beads show definite promise but are limited in supply. Fly ash, sisal scrap and Silvacon are of lesser interest and all other candidates should be disregarded. Sources and availabilities of the final reinforcement candidates are summarized in Table 2.6.

Table 2.6: Source and Availability of Final Reinforcement Candidates

Reinforcement	Source
Corn cobs	
1,500–2,000 tons/yr	Cornnuts Inc., Oakland, CA
1,500–2,000 tons/yr	Seed mills in California and Midwest

(continued)

Table 2.6: (continued)

Reinforcement	Source
Rice hulls	
3,000 tons/mo	Comet Rice Mills, Houston, TX
>150 tons/mo	C.E. Grosjean Rice Milling Co., San Francisco, CA
25,000–30,000 tons/yr	Shifflet Bros., Grindley, CA
25,000–30,000 tons/yr	Louisiana and Texas
Cotton waste	
Unknown	Unknown
Peanut shells	
350,000 tons/yr	Texas, Louisiana, Georgia, Alabama, Arkansas, Mississippi, Florida
3,000 tons/mo	Gold Kist Seed Mill, Comanche, TX
Wood shavings	
Unlimited	Northwest, South and Southeast
Silvacon	
Unlimited	Weyerhauser
Plastic scrap	
Unlimited	Unknown
Reject styrofoam beads	
Limited	Unknown
Fly ash	
30×10^6 tons/yr	Coal-fired furnaces

Source EPA 600/8-77-006

Fillers

The main purposes of a filler are to improve the properties and to reduce the use of more expensive materials in the making of a matrix composite. Calcium carbonate and alumina have been used as fillers in the past. This study evaluated the possibility of utilizing wastes from the paper and wood industries as well as municipal, industrial and mining wastes.

Filler Candidates: Fillers are primarily fine particles. In specific cases fillers can be very fine fibers. The filler provides a secondary reinforcing role as well as displacing matrix.

Ash — Ash is an industrial waste resulting primarily from the burning of coal. It is also generated by other processes, such as municipal incinerators, metal refining, etc. Fly ash is produced and readily available throughout the United States with the exception of the West Coast and the Texas-Louisiana area. It is fine, inert and performs well in a composite. The material will not support combustion.

Crushed Glass — Crushed glass is derived from industrial and municipal waste. It has recyclable value and, therefore, is economically more valuable than other waste products. The primary supply source at this time would be industrial as very few municipalities have the facilities for sorting their refuse. In all probability, the glass would have to be crushed by the user. The material will not support combustion.

Phosphate Slimes — Phosphate slimes are a waste product from phosphate mining and are limited to Florida. The particles recoverable from the slime may be used as filler. Experimental studies have been made with them in brick production. The slimes have a high moisture content that must be removed before they are usable. The economics of this process makes the slimes as a filler source noncompetitive with other fillers.

Silicate Waste — Silicate waste from paper processing is applicable as a filler. The source is very local with the processing technique yet to be developed.

Shredded Refuse — Shredded refuse is adaptable as a filler material. The availability is limited because few municipalities have sorting and shredding facilities. The organic characteristics of some of the refuse would possibly react with many of the matrices and may not age well over a period of years. The variety of particles shapes and sizes would also create a problem.

Waste Plastic — Waste plastic is derived from both municipal and industrial waste. The difference between waste plastic for filler and plastic scrap for reinforcement is the particle size. Also, the mechanical property requirements are much less demanding. Surface and material compatibility with the matrix is much more important. Because of the greater surface area, flammability would be of greater concern when used as a filler.

Wood Bark — Wood bark is a waste product from the lumber industry. The fine particularized material which is unsatisfactory as a reinforcement is an advantage as a filler. As in waste plastics, the large surface area developed by these particles could make flammability a problem. The density of the material could make uniform distribution through the more dense matrix a problem. The material is widely available.

Rice Hulls — Rice hulls are waste from rice harvesting. The size may require that they be crushed for use in a true filler application. As is, the hulls develop a good syntactic foam additive. The high silica content makes rice hulls a good filler. Although not completely inert, reaction with most matrix materials is not probable. Only minimal if any protection will be required from combustion and environment. The material is widely available.

Taconite — Taconite is a waste product from iron-ore processing. Its availability is highly localized. Experimental bricks and concrete have been made from it. It would make a good filler as it can be processed very fine, is inert to most matrices and will not support combustion.

Red Mud — Red mud is a waste from aluminum processing. The material is localized in areas of Texas, Arkansas, Alabama and Louisiana. Much less of this material is available than of taconite or phosphorus slimes. When processed the particles should make fine fillers. Concrete and bricks have been made from it on an experimental basis. The material is fine, inert to most matrices, and will not support combustion.

Coal Waste — Coal waste has a potential for producing alumina which is an excellent filler. Alumina fillers have been used by Material Systems for certain of their fire-rated products for some time. The process is experimental and offers future potential.

Foundry Ash — Foundry ash and dusts from arc furnaces and sand reclaimers have been used experimentally as fillers in epoxy resins. The supply will be localized with small outputs when compared to other candidates. The fly ash discussion will apply to foundry ash also.

Sawdust — Sawdust is a waste product of the lumber industry. The discussion on sawdust as a reinforcement applies here also with the exception that the fine particles are an advantage. The large surface area of this organic material could make flammability a problem. Uniform distribution through the composites could be a problem because of its density.

Miscellaneous — Material Systems Corporation has been using calcium carbonate and alumina as fillers in production of polyester glass reinforced laminates for some time. These are relatively inexpensive materials which work well.

Ratings of Properties: Filler candidates were evaluated against the following criteria: destructive reactivity and rate of reaction; temperature of decomposition (at least 750°F or 399°C); grindability and fineness of mesh; density; absence of aroma; performance with various matrices and reinforcement materials; and availability.

The rating system appears in Table 2.7. Table 2.8 shows the ratings of the fillers tested. These ratings are based on an examination of the literature. References may be found at the end of this chapter.

Table 2.7: Rating System for Fillers

	Points
Reactive to Matrix Material*	
Inert	5
Very slow (20 years)	4
Slow (15 years)	3
Medium (10 years)	2
Rapid (5 years)	1

(continued)

Table 2.7: (continued)

	Points
Decomposability	
Undecomposed to above 2000°F	5
Undecomposed below 2000°F	4
Undecomposed below 1500°F	3
Undecomposed below 1000°F	2
Undecomposed below 750°F	1
Grindability	
300 mesh or better	5
200–300 mesh	4
100–200 mesh	3
50–100 mesh	2
Less than 50 mesh	1
Density	
Specific gravity	5
Absence of Aroma	
None	5
Mild	2
Strong	1
Stench	0
Availability	
Available in usable state	10
Usable but in short supply	4
Raw material broadly available, collectable, process known	8
Raw material broadly available, collectable, process to be developed	7
Raw material broadly available, collection problems, process known	6
Raw material broadly available, collection problems, to be developed	5
Raw material availability localized, collectable, process known	3
Raw material availability localized, collectable, process to be developed	2
Raw material availability localized, collection problems, process known	1
Raw material availability localized, collection problems, to be developed	0

*In destructive sense.

Source: EPA 600/8-77-006

Table 2.8: Evaluation of Fillers

Filler	Reactive to Matrices	Decompos- ability	Grind- ability	Density	Absence of Aroma	Avail- ability	Score
Ash	5	5	5	3	5	8	31
Crushed glass	5	4	5	3	5	5	27
Phosphate slimes	3	4	5	4	2	2	20
Silicate waste	5	4	5	3	2	2	21
Shredded refuse	2	3	3	4	2	7	21
Waste plastic	3	1	5	4	5	1	19
Wood bark	4	1	4	4	2	8	23
Rice hulls	5	3	3	5	5	6	27
Taconite	4	3	5	3	5	3	23
Red mud*	4	3	5	3	2	2	19
Coal waste**	5	5	5	3	5	2	25
Foundry ash	5	5	5	3	5	2	25
Sawdust	3	2	5	5	5	4	24

*Aluminum ore
**Recovered alumina

Source: EPA 600/8-77-006

Fillers Selected for Application: The acid reaction of furfuryl alcohol, which will be discussed in the Matrices Section, requires the selection of nonneutralizing fillers. Therefore, the pH of the fillers may be important. The primary inorganic filler candidate is fly ash (pH 5.5) which may be used with both organic and inorganic matrices. The remaining inorganic candidates from Table 2.8 are not economically viable because of the limited locations of their sources. It is recommended that, because of flammability, only inorganic fillers be considered with organic matrices.

Final compositions from the inorganic matrices are nonflammable despite the utilization of large quantities of organic fillers and reinforcements. As a consequence, serious thought can be given to the use of scrap plastics extracted from dumps and manufacturers. Scrap styrofoam is most adaptable for formulation into syntactic foams. Other plastics of higher density could be made more suitable by shredding and/or grinding to increase surface area. The thermoplastic resins are especially useful since they melt within their confinement in the inorganic matrix to produce a true foam from a syntactic foam. If scrap plastic can be so used in the construction industry, the ecological and economic advantages would be considerable. This could eliminate in many instances the need for more costly photodegradable resins. This same fact permits the selection of wood bark, rice hulls and sawdust as filler candidates for the inorganic matrix.

Fly Ash — Fly ash was the primary candidate considered because of its universal availability. The first application was as a filler for polyester fiber glass reinforced composites. Samples were made on the MSC continuous laminate production process. Fly ash-filled specimens exhibited mechanical and physical properties

equivalent to calcium carbonate-filled specimens in addition to excellent retention of appearance after 1,500 hours of continuous exposure in an accelerated
weathering test.

Since transportation is the significant element of cost in both, only the amount
of utilization can be used for cost effective evaluation. Fly ash unfortunately exhibits a thixotropic behavior in polyester resin, which results in decreased viscos-
ity with application of pressure or force. This limits the concentration of material usable. Tests demonstrated that a maximum level of 75 parts per hundred of
resin can be used. This compares to 100 parts of calcium carbonate per 100 parts
of resin which is feasible. For a given amount of resin-filler mix, the fly ash would
require more resin and, therefore, be a less effective filler for inorganic waste
composites. Fly ash can be used as a one-to-one replacement for calcium carbonate or casting plaster when used as a filler with the MSC inorganic matrix.
There is a color problem if the material is to be exposed because the fly-ash products range from dark grey to almost black.

Though the optimum concentration of fly ash in the polyester matrix was lower
than the calcium carbonate in the same matrix, fly ash could be used in equivalent amounts to calcium carbonate in MSC's inorganic matrix. The overall performance of fly ash as a filler with either matrix was very promising. Fly ash obtained the highest rating of all the fillers evaluated (see Table 2.8). Calcium carbonate and fly ash cost about the same. Therefore, use of fly ash as a filler is
cost-effective only in that this use effectively disposes of a waste material.

Ineffective Fillers — The ineffective fillers were sawdust, paper pulp, waste paper
and computer cards. They were tested with conventional organic systems, the
waste organic system and the MSC inorganic matrix.

Matrix Materials—General

The matrix is a binder which integrates the filler and the reinforcement and
causes the composite to perform as a single material. This is accomplished by
chemical adhesion of the matrix to the surface of the reinforcement and the filler. Both organic and inorganic matrices were considered. Organic matrices offer
versatility in processing; inorganic matrices provide a high degree of nonflammability to the final product.

Matrix Candidates: Dialdehyde Starches — The dialdehyde starches are derived
from starch-producing vegetation, such as corn, and are reactive with protein-
type materials, such as animal blood. The source of supply for the raw material
is plentiful. Considerable exploration has been made with it for glue applications
for bonding plywood panels. The material requires pressure and time for cure
which limits it to a batch-type process. The interfacial adherence to reinforcements is unknown as is the reaction as a binder rather than an adhesive. The
flame resistance for building structures would not be as good as other candidates. The ability of the material to weather as an exposed matrix would also be
questionable.

Furfural and Furfuryl Alcohol — Furfural and furfuryl alcohol based resins are in use and have been utilized as molding compounds and matrices for reinforced composites. Quaker Oats Company has limited production on a furfuryl alcohol based resin (Quacor) where the furfural is derived from oat hulls. Furfural is unique in that it can be derived from a wide variety of sources, such as manure, oat hulls, rice hulls, corn cobs, bagasse (sugar cane), all types of cereal straws, bark and wood chips. The resin cures rapidly with minimal pressure which permits continuous processing. It is also nonflammable and generates very little smoke. The weathering would appear to be good, also. The mechanical properties are equivalent to or superior to polyester laminating resins.

Cellulose — Cellulose can be reacted in a variety of ways to create a binder. The material can be derived from wood waste, cereal straw and manure. It has been evaluated experimentally to produce particle board. The mechanical properties appear to be marginal for primary-type structures. The system requires heat, pressure, and time for cure which limits it to a batch process. It would not be very fire resistant and would generate smoke. The evaluation of its use in particle board would indicate poor weathering ability.

Phenols — Phenols have been a basis for a variety of resins for a number of years. The phenols are best derived from wood waste. The resin requires heat and pressure for cure but very little time. These factors can be adjusted if combined with furfurals. As it exists, it would be limited to a batch process. It should perform well as a flame-resistant material. Mechanical properties are good but the system will require modification for weathering.

Lignin Sulfonic Acids — Lignin sulfonic acids are derived from the residues left after the kraft and bisulfite treating for wood pulp. There are large quantities of these materials now available and unused. The lignin is another source for phenolic resins and can be reacted with furfurals or formaldehyde.

Inorganic Resins — Inorganic resins are generally of the cement variety, which requires a refractory or fired-type system. Material Systems Corporation has developed an inorganic resin, derived from magnesium oxychloride and sulfates, that is cured at room temperature. This material is lightweight (0.045 lb/in^3), has excellent mechanical properties, is fire resistant and does not generate smoke. The material is formulated from seawater-derived chemicals. Although it is not a waste product, it does not expend natural resources.

Ratings of Properties: The matrix materials were rated on: curability temperature; absence of aroma; processability (time required, pressure and temperature); physical state; toxicity; decomposability; color; and, availability. A detailed explanation of the meanings assigned to these terms and the rating system employed is found in Table 2.9. Table 2.10 summarizes the ratings and gives the final scores for the matrices considered. References to the literature on which these ratings are based are found at the end of the chapter.

Table 2.9: Rating System for Matrices

	Points
Curability, °F	
Ambient–150	5
151–250	4
251–350	3
351–450	2
451 and over	1
Noncurability	0
Absence of aroma	
No odor in precursor compound or final form	5
Mild odor in precursor compound and none in final form	4
Processability	
Time required, min	
2–10	5
10–12	4
12–14	3
15–60	2
$<2, >60$	1
Pressure, roller, psi	
0–15	5
16–25	4
26–50	3
51–100	2
>100	1
Temperature, °F	
Ambient–150	5
151–250	4
251–350	3
351–450	2
450 and over	1
Physical form	
Liquid	5
Soluble solid	4
Insoluble solid, fusible below 350°F	3
Insoluble solid, fusible below 500°F	1
Inprocessable, by standards used	0
Toxicity	
Nontoxic	5
Noxious	3
Toxic	0

(continued)

Table 2.9: (continued)

	Points
Decomposability, °F	
Undecomposed to 600	5
Undecomposed to 550	4
Undecomposed to 500	3
Undecomposed to 400	2
Undecomposed below 400	1
Color	
None	3
Light	2
Dark	1
Black	0
Availability	
Available in usable state	10
Usable but in short supply	4
Raw material broadly available, collectable process known	8
Raw material broadly available, collectable, process to be developed	7
Raw material broadly available, collection problems, process known	6
Raw material availability localized, collectable, process known	3
Raw material availability localized, collection problems, process known	1
Raw material availability localized, collection problems, to be developed	0

Source: EPA 600/8-77-006

Table 2.10: Matrix Ratings

	Curability	Absence of Aroma	Time	Pressure	Temperature	Physical Form	Toxicity	Decomposability	Color	Availability	Score
Dialdehyde/protein starches	5	5	1	1	5	3	5	1	1	8	35
Furfurals (manure)	5	4	5	5	5	5	5	5	0	6	45

(continued)

Table 2.10: (continued)

	Curability	Absence of Aroma	Time	Pressure	Temperature	Physical Form	Toxicity	Decomposability	Color	Availability	Score
Furfurals (rice hulls, bagasse)	5	4	5	5	5	5	5	5	0	8	47
Inorganics (cement)	5	5	1	5	5	3	5	5	2	10	46
Cellulose (reactants)	3	4	5	2	3	4	5	1	2	6	35
Phenols	3	4	5	1	3	5	5	5	1	6	38
Lignin	3	4	5	2	3	5	5	3	1	7	38

Source: EPA 600/8-77-006

Matrices Selected for Application: Furfural, phenols, and inorganic matrices offer the most potential and are in a sufficient level of development to permit their
consideration here.

The phenol family of resins based on the condensation polymerization of a phenol with an aldehyde are versatile and strong. The most common resin is based
on phenol and formaldehyde. Many variations can be synthesized from these
two reactants. One possible variation of the phenolic family is to replace formaldehyde with different aldehydes. By and large this route has not been pursued
vigorously because of economics; these aldehydes are all more expensive than
formaldehyde or processing of the resin is more difficult because, for example,
of decreased solubility in low-boiling solvents such as isopropanol.

In light of our interest to utilize waste materials, phenolic resins based on furfural appear to be particularly attractive. Resins based on the furan ring system
have excellent nonflammability and very low smoke formation. Furfuryl alcohol
is made by hydrolysis and dehydration of pentoses in rice hulls, corn cobs, oat
hulls, manure, and other sources to afford furfural which is then hydrogenated.
Furfural as such is also highly reactive and condenses with phenols to give resinous products.

Accessory investigations conducted on the inorganic matrix have demonstrated
definite potential for a variety of waste materials. Of particular interest are cotton waste, shredded paper, wood-bark fibers, sisal waste, ground styrofoam scrap,

rice hulls and electric hopper fly ash. Those materials which are highly absorptive, e.g., bark fibers and sisal waste, lead to high density compositions because of absorption of the matrix; this can be overcome either by foaming or preparation as a syntactic foam.

Most of the above waste materials show possible use as nonflammable wood substitutes. Preliminary studies indicate excellent nailability, sawability and screw retention and at a materials cost less than prices for wooden 2" x 4" stock. Compositions using rice hulls show excellent heat insulation. After 2 hours of exposure to propane air torch impinging perpendicular to the face of a 1-inch thick sample, heat penetration was insufficient to char a piece of masking tape on the rear face of the sample.

Inorganic — The inorganic matrix is produced from constituents removed from seawater. The large available quantity of the basic raw materials and the ability for the matrix to react with compatibility with a variety of waste materials make it a prime candidate for this program. The resulting composites have a higher modulus than those from organic matrices and are nonflammable. This makes the material applicable to high-rise structures.

Inorganic matrices selected for application were the MSC inorganic resins and commercial cements. Organic and inorganic matrices and their development will be discussed in further detail below.

Organic Matrices

Furfural-type matrices were selected as the most promising organic system. The selection was based on considerations above, which may be summarized as follows:

Some of the most versatile and strong resins commercially available are based on the condensation polymerization of a phenol with an aldehyde. Though formaldehyde is normally used, it is possible to replace this chemical with other aldehydes. In practice this is rarely done because of expense and technological difficulties in processing. Furfural and furfuryl alcohol based resins are in use and have been utilized as molding compounds and matrices for reinforced composites.

Furfuryl alcohol is made by hydrolysis and dehydration of pentoses in rice hulls, corn cobs, oat hulls, manures, etc. to produce furfural which is then hydrogenated. Furfural in turn is highly reactive and known to condense with phenols to give resinous products.

Chemically the pentosan (from oat hulls, corn cobs and rice hulls) is hydrolyzed to pentose which, in turn, is cyclized to furfural (equations 1 and 2, respectively, shown on the following page).

Equation 1

$$\text{pentosan} \xrightarrow[\text{H}_2\text{O, H}^+]{\text{hydrolysis, hot HCl}} \begin{array}{c} \text{H} \\ | \\ \text{C}=\text{O} \\ | \\ \text{H}-\text{C}-\text{OH} \\ | \\ \text{H}-\text{C}-\text{OH} \\ | \\ \text{H}-\text{C}-\text{OH} \\ | \\ \text{H}-\text{C}-\text{OH} \\ | \\ \text{H} \end{array}$$

pentosan

(from oat hulls,
corn cobs, rice
hulls)

pentose

Equation 2

$$\begin{array}{c} \text{CHO} \\ | \\ (\text{CHOH})_3 \\ | \\ \text{CH}_2\text{OH} \end{array} \xrightarrow[\text{ring closure}]{-3\text{H}_2\text{O}} \text{furfural}$$

furfural
(2-furancarboxyaldehyde)

Furfural condenses with phenols to give resinous products in the manner illustrated on the following page.

It would be very useful to obtain a construction material based on furfural-phenol resins obtained from waste materials without the cost-increasing step of isolating the reactants. The in situ reaction of the furfural generated would also eliminate the cost of catalytic hydrogenation to furfuryl alcohol and the need to add presynthesized aldehyde to the phenol-containing wood waste.

The process was initially visualized as permitting the furfural to remain in solution and then adding phenol-containing wood waste material or lignins from wood pulp waste to form furfural-phenol resins. It was thought that by finely dividing the rice hulls, corn cobs or other sources of pentose prior to reaction, it would be possible to allow these fibrals to remain in the material to act as additional fillers. If this did not prove feasible, then the resin would be isolated, and the material formed and heated to finish the condensation.

Three approaches to the use of a furfural-phenol matrix were considered and will be discussed in detail. They are: development of a matrix using a commercial furfuryl alcohol source with waste materials chosen for reinforcement and filler candidates as an evaluation of furfural potential in construction; a three-step in situ formation of furfural with addition of organic resins or resin precursors; a simpler two-step process for in situ formulation of furfural from waste without added organic resins or resin precursors.

As shown in the following, the phenol reacts with the furfural to form an ortho- or para-hydroxyfurfural phenol. The hydroxyfurfural phenol then reacts with another molecule of phenol, resulting in the loss of one molecule of water to form a compound in which the two rings are joined by a furan-substituted carbon. This process continues to yield a product of high molecular weight. Since three positions of each phenol molecule are susceptible to attack (namely, the 2, 4 and 6 carbons or the 2 ortho and the 1 para positions), the final product contains numerous crosslinks and hence has a rigid structure.

Development of a Matrix Using a Commercial Furfuryl Source: The formulation of the resin was tested using Quacor, a furfuryl alcohol-based resin. This gave the opportunity of testing a resulting matrix material theoretically similar to the expected in situ resin produced by either the two- or three-step process.

A series of commercial formulations were prepared (Tables 2.11 and 2.13). Two experimental runs were conducted on the MSC continuous process machinery. The first run used resin mixes twice as viscous as that of the production polyester mix. Line speed was 3 feet per minute and production speed was between 5 and 10 feet per minute. Three ovens were used at temperatures of 77°, 82° and 99°C, respectively. None of the formulations were fully cured after treatment in oven 3. After overnight air-cure and post curing at 127° and 141°C for ten minutes at each temperature (A) and (B) were fully cured. Table 2.12 shows the results of evaluated variations in fillers and catalysts. Oven 1 was set at 71°C, oven 2 at 102°C and oven 3 at 177°C. All samples appeared well cured after oven 3, though some samples were post cured at 177°C for two hours. The results of mechanical and flame spread tests are shown in Tables 2.12 and 2.14.

Table 2.11: Formulations for Run 1*

For-mula	Resin**	Solvent	Catalyst**	Filler
	. . . . (grams)			
A	RP100A (2,000)	furfuryl alcohol (100)	RP104B (60)	Huber 35*** (1,200)
B	RX300 (2,000)	furfuryl alcohol (100)	RP104B (60)	Huber 35*** (1,200)
C	RP100A (2,000)	furfuryl alcohol (100)	RP104B (60)	CP† (1,800)

  *Each formulation also included 25 grams of TiO_2 in furfuryl alcohol (75% TiO_2, 25% furfuryl alcohol).
  **Quacor.
***Huber 35 is a fine clay with acidic pH.
  †Casting plaster.

Source: EPA 600/8-77-006

Table 2.12: Evaluation of Run 1 (Formulations A and B)

Formulation	Density (lb/m^3)	Smoke*	Flame Spread**	Glass Fiber (%)	Tensile Strength (psi)
A	0.052	5	25	29	5,240
B	0.069	0	17	28	5,544
Control***	—	400	100	—	2,000–5,000

  *National Bureau of Standards Technique (American Instrument Co., Smoke Density Chamber).
  **ASTM E-84-70 Test (modified).
***Commercial building materials.

Source: EPA 600/8-77-006

Table 2.13: Formulations for Run 2

For- mula	Resin*	Solvent	Catalyst*	Filler
	. . . .	(parts per hundred	of resin)	. . . .
D	RP100A (100)	furfuryl alcohol (5)	RP104B (3)	Huber 35 (60)
E	RP100A (100)	furfuryl alcohol (5)	RP104B (3)	Huber 35 (80)
F	RP100A (100)	furfuryl alcohol (5)	RP104B (3)	Huber 35 (100)
G	RX300 (100)	furfuryl alcohol (5)	RP104B (3)	Huber 35 (60)
H	RP100A (100)	furfuryl alcohol (5)	RP104B (3)	C-31** (60)
I	RP100A (100)	furfuryl alcohol (5)	RP104B (4)	C-31** (60)
J	RP100A (100)	furfuryl alcohol (5)	RP104B (4)	Huber 35 (60)
K	RP100A (100)	furfuryl alcohol (5)	RP104B (4)	Huber 35 (60)

  *Quacor.
**Alumina hydrate.

Source: EPA 600/8-77-006

Table 2.14: Evaluation of Run 2 (Formulations D through K)

| | . . . . Flame Spread . . . . | | . . Tensile Strength, psi . . | |
Formulation	As Cured	Postcured	As Cured	Postcured
D	37	16	6,850	8,015
E	20	12	5,480	6,020
F	20	25	3,680	4,050
G	16	18	7,380	6,310
H	31	18	5,080	4,890
I	33	18	4,175	4,780
J	33	27	3,490	3,560
K	22	18	7,630	7,600
Control*	. . . . . . 100		. . . . 2,000–5,000	

  *Commercial building material.

Source: EPA 600/8-77-006

Conclusions — It was concluded that furfural is processable on the production system and will develop a product equivalent to or superior to the presently qualified product. The studies indicated no insurmountable difficulty in processing composites based on matrix resins using the furan ring system.

To prepare an aesthetic surface for use as exterior wall panels, it was found most effective to add crushed rock, glass, plastic, etc. to the composite on the belt, and then cure the entire system.

Three-Step Process of In Situ Formation with Additives: As indicated, furfural can be derived from rice hulls or corn cobs by acid hydrolysis under pressure. The purpose of this study was to determine if pressure was really necessary; and, determine yield of furfural at lower pressures. The additives were used to interact with the furfural, and/or stimulate furfural formation, and/or reinforce and absorb excess furfural.

It was theorized that a novolak resin would be formed in situ by refluxing rice hulls (source of furfural) with wood bark (source of phenol) at atmospheric pressure. Addition of a furfural or hexamethylenetetramine seed would produce further crosslinking. After preparation, rice hulls were refluxed with dilute hydrochloric acid followed by addition of phenol and further refluxing. The mix was air dried; hexamethylenetetramine was added and the resulting material molded at 150°C and 250 psi. There was no flow, the molding was resin-starved and easily breakable.

A second series of experiments was carried out refluxing the rice hulls in dilute hydrochloric acid with phenol present initially. Molding trials were conducted on the hydrolysis mixtures after addition of Silvacon 412 as a filler and 10% dry weight of chopped glass fibers as reinforcement.

Tests performed on the hydrolysis mixture did not determine the exact yield of furfural. However, it was concluded that with an approximate 3 to 6% acid concentration and refluxing at 100°C for 15 to 20 hours, it was possible to produce enough furfural to give a moldable material. A lower acid concentration (1%) and shorter reflux time (3 to 5 hours) did not produce a moldable product.

Successful resins were also obtained by refluxing rice hulls or corn cobs without bark or other phenolic materials present. After hydrolysis, Silvacon 412 was added to absorb excess furfural and act as a filler. Addition of shredded newspaper reinforced the composite which was cured for 20 minutes at 150°C and 500 psi.

The effect of different concentrations of wood bark on the hydrolysis mixture was also investigated. Addition of hexamethylenetetramine improved the integrity of the moldings. Table 2.15 gives various formulations for the hydrolysis mixture and Table 2.16 gives formulations for various molding mixtures.

The mixtures shown in the tables produced crosslinked resins, insoluble in water and retaining much of their strength after 24 hours of water immersion. An attempt to produce moldings by adding alkali after initial acid hydrolysis was not successful, producing water-soluble resins.

The yield of furfural was investigated under various reaction conditions including reaction time, change of acid and mechanical agitation. The amount of furfural was determined by titrametric analysis using sodium bisulfite.

The yields of furfural were studied after 3, 10 and 20 hours. It is not certain that the reaction came to equilibrium kinetically. After 20 hours, rice hulls gave a yield of 4.13% furfural and corn cobs yielded from 3.27 to 10.93%. Mechanical stirring did not improve the yield of furfural. Replacing hydrochloric acid with sulfuric acid did not alter the yield of furfural produced from rice hulls. The yield from acid hydrolysis of corn cobs was 50% lower with the sulfuric acid.

All compositions discussed were compression molded in duplicate (20 minutes at 150°C and 500 psi) and dried overnight at 40°C in an air-circulating oven. The samples measured 1" x 6" and were approximately ¼" thick. It was found that:

> Modulus of rupture increased with density for mixtures containing no wood bark, and a high proportion of wood bark, rice hulls/wood bark, and corn cobs/wood bark;
>
> addition of newspaper did not seem to improve modulus of rupture, and in some cases even lowered density and strength;
>
> addition of furfural (samples C, F) or addition of furfuryl alcohol (G, H) did not improve the strength.

Table 2.15: Composition of Hydrolysis/Condensation Mixtures

Mix No.	Corn Cobs (g)	Rice Hulls (g)	Wood Bark (g)	HCl (ml)	Water (ml)	Silvacon 412* (g)
1	120	—	—	12	200	50
2	120	—	60	12	200	70
3	120	—	90	12	200	70
4	120	—	120	12	220	60
5	—	30	—	3	115	40
6	—	30	15	3	115	30
7	—	30	22.5	3	115	30
8	—	30	30	3	115	30

*Added after completion of hydrolysis.

Table 2.16: Formulation of Molding Mixtures

Sample	Wet Mixture* (g)	Furfural (ml)	Furfuryl Alcohol (ml)	Newspaper (g)
. . . . Mixtures 1 and 5				
A	35	—	—	—
B	35	—	—	3
C	35	1	—	2
. . . . .Mixtures 2, 3, 4, 6, 7 and 8				
D	24	—	—	—
E	—	—	—	2
F	24	1	—	2
G	24	—	1	2
H	24	—	2	2

*Wet mixture is the hydrolysis mixture plus Silvacon.

Source: EPA 600/8-77-006

Two-Step Process of In Situ Furfural Formation from Wastes Without Additives:
It was discovered that after acid treatment cellulose and pentosan containing materials yield a binder during molding. Initial work was conducted on wheat straw, rice hulls and corn cobs. Acids used were 3% solutions of hydrochloric acid, phosphoric acid, oxalic acid, chromic acid, p-toluene sulfonic acid and hydrochloric acid with 1% aluminum chloride. The materials tested were soaked in acid solution for an arbitrary 30 minutes, after which they were dried at room temperature or oven-dried at 50° to 60°C. The treated materials were molded for 5 minutes at 120° to 150°C and 500 psi.

The p-toluene sulfonic acid was most successful; oxalic acid and boric acid failed to catalyze binder formation; chromic acid and the hydrochloric acid plus aluminum chloride mixture caused charring. Table 2.17 summarizes acid treatment effects.

Table 2.17: Acid Treatment for Short Periods

Sample	Material	Acid Treatment Time (min)	Temp (°C)	Molding* Time (min)	Pressure (psi)	Density	Rupture Modulus (psi)
YT-64	Ash + 3% H_3PO_4	1	24	3	300	0.79	1,205
YT-64	Ash + 3% H_3PO_4	1	24	3	500	1.08	2,023
YT-64	Ash + 3% H_3PO_4	1	80	3	300	0.78	993
YT-64	Ash + 3% H_3PO_4	1	80	3	500	1.10	2,570
YT-46	Rice hulls + 3% p-toluene sulfonic acid	1	24	5	500	**	**
YT-46	Rice hulls + 5% p-toluene sulfonic acid	5	60	5	500	1.10	1,308

*Temperature of 140°C.
**Dry, falls apart, no resin formed.

Source: EPA 600/8-77-006

These experiments clearly demonstrate the feasibility of industrial processing. In any specific case, optimal treatment parameters should be investigated, depending on the types of wood and particle size distribution.

Cotton waste was successfully molded with hydrochloric acid, phosphoric acid and p-toluene sulfonic acid. The main source of binder seemed to be the dried stalks and flower pods. Wheat straw composites did not weather well, containing a great deal of pith not removed by initial blending. Wood wastes gave excellent results on treatment with phosphoric acid, giving moldable materials without need of an added binder. Wood wastes of particle size less than 4 mesh gave the best final products.

Testing — The molded wood specimens and rice hull moldings were submitted to an accelerated weathering test carried out in an Atlas Electric Weatherometer Model HVDC. The samples were compared to commercial and industrial grade particle board (44 lb/ft^3 and 55 lb/ft^3 density, respectively). The properties compared well, though the specimens were not intended for external use. Samples with mixed size particles showed the best surface condition after weatherometer testing.

Two flammability tests were perfomed on: industrial grade particle board (the control); molded rice hulls (YT-46); molded white pine (YT-58); and, molded ash (YT-64). The flame-spread test (Test 3030) results showed that the molded rice hulls were the least-flammable product. The industrial particle board was the most flammable of the samples (Table 2.18). The molded wood samples were self-extinguishing. The smoke generated by the molded rice hulls was very low. Again, the particle board produced the most smoke.

Nail and screw retention tests of the wood waste moldings were conducted to determine material workability. The results were equivalent to those for industrial particle board. Rice hull moldings showed inferior nail and screw retention. A summary of all properties of the molded materials is found in Table 2.18.

The molded wood waste and rice hulls showed good mechanical properties without an external binder, when molded at pressures above 300 psi. A pressure of 500 psi gave the best results. It was felt that the addition of an external binder might reduce the need for high pressure. The binder should be reactive at low pH and be inexpensive.

Incorporation of ITT Rayoner Binders HT-115 and Raylig-A1 — Wood particles and rice hulls were soaked in a 10% aqueous solution of HT-115. The excess was decanted, the particles dried, soaked in 3% phosphoric acid and dried following removal of excess acid. The particles were molded at 150°C and 500 psi for 5 minutes. Both rice hulls and ash particles receiving the same treatment were dry and broke more easily than without addition of HT-115.

Soaking in a solution of Raylig-A1 and 3% phosphoric acid was followed by molding at 150°C and 500 psi for 5 minutes. Though rice hulls showed 30% improvement in strength, when the molded specimens were put into water, they softened and were easily broken.

Inorganic Matrices

The studies in this task involved two types of matrices and two types of composites. The matrices considered were an MSC inorganic matrix derived from magnesium oxychloride and sulfates and various classes of commercial plasters. The MSC system is more expensive than the plaster, but is stronger and more resistant to environmental effects. The plaster systems are less expensive and more processable, but must be protected from moisture.

Table 2.18: Properties of Molded Materials Without External Binder

	Sample									
	YT-126	YT-46	YT-58C	YT-61C	YT-63C	YT-64C	YT-33	YT-49	YT-51	Control
Waste material	peanut shells	rice hulls	pine	alder	redwood	ash	corn cobs, rich hulls	wheat straw, rice hulls	cotton waste	particle board*
Acid	phosphoric	p-toluene sulfonic	phosphoric	phosphoric	phosphoric	phosphoric	hydrochloric	p-toluene sulfonic	phosphoric	—
Molding, 0.3″ thick										
Temp, °C	170	150	150	150	150	150	150	130	150	—
Time, min	15	5	3	5	3	3	5	5	8	—
Pressure, psi	500	500	500	500	500	500	500	500	500	—
Density, g/cm^3	1.00	1.08	1.06	1.03	1.11	1.02	0.95	1.14	1.09	0.88
Rupture modulus, psi	2,400	1,322	2,297	2,148	3,236	3,188	1,034	1,965	1,327	1,500
Straight nail pull, lb	—	13	39	—	—	67	—	—	—	56
Straight screw pull, lb	—	130	252	—	—	378	—	—	—	296
Flame spread	—	58	95	—	—	123	—	—	—	127
Smoke number	200	51	315	—	—	198	—	—	—	345
Water soak, 9 days										
Weight gain, %	—	27	23	39	54	29	—	—	—	64
Thickness gain, %	15	13	12	21	11	9	—	—	—	22
Hardness, Shore										
Before test	80	64	75	64	71	80	—	—	—	70
After test	60	55	40	36	63	58	—	—	—	50
Weatherometer, 350 hr										
Weight loss, %	—	17	18	20	17	30	—	**	**	14
Thickness gain, %	—	27	4	25	3	4	—	***	†	22

*Industrial. **Badly weathered after 115 hours. ***Warped fibers exposed. †Swollen.

Source: EPA 600/8-77-006

Unlike the organic material, an elemental panel of an inorganic system does not offer a product. Instead, the materials had to be directed towards a functional application. All such applications require at least two elements. One element is a high density surface for strength, wear, and appearance; and the other is a low density core for stiffness, weight reduction, insulation, and cost. Therefore, this program developed a high density structural composite, defined here as a laminate and a low density core composite, defined here as a foam

Laminate Development: Magnesium oxychloride was used in the MSC inorganic matrix. It has been used for floor construction and interior stucco surfaces for many years and MSC has previously studied its use as an efficient matrix.

The matrix was produced on MSC continuous processing machinery. Glass fibers were used as the reinforcement. The material was deposited on a tray and allowed to cure at room temperature overnight. One-half was covered with an impermeable Mylar film. The panel was then removed and permitted to continue its curing at room temperature for 28 days.

Figure 2.3, on the following page, shows the tensile strength of the machine-deposited laminate after testing at 6, 11, 18 and 28 days. The higher values for days 6 and 11 are questionable and may be attributed to test scatter. These results show that it is feasible to process the inorganic matrix continuously when a faster cure is developed.

A number of waste materials were tested as reinforcers. They included rice hulls, wood, Silvacon, paper, straw and cotton waste. The glass fibers were so superior to the wastes in performance that other reinforcements were disregarded. Systems, such as paper, which deteriorated when wet were completely unsatisfactory. Since the laminate is only part of the inorganic product, a limited utilization of an inexpensive commercially available material was considered consistent with the study.

Studies Conducted on the Laminate — Figure 2.4a shows the effect of fiber length on strength. As can be seen, the longer the fiber the greater the strength. Two inches is the practical limit for processing. The superiority of a two-inch fiber is further demonstrated in Figure 2.4b, which evaluates the effect of fiber content. Since the interfacial shear strength of the inorganic matrix is low compared to that of a polyester, a longer fiber would be expected to develop greater strength.

The tensile values were recorded in pounds per inch of width. Thus, variance in thickness was not accounted for, resulting in the test scatter shown. On an analytical basis, a higher fiber content should develop greater strength. However, under certain processing conditions and with certain matrices, a saturation point is developed where additional fibers provide limited improvement.

The susceptibility of inorganic laminate fabrications to moisture was also evaluated. After water immersion, the laminate deteriorated in both strength and in

Figure 2.3: Tensile Strength of Machine-Deposited Laminate

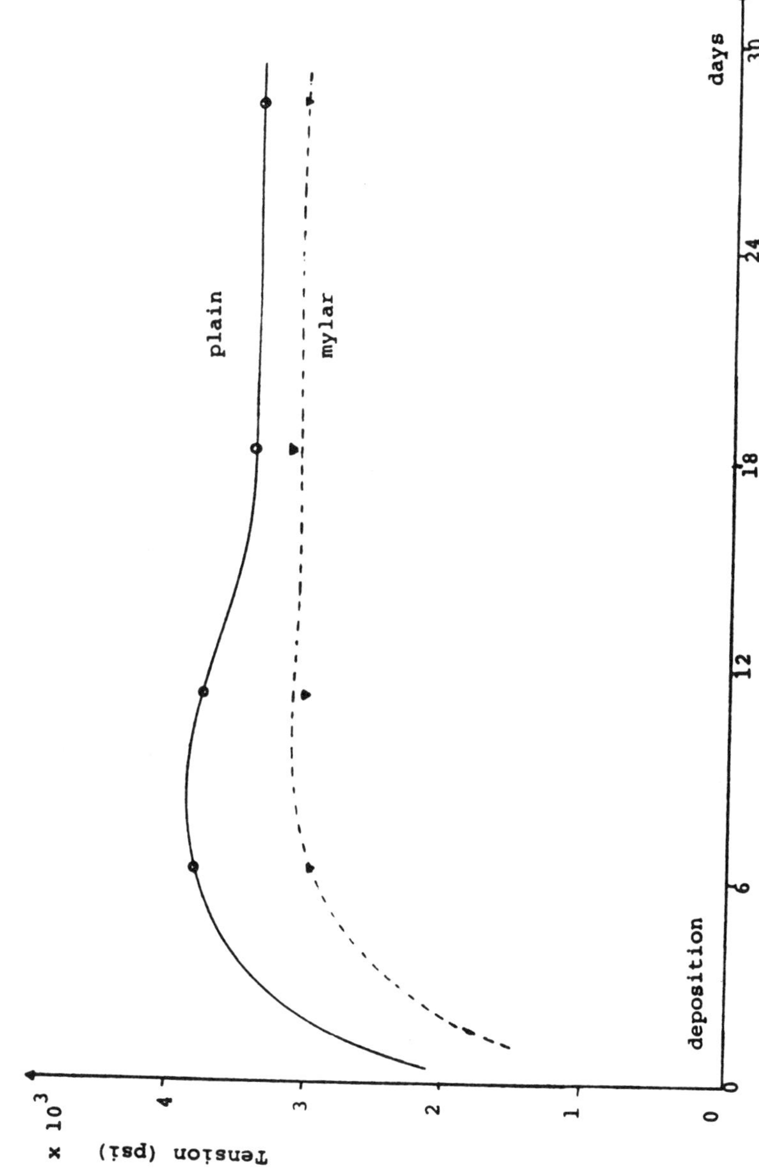

Source: EPA 600/8-77-006

Figure 2.4: Effect of Fiber Length and Glass Content on Laminate Strength

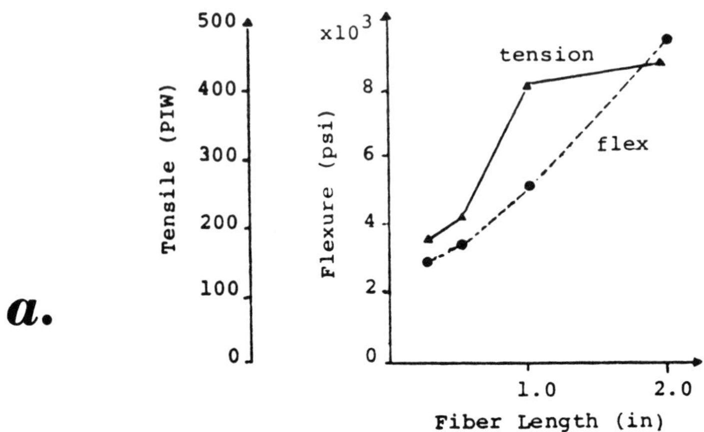

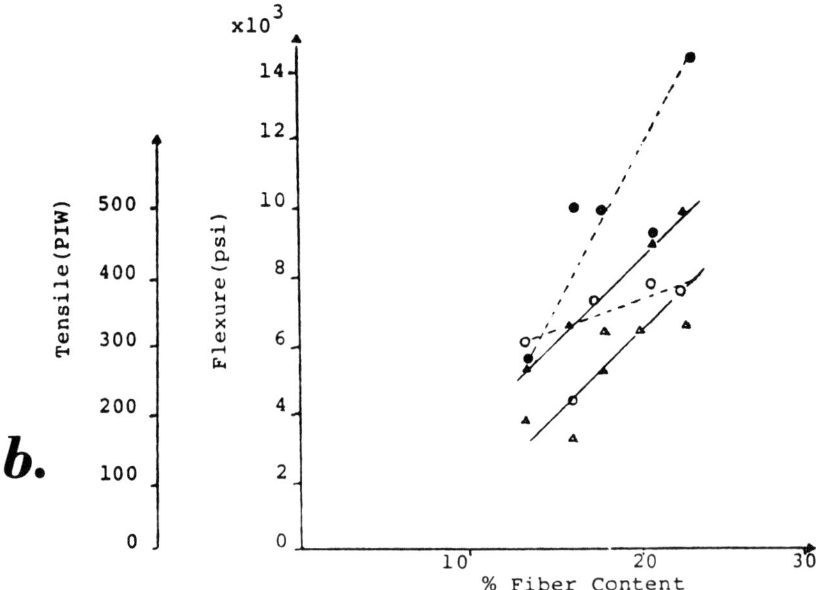

(a)   Effect of fiber length.
(b)   Effect of glass content.

Source: EPA 600/8-77-006

stiffness. In order to improve moisture resistance, a number of organic polymers were incorporated into the laminate. Addition of polyurethane resulted in the greatest improvement in moisture resistance. Tests were also performed on surface seals; alkyd paint was most effective if maintained on the surface.

The relationship of tensile stress to strain for the inorganic laminate is shown in Figure 2.5. There is a clearly defined elastic region with a yield point followed by a very long plastic region. This type of characteristic is particularly good for building construction. If the yield point is exceeded, there exists a very long period of deformation before failure. This period permits corrective action to be taken before failure occurs.

In summary, these laminates demonstrate highly desirable building properties. In addition to strength, the laminate will neither burn nor smoke, it is inexpensive, and the raw materials are freely available.

Foam Development: Initial studies focused upon development of a medium density foam for use as a wood substitute. Desirable properties for the composite were considered to be nonflammability, lower cost than wood, and similar structural properties.

Magnesium oxychloride and casting plaster were used as the matrices while the fillers and reinforcers evaluated included rice hulls, cotton waste, scrap styrofoam, electrostatic precipitator fly ash, Silvacon 412, and ¼-inch chopped glass. The electrostatic precipitator fly ash was supplied by the Environmental Protection Agency. Silvacon 412 is a Douglas fir bark fiber by-product, which has an interesting needlelike crystalline form and consists of almost equal parts of cellulose and lignin. The geometry of the Silvacon can contribute to toughening of brittle materials. Rice hulls are a voluminous filler with an apparent density of about 0.125 g/cm^3, so that any material containing rice hulls will have this minimum density. Any additional material that will fill voids between the hulls serves to increase the apparent density.

Most construction systems use 2" x 4" wood profiles for door and window framing which can warp and pose problems. A substitute for these profiles must be light, inexpensive, nonwarping and available. In order to test the nailability of the composites formulated, two nailability tests were performed: (a) the straight nail pull (Type 1 test); and (b) the bending nail pull (Type 2). Composites successful in the Type 1 were also evaluated under the Type 2 test.

Table 2.19 gives the results of these tests for the various composites formulated. For all compositions, the rice hull reinforcement (dry fraction) and the binder-filler (wet fraction) were separately premixed. Wheat straw was evaluated as a replacement for the glass fiber reinforcement. As the straw proportion increased, mixing became more difficult, density was reduced by as much as 17%, and nail retention reduced by up to 40%.

Figure 2.5: Stress-Strain Diagram for MSC Inorganic Matrix Composite Reinforced with Glass Fiber

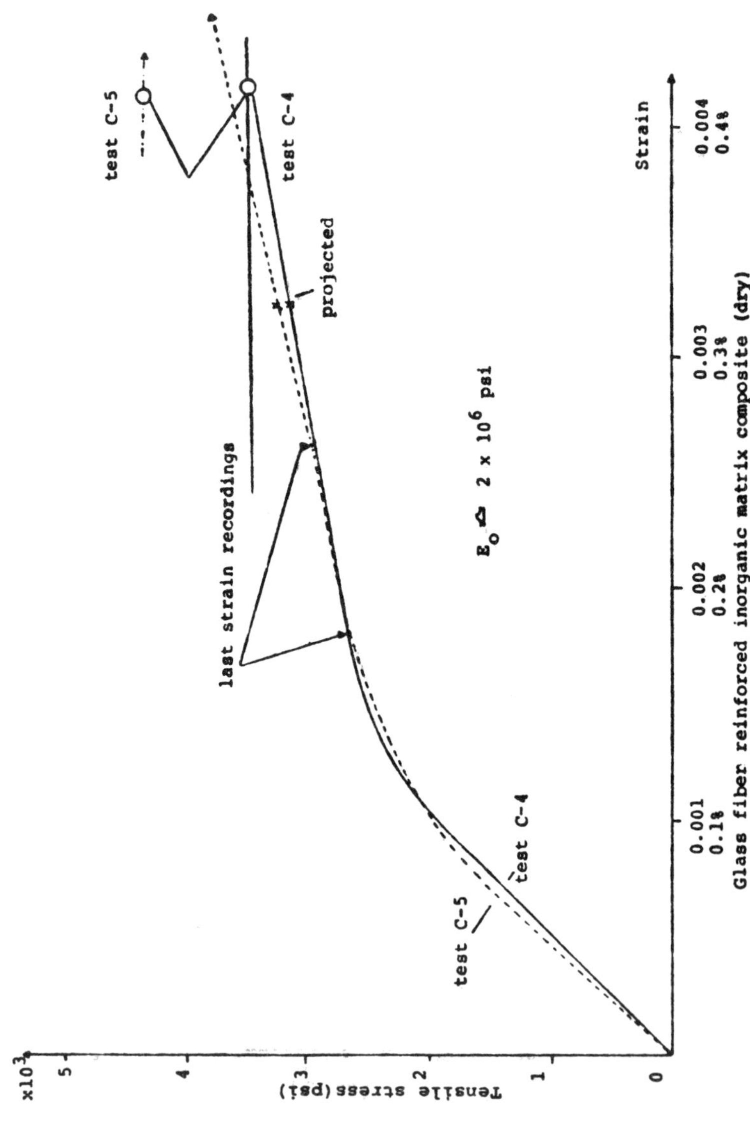

Source: EPA 600/8-77-006

Table 2.19: Formulations and Nail Retention of Nailable Wood Replacements

	Mixture											
	RH-21	RH-26	RH-27	RH-28	RH-29	RH-30	RH-31	RH-32	RH-33	RH-34	RH-35	RH-54
Component, parts by wt												
Rice hulls	100	50	100	100	100	100	100	100	100	100	90	100
Styrofoam (beads)	—	25*	—	—	—	—	—	—	—	—	5	—
1" Glass fibers (636AB)	5	5	5	—	5	5	5	5	5	5	5	15
Cotton waste	—	—	—	—	10	20	—	—	—	—	—	—
Proprietary binder	40	40	40	40	40	40	40	40	40	40	40	40
Water	130	200	200	160	200	200	200	200	260	260	250	225
Casting plaster/gypsum	—	150	300	—	300	350	300	200	200	100	300	240/60
Fly ash	200	150	—	200	—	—	—	50	100	150	—	—
Density, g/cm^3	0.35	0.58	0.58	0.38	0.53	0.64	0.69	0.64	0.61	0.47	0.70	0.65
Nail retention test, Type 1**												
Top, lb	16.0	20.6	8.3	10.6	8	18.6	34.6	11.3	14.6	6.6	15.0	41
Bottom, lb	20.6	19.3	14.3	15.6	15.6	24.0	51.0	23.6	17.6	10.6	22.6	41.6
Nail retention test, Type 2***												
Bottom, lb	—	—	—	—	—	—	195	—	—	—	225	—
Side, lb	—	—	—	—	—	—	225	—	—	—	190	—

*Styrofoam was shredded waste beads for this formulation.

**Straight nail pull.

***Bending nail pull. Results were recorded when nail started cutting along the beam, no nail was pulled out.

Source: EPA 600/8-77-006

The effects on nailability of increasing the amounts of plaster and glass fibers were also evaluated. Increasing the plaster increased the density but had no effect on nail retention. Increased amounts of glass fibers reduced density and increased nailability, but mixing became more difficult. Dry and wet mixing were carried out with a jiffy mixer causing no significant changes from hand-mixed materials. To overcome mixing difficulties, ¼" glass fibers (with finish) were added and the density was reduced, but with no increase in nailability.

In order to reduce process time, the effect of adding gypsum plaster to the casting plaster was evaluated. Introduction of as much as 15 parts of gypsum plaster caused hardening retardation of over two hours. Mixtures containing gypsum alone showed reduced nailability and density.

Compositions with Insulation Potential — The materials tested were fire resistant and low in smoke generation, and would probably be good insulators of low density. Keeping this application in mind, a number of binders were evaluated against the following criteria: expense, efficiency in bonding, ability to disperse or emulsify in water, ability to harden on drying.

A number of matrix binders were tested including water glass, acrylic latex, and wood bark extract. None of these binders were successful. Table 2.20 shows those compositions which showed structural integrity and would not ignite under a propane torch.

Table 2.20: Compositions* and Properties of Rice Hull Insulating Materials

	. . . . Composition	
	RH-8	RH-12
Component, parts by wt		
Rice hulls	100	100
MSC proprietary binder	40	40
Fly ash	—	200
Calcium carbonate	200	—
Water	150	150
Properties		
Density, g/cm^3	0.31	0.37
Compressive strength, psi	~100	~100
Material costs, \$/ft^3	1.02	1.02

*Compositions selected on the basis of structural integrity
  and nonflammability.

Source: EPA 600/8-77-006

These binders were prepared by blending the MSC proprietary binder with water, slowly adding the filler and blending for an extra minute. The mix was poured on rice hulls, mixed well, placed into a metal mesh mold and dried at 50°C or above.

The compositions were subjected to the NBS smoke test and a modified E-84 flame-spread test. Both smoke density and flame-spread test results showed very good fire resistance. As they are also inexpensive and light, they seem to have good potential as insulation materials.

While the rice hulls were a cheap, satisfactory and plentiful filler-reinforcement for the composite, a number of other fillers were tested. These included magnesium chloride, magnesium oxide, calcium carbonate, fly ash, casting gypsum. Both fly ash and calcium carbonate seem to be good candidates for a fireproof filler. Casting gypsum also appears satisfactory. Other insulating fillers tested were mineral rock wool, glass wool, vermiculite perlite and polystyrene foam beads.

Additional binders, fireproofing agents and reinforcements were studied as components for a fireproof insulating material. Vinyl flat and water glass proved to be unsatisfactory binders, while the MSC proprietary binder was most successful with a combination of rice hulls and inorganic fillers. Glass fibers and cotton waste were both considered as reinforcement. The one-inch long glass fibers gave best results with the rice hull mixtures. Composites containing oil starch finished fibers out-performed composites containing silane finished fibers in strength and integrity. The cotton waste reinforced materials developed mold and presented mixing problems, though they showed improved strength and nailability. None of the fireproofing agents tested were compatible with the formulations.

In addition to the compositions RH-8 and RH-12, three other compositions showed promise, as can be seen from Table 2.21.

Table 2.21: Rice Hull Syntactic Foams

| | . . . . .Composition . . . . | | | | |
	RH-8	RH-12	RH-21	RH-31	RH-46
Component, parts by wt					
Rice hulls	100	100	100	100	100
1″ Glass fibers	—	—	5	5	5
Proprietary binder	40	40	40	40	40
Calcium carbonate	—	—	—	300	400
Fly ash	—	200	200	—	—
Water	150	150	130	200	260
Properties					
Density, g/cm^3	0.31	0.37	0.35	0.69	0.74
Compressive strength, psi	100	100	350	700	1,200
Flame spread	28	24	24	12	7
Smoke density	72	48	48	15	10
Material cost, $/ft^3	1.02	1.00	1.02	1.50	1.60

Source: EPA 600/8-77-006

A series of tests were performed on RH-31 material 0.5", 0.83" and 1.09" thick to determine the char depth, burn through and back temperature. Samples were placed vertically in a 4" x 4" gypsum board with a 2" x 2" hole in the center. A thermocouple was attached to the center by means of a steel strip. A propane torch with ¾" nozzle was directed 5 inches away from the sample surface with gas pressure about 27 psi. The temperature was adjusted to 1600°F.

It was found that the insulation effect was not linear with thickness because the properties of the developing char were different from the nonburned material. There was a 100°F drop in temperature at the thermocouple placement (center of board) after the temperature peaked, attributable to the superior insulating properties of the char. This temperature peak was not reached by the 1" sample within a two-hour period.

Weathering Tests: Although rice hull syntactic foams should not be exposed to outside conditions or high humidity, the effect of adverse conditions on these materials was evaluated The materials were soaked in water up to 7 days. Weight, compression strength and nail pull changes were checked. Accelerated weathering up to 400 hours was also carried out. Due to the construction of the weatherometer chamber, which does not allow samples thicker than one-half inch, only weight changes could be measured. Water soak data (Table 2.22) showed a higher density material, which means more plaster absorbed less water. RH-21 which included just fly ash absorbed the highest amount of water.

Table 2.22: Water Soak and Accelerated Weathering Data

Test	. . . . Composition		
	RH-21	RH-31	RH-46
Water soak			
Weight picked up, %			
2-hr soak	49	36	29
24-hr soak	51	37	31
168-hr soak	52	46	36
Compressive strength, psi			
Control	350	700	1,200
2-hr soak	96	390	390
24-hr soak	38	340	370
168-hr soak	21	250	360
Nail pull, lb			
Control	18	43	45–70
2-hr soak	6	19	16
24 hr soak	4	27	25
168-hr soak	3	22	30
Weatherometer			
Weight loss, %			
200 hr	3	9	12
400 hr	6	21	19

Source: EPA 600/8-77-006

Fly-ash containing materials drastically lost their compression strength and nail-pull resistance. Plaster-containing materials lost strength and suffered from lowered nail-pull resistance, but to a lesser extent. No significant difference was noted due to increased amount of plaster. Weatherometer data showed weight loss, which indicated leaching out of either fly ash or casting plaster. After drying, the samples were firm and not warped.

It was also noted that mold growth can occur on rice hull syntactic foams. This required a study to find proper and effective fungicides to retard mold growth, under humid or wet conditions. Samples of the rice hull foams were inoculated with species of fungi in order to test the efficacy of various fungicides. The fungi inoculated were: *Penicillium roquefortii, Aspergillus niger, Chaetomium globosum* and *Aerobacter nerogenes.* Untreated samples had a profuse growth of naturally occurring *Aspergillus* sp. It was found that 0.6 to 1.0 part by weight (with 100 parts rice hulls) of Busan 30-1 was very effective in retarding mold growth. Busan 30-1 contains 2-(thiocyanomethylthio)benzothiazole.

Summary and Conclusions: There are a variety of inorganic matrix laminates and foams of waste materials which can be used competitively in the construction industry. The insulating material discussed contains three major components:

> (1) rice hulls as a filler-reinforcement;
> (2) inorganic filler to add fireproofing properties and
>   act as a binder;
> (3) matrix binder which may be inorganic or organic to
>   hold the other components together.

Rice hulls are a good filler-reinforcement due to their low apparent density, low cost, rough surface easily bondable, silica content which lowers flammability, and abundant supply throughout the world. The MSC proprietary inorganic binder is a successful matrix for combinations of rice hulls and inorganic fillers.

PRODUCT DEVELOPMENT

General Considerations

Code Qualification: All new materials and structural components intended for use in residential construction in the United States must be approved under one of the three major model codes, UBC (Uniform Building Code), BOCA (Building Officials Conference of America Inc.), or the SBC (Southern Building Code). In addition, FHA (Federal Housing Administration) and VA (Veterans Administration) approval may also be required if the product is involved in construction projects financed by these agencies.

During the last few years several states have passed so-called "Factory Built Housing Laws." Under the provisions of these laws the state can approve new industrialized building systems and components. This approval must be honored by local building officials without enforcement of local regulations on those aspects of the construction specifically approved by the state. All other aspects must meet local code requirements. Since most Factory Built Housing Laws specify the use of one of the three model codes as the basis of performance criteria, the requirements for qualification of new materials and building components under the state approval is practically the same as those under the model codes. The state approvals do not supersede FHA or VA approvals.

In the following discussion typical requirements for qualification under UBC and FHA regulations will be outlined for various building components utilizing new materials and/or new methods of construction.

UBC and FHA Requirements — The UBC is the most widely used model code in the country and it has the most stringent design criteria among the model codes in such critical areas as earthquake and fire safety. The UBC is controlled and published by the International Conference of Building Officials (ICBO), which maintains a permanent Research Committee for the purpose of evaluating applications for UBC acceptance of new materials and construction methods. The ICBO Research Committee has certain standard requirements for new materials for specific applications; however, in most cases when new construction methods are proposed in combination with new materials the Research Committee staff will specify the supporting technical data required for approval. The sponsor of the proposed product is required to generate actual test data or the engineering calculation. This data must be certified by an independent test laboratory or qualified independent engineer or architect.

Upon review and acceptance of the supporting data, the Research Committee staff prepares its recommendations for approval, which the full community acts on in their regular monthly meetings. If approval is granted, an ICBO Research Committee Recommendation Bulletin is issued and is distributed to all members of ICBO, which includes most local building departments. Although the local building officials are not obligated to approve the use of a new material or construction method covered by an ICBO Bulletin, in most cases the bulletin assures local acceptance of the product or method of construction.

FHA acceptance of new materials and construction methods is granted through the issuance of Structural Engineering Bulletins. The supporting technical data required for FHA approval is much the same as that required by ICBO. In the case of FHA, the data submitted by the sponsor is evaluated by the HUD/FHA Central Offices, Architectural and Engineering Standards staff in Washington, DC. When issued the SEB is distributed to all FHA field offices nationwide and assures local acceptance of the new product in FHA insured construction.

The supporting data required by ICBO and FHA for qualification of new materials and/or construction methods varies widely depending on the nature of the product being considered. For the purpose of the following discussion, it will be assured that the materials being developed will be used in prefabricated, sandwich panel structural building components.

Material Qualification — If new materials are considered for use as stressed skins or loadbearing core of sandwich panels, the first step in their qualification is to conduct sufficient testing to establish a reliable level of minimum mechanical properties to be used in engineering design calculation and to serve as the criteria for material acceptance in production quality control.

The most important mechanical properties are the following: tensile strength, modulus of elasticity, compressive strength and shear strength. In addition to the requirement to establish the mechanical properties listed, the material must meet fire safety and durability requirements depending on intended use and exposure.

Exterior wall-facing materials must be tested for: flame spread, smoke generation, water permeability, weatherability. Interior wall-facing and core materials must be tested for flame spread and smoke generation. In addition to these test requirements, the use of new facing and core materials will be necessary, in most cases, to requalify the adhesives used in factory and field assembly of the panel components.

Adhesive qualification required the following tests: block shear test after accelerated aging, lap shear test after accelerated aging, flatwise tensile test after accelerated aging, creep test before and after accelerated aging at room temperature and at elevated temperature, and block shear test after high humidity mold environment aging.

Structural Component Qualification — Exterior Loadbearing Wall Panels: The ability of a proposed wall design to withstand the various loads due to wind, earthquakes, snow, etc. can be shown analytically by use of well-known engineering principles in the case of simple, conventional designs utilizing standard building materials with well established mechanical and physical properties. However, in the case of complex sandwich panel construction utilizing new materials, actual full-scale physical testing is the only reliable way of establishing design load capacity.

The tests required are the following: axial compression test, transverse load test, racking shear test and impact test. Each test must be conducted on a minimum of three specimens and if the test results have more than 15% variation, a total of five specimens must be tested. In addition to the structural tests, exterior walls must also pass a minimum 20-minute loadbearing fire endurance test (this is an FHA requirement only).

Interior Loadbearing Wall Panels: The tests required of interior loadbearing walls are the same as those for exterior walls with the exception of lower load requirements in case of transverse loading, since the interior walls are not exposed to direct wind loading.

A special core interior wall is a party wall separating two dwelling units. Party walls usually require a minimum of one-hour fire rating and acoustical performance of STC 50 or better. The fire rating can only be verified by actual fire test.

Acoustical performance, however, can be derived by comparison of the proposed wall design with similar construction previously tested.

Interior Non-Loadbearing Wall Panels: The only requirement is to demonstrate 5 pounds per square foot transverse load capacity.

Roof Panels: Roof panels are generally designed for a specific span to withstand various magnitude live loads in addition to their own weight (dead load) within the allowable deflection limits. Transverse loading tests under short-term and long-term (creep) loading conditions must be performed for each combination of span and design live loads.

In addition to the structural tests, roof panels must be tested for roof fire classification A, B, or C unless the roofing material and sheeting has previously been classified. If the underside of the roof panel is used as the finished ceiling, it also must be able to pass a 15-minute roof/ceiling fire endurance test (FHA requirement only).

Of course, any roof panel system must be impervious to water. There is no specific test requirement for water penetration, but general industry standard is 20-year service life without reroofing.

Floor Panels: As in the case of roof panels, floor panels are designed for specific spans and live loads. Therefore, transverse loading tests under short and long duration loading conditions must be conducted for each specific continuation of span and design loads for which the panels are intended to be used. Floor panels must also be tested for concentrated load-bearing capacity.

Fire endurance test requirements depend on the type of dwelling in which the floor panels will be used. Single family homes must have 15-minute rated ground floor and 20-minute rated floor/ceiling assemblies (FHA requirement only). Apartment houses with separate occupancy of upper and lower units must have minimum 1-hour rated floor/ceiling assemblies.

Estimation of Development Costs: The estimation of development costs for a product is complex and prone to error. There are many steps involved in development. The best approach to establishing costs would be as follows:

> The cost for each step, assuming 100% achievement of projected results, should be estimated with maximum accuracy.
>
> A factor of error should be applied. This factor, where possible, would be derived from similar type development.

The factors of error are established in the following discussion. This study will be based on the assumption that a laboratory scale process has been established to process the material. This process will have defined the parameters within which the manufacturing process and resulting product will be developed. The subsequent steps to product development and their associated factors for error in cost projection are discussed in the following text.

Selection and Development of a Manufacturing Process — Relationship of Time, Pressure and Heat: All composite material systems are processed by the manipulation of these parameters. Under special cases humidity and atmosphere could be involved to complicate matters. Most processes such as continuous lamination, molding, extrusion, and pultrusion are variable with time. Therefore, if a specific process was selected and the time relationship varied, it would have minimal effect on the process. The resulting effect on cost would only be that necessary to establish the correct time relationship. A typical manufacturing process development program including machinery for a pilot plant could range between $300,000 and $500,000. A time study on a continuous processing line equivalent to that at MSC would require a maximum of four one-half hour runs at about $500 per run for material, people and set up. This would have less than 1% effect on total cost.

Heat variable has little effect on the cost of the technique unless temperatures in excess of $400°F$ are involved. The materials processed in this study require lower temperatures. Therefore, any selected heat source would be capable of accepting a variable. The only cost involved would then be a study of temperature variables on the pilot plant. This would require more runs of longer duration. A temperature study could require eight one-hour runs. This could have a possible 3% effect on the total cost.

Pressure has a much more serious effect on certain processes. In molding, extruding and pultruding it affects the capacity required. On a continuous lamination machine it affects the method of application. The products under evaluation here are of a large geometry. The increase in pressure then has an exponential effect. The equipment cost would conservatively be $5,000 per additional psi, up to 5 psi. The cost would increase to $10,000 per additional psi up to 10 psi, and $12,000 per additional psi up to 15 psi. Pressure above this would be limited to smaller specialty products. Modification to pilot plant design and installation would be in the $6,000 to $7,000 range.

If the pilot plant is in the same price range as above, then the percent effect on cost can be estimated as follows:

Pressure Variable Effect on Cost

Pressure Range (psi)	Effect (%)	C_o*
0–5	10	0.10
5–10	20	0.20
10–15	28	0.28

*C_o is the pressure dependent cost variable.

As the pressure increases so does the price of the pilot plant; $300,000 would be used for a base estimate for 0 to 5 psi, $400,000 for 5 to 10 psi and $500,000 for 10 to 15 psi.

Humidity and atmosphere controls within the process affect cost dramatically. If such a control is required, it is recommended that a factor of at least 50% be utilized on the total cost.

Therefore, the factor (k) for time, pressure, heat, and atmosphere can be summarized as follows:

$$k_1 = 0.01 + 0.03 + C_O$$

Or, if atmosphere is involved,

$$k_1 = 0.01 + 0.03 + C_O + 0.5.$$

Thus, when atmosphere is involved

$$k_1 = 0.04 + C_O \quad \text{or} \quad k_1 = 0.54 + C_O$$

General Design of Techniques: In order to estimate the development costs, the estimators require knowledge of the techniques that will be utilized. Variations in the techniques would have been accounted for in the original estimate and no additional factors would be required.

Range of Product Possibilities: The variations would primarily involve geometry. This in turn would affect shapes, forms, tools. In a typical wall panel, there could be at least three changes before development. The cost of typical in-line process tools and trimmers plus set-up charges are approximately $10,000 per change. However, at least 30% would be reusable equipment. The effect on total cost could be as much as 7%. The k_2 factor would then be 0.07.

Technique Selection: The experimental set up for most techniques using a qualified facility would be an estimated $25,000. The worst condition possible would be that the technique would not work. Assuming at least 10% of the cost would be in equipment, such a failure would have an effect on the total cost of 8%. The k_3 factor would then be 0.08.

Full-Scale Experiments: Although a reasonable test program can be planned ahead of time, developed variables will create changes. Experience at MSC indicates that preplanned experimental studies on machinery and process can vary as much as 23% on the average. Therefore, the k_4 factor would then be 0.23.

Review of Results and Selection of a System: At this point there will be a considerable amount of data available. The selection will be based on achieving maximum reliability consistent with cost. This step will not create any variables that require consideration in the cost estimate.

Construction of a Full-Scale Pilot Plant: This will be an expansion of the experimental study. It will include automation, controls, and some scale-up. In addition, recent experience has shown that considerable inflation of outside purchased parts can be expected from the date of estimate to construction. Finally, there will be some parts that will not function as planned and will require modifications. Experience indicates that in a complex pilot plant the above variances may increase the cost as much as 34%. Therefore, the k_5 factor would then be 0.34.

Evaluation Runs and Modifications: Once evaluation runs are conducted, certain design and process changes become apparent. This is particularly true of a complex system. The effect on cost from historical data at MSC can be as much as 5%. Therefore, the k_6 factor would then be 0.05.

Development of Quality Control Procedures: These are known approaches that can be applied to any technique. There are no cost variance implications involved.

Summary: The total factor, K_I, that can be applied to an estimate for the selection and development of a manufacturing process can be developed as follows:

$$K_I = 1 + k_1 + k_2 + k_3 + k_4 + k_5 + k_6$$

When no atmosphere control is required,

$$K_I = 1.81 + C_O;$$

and when atmosphere control is required,

$$K_I = 2.31 + C_O.$$

Design and Qualification of a Product — Selection of a Product: The product selection is based on marketing evaluation. If the selection is a poor one, then the entire development program is jeopardized. In that case, the effect on cost variance would approach 100%. For the purpose of this study, it is assumed that the market selection is adequate to good. In this case, there would be no effect on the development cost.

Design of a Product: In the design of a new product from new materials there are always unexpected developments. Studies of case histories show both under-variances and over-variances resulting in an average of 5% increase in design cost. Therefore, the k_7 factor would be 0.05.

Construction of Prototype Models: There are considerable series of case histories to evaluate variances on prototype construction. The variance results from misjudgment in fabrication time, designs that require modification, and miscalculation in material cost. The percent of variance increases with the lower the projected prototype cost. To establish the variance factor here, the total of several project estimates were compared with the total of their actual cost. The study included three prototype houses and one set of prototype panels. The total estimated budget for these four was $56,690 and the actual total direct cost was $67,113. This results in an 18% increase over the budget. Therefore, the k_8 factor can be established as 0.18.

Evaluation, Modification and Reevaluation of the Prototypes: This evaluation would be analytical for cost and aesthetic characteristic and experimental for mechanical and physical properties. The major variances occur where there is a system failure and modifications and subsequent reevaluation must be done. Case histories would indicate a potential variance of 19%. Therefore, the k_9 factor would be 0.19.

Construction of Specimens, Qualification Tests, Analyses, Modifications and Retests: This is an outside evaluation of the product, usually on a larger scale than the previous tests. Since the evaluation is different, experience would indicate this factor would be a duplicate of the one above. Therefore, the k_{10} factor would be 0.19.

Submission of Results to Specific Agencies: The above data has to be placed in report form and submitted in a prescribed manner to a particular qualifying agency. The cost for this can be closely projected. There would not be a variance of any consequence.

Coordination with the Agency: The coordination, until receipt of approval, involves personalities and the particular characteristics of the agency. Experience would indicate that a 15% cost variance on the estimate should be included. Therefore, the k_{11} factor would be 0.15.

Summary: The total factor, K_{II}, that can be applied to the design and qualification of a product can be developed as follows:

$$K_{II} = 1 + k_7 + k_8 + k_9 + k_{10} + k_{11}$$

Then,

$$K_{II} = 1.76.$$

Application of Product to Market — Review and Selection of a Market: The various markets for the product or products are reviewed. A selection is then made of the ones that offer the most potential. The cost of such a market survey is a controlled one. That is, a given number of manhours are expended to collect data and at the completion of the manhours the data is reviewed and a selection made. No overrun factor need be considered.

Evaluation of Methods of Market Penetration: This is a controlled study also. An established amount of manhours is expended to collect data on various marketing methods. At the end of this expenditure, the data is reviewed and summarized for a selection. No overrun factor need be considered here also.

Selection of a Method: The above information is used to select a method that offers the greatest return on development investment plus market investment.

This is accomplished within the framework of a controlled program so an overrun is not probable.

Approach to Market: In most cases this will involve prototypes and models. K_{II} should be applied to these specific investments. This marketing effort is to some degree controlled. Periodic evaluation of results permits corrections and redirection and thus reduces potential overruns. Without such periodic checks a variance of 100% could easily be achieved. By carefully controlling the program it may be possible to restrict potential variances to 20%. Therefore,

$$K_{III} = 1.20.$$

Product Acceptance — First Level Acceptance: This is the reaction of the distributor, builder or user. These individuals generally will not use the product as is unless it has an acceptance record. Therefore, it will always be necessary to collect their comments for action if sales are to be made. This is, again, a controlled program with limited probability of variance.

Reaction: A review of the above comments will be made and reactions will be initiated under marketing, engineering, and production guidance. An estimate can be made for this cost. However, the variance can be extreme. It is recommended that a k_{12} factor of 0.30 be used.

Second Level Acceptance: This is the reaction of the consumer. Again, this will be a controlled program of a survey type. The results will, in most cases, be less dramatic than the first level survey, which has already provided a high degree of consumer acceptance. No variance factor need be considered.

Reaction: Since the major corrections have already been made, the actions required will be minimal in nature. However, it will be very difficult to estimate these costs. A variance factor of $k_{13} = 0.10$ should be used.

Summary: The estimate for product acceptance can be controlled with the exception of corrective actions required. Therefore,

$$K_{IV} = 1 + k_{12} + k_{13}$$

Then,

$$K_{IV} = 1.40.$$

Application of Factors of Cost —

> Selection and development of a manufacturing process
>> Estimate of cost (A)
>> Computed probable cost (C_A)
>>> $C_A = AK_I$
>>>> $K_I = 1.81 + C_O$ (no atmosphere control required)
>>>> $K_I = 2.31 + C_O$ (atmosphere control required)

Design and qualification of a product

    Estimate of cost (B)
    Computed probable cost (C_B)
      $C_B = BK_{II}$
        $K_{II} = 1.76$

Application of product to the market

    Estimate of cost (C)
    Computed probable cost (C_C)
      $C_C = CK_{III}$
        $K_{III} = 1.20$

Product acceptance

    Estimate of cost (D)
    Computed probable cost (C_D)
      $C_D = DK_{IV}$
        $K_{IV} = 1.40$

Organic Matrix Products

There are a variety of products conceivable from the organic materials developed here. The ones evaluated in this program with the most promise are structural board, replacement for sheet rock, lumber substitute, and fire doors. Each of these will be discussed in detail.

Structural Board: Structural board is a direct substitute for commercial grade particle board (chip board). Formulations utilizing organic materials are presented in Table 2.18. These materials can be produced in various densities and strengths, as can commercial particle board. The 55 lb/ft^3 density commercial grade particle board was used as the competitive standard. It has the following characteristics:

Modulus of rupture, psi	1,500
Straight nail pull, lb	56
Straight screw pull, lb	296
Flame spread	127
Smoke number	345
Water soak (7 days)	
Weight gain, %	64
Thickness gain, %	22
Shore hardness, D	
Before soak	70
After soak	50
Weatherometer (350 hr)	
Weight loss, %	14
Thickness gain, %	22
Shore hardness, D	
After weathering	50

As can be seen in Table 2.18, organic materials show promise as a replacement for commercial grade particle board. It should be noted that each composite is presented in the density providing maximum strength but that densities vary in production in terms of modulus of rupture. Most materials are of acceptable strength or are superior to the commercial particle board. The corn cob product, however, shows lower strength than the commercial board. The higher the modulus of rupture, the more desirable the product.

The smoke generation criterion calls for lower figures to demonstrate good qualities. Rice hull materials are far superior to commercial particle board. Peanut shells are almost as promising as rice hulls. The data is summarized in Table 2.23.

Table 2.23: Smoke Generation Properties

	. . . . Formulation			
	YT-46	YT-58-C	YT-126	Control
Material	rice hulls	pine	peanut shells	*
Smoke number	51	315	200	345

*55 lb/ft^3 commercial grade particle board.

Source: EPA 600/8-77-006

Costs — Two commercial particle board processes are shown in Figure 2.6. The wet process is the most firmly established method for the manufacture of hard, semihard and insulation board products. It has been in use for more than 40 years, in the course of which considerable practical experience has been gained. The experience, the simplicity of the method, and the constant improvement of machinery, enables preset product capacity and quality to be reached easily and quickly. The wet method is used for production lines with daily fiberboard outputs ranging from 20 to 250 tons, in thicknesses varying from 2 mm for hard to 25 mm for insulation board.

The dry method is characterized by high production output, implying a lower production cost per ton of board. Board characteristics and thicknesses can be varied over a wide range and the production output is not appreciably affected when thicker board is produced.

The waste process is shown in Figure 2.7. The rice hulls or peanut shells are fed into a storage area from which measured amounts are transported to the resin wash. From the resin wash, the material goes to a wet preformer. The preformed billets are then passed through a dryer to remove excess water. The dry billets are then pressed, posttreated and trimmed. Equipment cost for a waste process particle board plant would be about 78% of that of a conventional plant.

Assuming that the waste material is converted into the product at the waste material source, comparative costs for rice hull materials, peanut shell materials, wood chips, and commercial particle board are shown in Table 2.24.

Figure 2.6:　Processes for Commercial Particle Board Manufacture

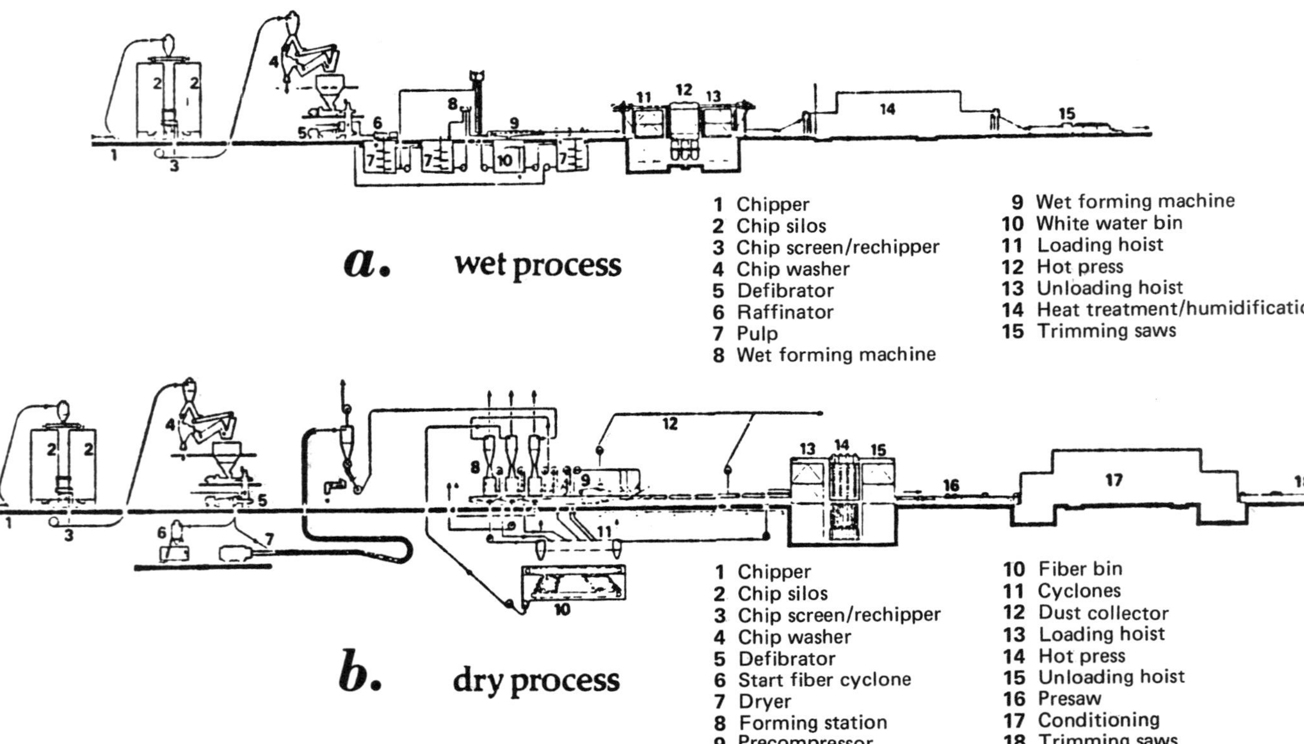

Source:　EPA 600/2-78-092

Figure 2.7: Waste Process for Panel Board

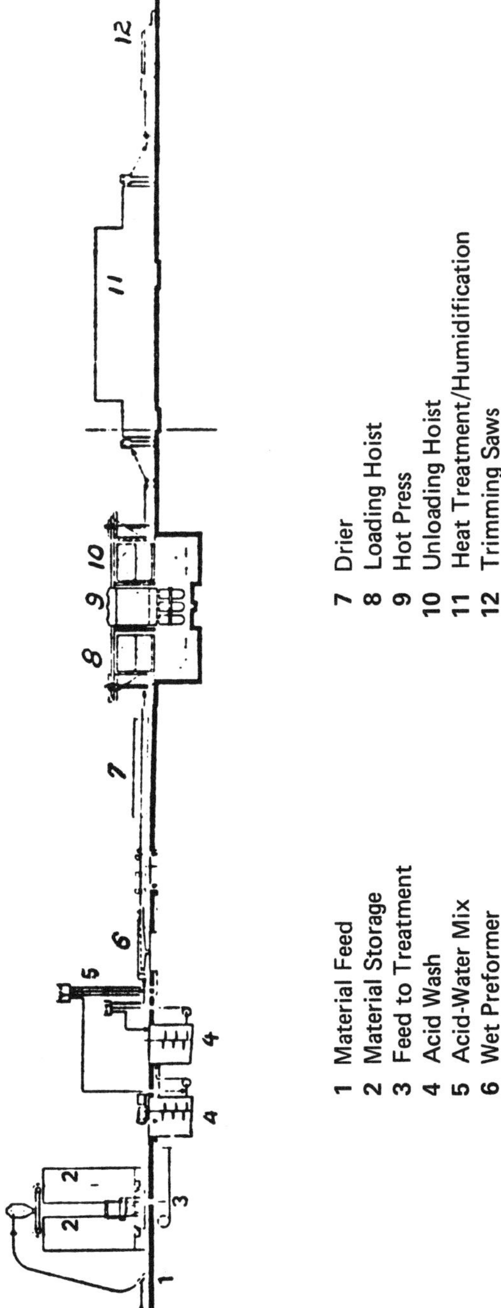

Source: EPA 600/2-78-092

Table 2.24: Comparative Costs of Products

	Rice Hulls	Peanut Shells	Wood Chips	Commercial Particle Board
	. . . . (dollars)			
Material	0.632	0.898	0.881	1.133
Manufacturer's (1.67)	1.055	1.501	1.471	1.797
Retailer's (1.25)	1.318	1.876	1.838	2.246
At retail (1.54)	2.031	2.889	2.832	3.459

Source: EPA 600/8-77-006

In the table, for the three different elements in the manufacturing series, a built-in rule-of-thumb index was supplied by the manufacturer, i.e., for rice the material cost is $0.632, the manufacturer buys it for 66% more from the supplier (1.67 factor number) which makes his cost $1.055 ($0.632 x 1.67). The rule-of-thumb index from manufacturer to retailer is 1.25 (25% increase in cost); hence cost to retailer is $1.318 ($1.055 x 1.25). The retailer takes his profit (54%), making the retail cost $2.031 ($1.318 x 1.54). The same considerations were taken into account in Tables 2.28 and 2.29.

Cost Analysis for a Commercial Structural Board

Assumed plant cost is $8.27 million for production of 200 tons/day, or 55 million square feet of ½ inch board per annum at 45 lb/ft^3 density.

Assumed material cost is $0.007/lb for rice hulls, $0.011/lb for peanut shells, $0.010/lb for wood chips.

Assumed retail price is $0.031/lb, using commercial figures for particle board at 55 lb/ft^3.

Assuming fixed operation costs per year for plant capacity of:

Labor	$374,000
Other direct costs*	292,600
Indirect costs	283,800
Depreciation of 10%	827,000
Total costs per year	$1,777,400
Costs per day	6,836

*Not including material.

Break-even production rate would be:

For rice hulls the cost retail differential =

$$\frac{6,836/\text{day}}{0.024/\text{lb}} \times \frac{67 \text{ lb/ft}^3 \text{ rice hulls}}{55 \text{ lb/ft}^3 \text{ commercial}} = 346,978 \text{ lb/day}$$

For peanut shells the cost retail differential =

$$\frac{6{,}836/\text{day}}{0.020/\text{lb}} \times \frac{62 \text{ lb/ft}^3 \text{ peanut shells}}{55 \text{ lb/ft}^3 \text{ commercial}} = 385{,}302 \text{ lb/day}$$

For wood chips the cost retail differential =

$$\frac{6{,}836/\text{day}}{0.021/\text{lb}} \times \frac{63 \text{ lb/ft}^3 \text{ wood chips}}{55 \text{ lb/ft}^3 \text{ commercial}} = 372{,}873 \text{ lb/day}$$

Assuming full production, facility costs are based on 200 tons/day at 45 lb/ft^3. The plant production is limited by volume, not density, i.e., denser panels of 60 lb/ft^3 would mean production of 267 tons/day.

Profits would be as follows:

Rice hulls: 534,000 (0.024) (55/67) = $10,520/day sales – $6,836/day cost which equals $3,684/day profit or $957,840/annum (260 days).

Peanut shells: 534,000 (0.020) (55/62) = $9,474/day sales – $6,836/day cost which equals $2,638/day profit or $695,880/annum (260 days).

Wood shavings: 534,000 (0.021) (55/63) = $9,790/day sales – $6,836/day cost which equals $2,054/day profit or $768,040/annum (260 days).

The following table, Table 2.25, gives the costs for commercial plants in comparison with rice hulls or peanut shell plants, using figures for 1967 and converting to particle board plant costs for 1975. It is assumed that the inflation rate on equipment costs has been 3 since 1967 and 2 on other costs.

Table 2.25

Conventional Wood Shaving Plant		Rice Hull or Peanut Shell Plant	
Unloading and storage	$ 120,000	Unloading and storage	$ 120,000
Milling and drying	190,000	Acid wash	100,000
Bending and forming	490,000	Forming and drying	150,000
Press line	1,020,000	Press line	1,020,000
Finishing section	350,000	Finishing section	350,000
Auxiliary equipment	270,000	Auxiliary equipment	175,000
Total equipment cost	$2,440,000	Total equipment cost	$1,915,000

Source: EPA 600/8-77-006

Estimated particle board plant cost in 1975 is $3.2 million plus $135,000 per million square feet of annual production. Therefore for a 200 ton per day plant (55 million square feet annual production), the cost would be $3.2 million plus 55 times $135,000 or $10.6 million.

Production for five-year pay-off:

$$\text{Cost per day } (8.27 \times 10^6)/(5 \times 260) + 6{,}836 = \$13{,}198/\text{day}$$

Production required for rice hulls:

$$
\begin{array}{rll}
13{,}198/0.024\ (67/55) = & 669{,}898 & \text{lb/day} \\
= & 355 & \text{tons/day} \\
= & 7{,}499 & \text{panels/day}^* \\
= & 62 & \text{MM ft}^2/\text{year}^{**}
\end{array}
$$

Production required for peanut shells:

$$
\begin{array}{rll}
13{,}198/0.020\ (62/55) = & 743{,}887 & \text{lb/day} \\
= & 372 & \text{tons/day} \\
= & 8{,}891 & \text{panels/day}^* \\
= & 74 & \text{MM ft}^2/\text{year}^{**}
\end{array}
$$

Production rquired for wood shavings:

$$
\begin{array}{rll}
13{,}198/0.021\ (63/55) = & 719{,}890 & \text{lb/day} \\
= & 360 & \text{tons/day} \\
= & 8{,}572 & \text{panels/day}^* \\
= & 71 & \text{MM ft}^2/\text{year}^{**}
\end{array}
$$

*Panels = ½" x 4' x 8'.
**Board = ½".

The developed waste process is a marginally viable venture. The break-even rate is 180 tons per day or 35 million square feet of ½" board per year; 1,093,750 4' x 8' panels per year. Full production of 267 tons per day, or 79 million square feet of ½" board, or 2,483,624 4' x 8' panels per year would be required.

Based on the cost analysis, retail prices for the waste material based particle board would be 58 to 84% of that of commercial particle board.

In order to reduce shipping costs for waste materials, MSC developed a process which reduces the bulk of the material by converting it to low density billets. In this process the waste is treated with acid and then heated and dried. Through this process, shipping costs can be reduced from $0.014 per pound to $0.005 per pound.

This analysis of costs precludes consideration of labor and equipment amortization, which is assumed to be the same regardless of the material processed. As shown previously in Table 2.24, waste material based panels can be produced at 35 to 68% of the cost of commercial particle board. If the cost of transportation within a 500-mile radius is included, then production costs would increase by 50 to 70%, a factor which also applies to particle board manufacture.

Design and Qualification: The design involves material selection. Table 2.26, on the following page, summarizes the cost per material per thickness. The inference is that the cost will range from $7,870 to $13,851 per product, depending upon the degree of problems that occur.

Table 2.26: Design and Qualification Cost per Organic Material Panel Product

	Dollars
Technical services (includes burden)*	2,800
Required tests	
Mechanical properties	1,000
Flame spread	500
Smoke generation	300
Recommended tests	
Weathering	400
Water permeability	200
Materials	50
Press time	50
Tooling	1,000
Filing fees	570
Travel and support	1,000
Estimated cost	7,870

$$\text{Probable cost} = \text{Estimated cost } (K_{II})^{**}$$
$$= 7{,}870 \ (1.76)$$
$$= 13{,}851 \text{ per product}$$

*Rate is $21 per hour.
**K_{II} was estimated in the General Considerations section.

Source: EPA 600/2-78-092

Development of the Manufacturing Procedure: This involves the plant facility, optimization and productization of the panel to give reliability and minimum cost possible. The process can utilize an existing particle board facility and its equipment. Therefore, no equipment development is involved.

Only processing procedures require development. This, of course, requires the use of an existing particle board line. The cost of manufacturing standard board is approximately $0.037 per square foot. If it is assumed that an economically viable operation produces 70,000,000 square feet of board per year, then the operation cost per hour is $1,248. Conservatively, it can be assumed that the operational line cost for development is $1,500 per hour. The cost of scale-up studies, pilot runs, and production start with adjustments to product needs are estimated in Table 2.27, presented on the following page. The estimated cost range is $285,490 to $596,674.

Table 2.27: Development of Manufacturing Procedure for Waste Process

	Dollars
Scale-up studies	
Technical services*	6,720
Process line cost, 1,500/hr	12,000
Material cost	50
Total	18,770
Pilot run	
Technical services*	13,440
Process line cost, 1,500/hr	60,000
Material cost	800
Total	74,240
Start-up and adjustment to product needs	
Technical services*	10,080
Process line cost, 1,500/hr**	180,000
Material cost**	2,400
Total	192,480
Total estimated cost	285,490

$$\begin{aligned}
\text{Probable cost} &= \text{Estimated cost } (K_I)^{***} \\
&= 285,490\,(2.09) \\
&= 596,674
\end{aligned}$$

*Includes burden.
**Assume 75% of product marketable.
***K_I was estimated in the General Considerations section.

Source: EPA 600/2-78-092

Application of the Product to the Market: This cost would depend on the organization involved. In all probability, an adequate job could be accomplished for a cost of $50,000 to $60,000.

Product Acceptance: Product acceptance should be accomplished with a minimal effort. The product is similar in appearance, quality and performance to the existing commercial product and would have ICBO and FHA approvals. Acceptance in this case would be made on price only.

In summary, to get this product on the market a cost of $343,360 to $670,525 would be required. If only wood materials are compared, there is a material saving of $0.025 per square foot of ½-inch board. If only half is passed on to the customer, a 70,000,000 square foot production output would yield $875,000 savings in one year. Based on this analysis, the product development cost can be absorbed in one year and still offer the product on the market at a much lower price than the commercial product.

Sheetrock Replacement: Sheetrock, dry wall or gypsum board are inexpensive and fire resistant, but highly susceptible to damage from impact or water. Fire tests were performed on a rice hull panel, peanut shell panel, commercial panel and sheetrock, for a period of about 20 minutes (although times varied because of difficulties in controlling the fire). As a result, sheetrock was rated for 24 minutes, commercial particle board less than 20 minutes, rice hull materials for 27 minutes, and the peanut shell panel just less than 20 minutes. The commercial board burned most readily, and the peanut board began burning after 15 minutes. The rice hull panel did not smoke or burn. The rice hull panel was superior to sheetrock in performance, and was intact after the fire. Both the rice hull panel and the peanut shell panel were superior to the commercial particle board. It is believed that a commercial product with comparable properties to sheetrock could be manufactured from rice hulls.

Screw and nail retention qualities of the organic panels are equivalent to sheetrock. The rice hull and peanut shell panels are more durable, more crack resistant and easier to work than the sheetrock. The greater flame resistance of the rice hull panels may give them a competitive edge over the slightly cheaper sheetrock panels.

Costs — Table 2.28 compares the costs of materials made from peanut shell or rice hull composites with the costs of manufacturing sheetrock (board size, ½"-thick, 4' x 8').

Table 2.28: Comparative Costs for Sheetrock Substitutes, $

	Rice Hulls	Peanut Shells	Sheetrock
Material cost	0.519	0.737	0.508
Cost to manufacturer (1.67)	0.867	1.231	0.848
Cost to retailer (1.25)	1.083	1.538	1.060
Cost at retail (1.54)	1.668	2.369	1.632

Table 2.29: Comparative Costs of Panels of Equivalent Strengths, $

	Rice Hulls (½ inch)	Peanut Shells ($^{3}/_{8}$ inch)	Sheetrock (½ inch)
Material cost	0.519	0.583	0.508
Cost to manufacturer (1.67)	0.867	0.973	0.848
Cost to retailer (1.25)	1.083	1.217	1.060
Cost at retail (1.54)	1.668	1.874	1.632

Source: EPA 600/8-77-006

Rice hull sheets could be cost-competitive with sheetrock, but peanut shell composites are more expensive. If, however, boards of equivalent strength are compared rather than boards of the same size, then the rice hull panel appears even more economically competitive with the sheetrock. As shown in Table 2.29 the rice hull panel weight of 73 lb/ft^3 was compared to the 80 lb/ft^3 of sheetrock and 58 lb/ft^3 of peanut shell panels.

The waste process is marginal economically if the product is sold on a direct cost basis with sheetrock. If the superior qualities of the organic panel permit a higher sales price, then the product becomes economically feasible. The cost required to advance the product from concept to market is as discussed for particle board.

Design and Qualification: Engineering consideration must be given to thinner panels for the higher strength and more expensive materials. These tradeoffs can be accomplished by analytical methods. In all other aspects figures for particle board in Table 2.26 would apply. Cost for this activity would then range from $7,870 to $13,851, depending on the problems involved.

Development of Manufacturing Procedure: This step should be less complex than with the particle board since mechanical properties are less important. Press time is faster, which will reduce cost also. Since an existing particle board facility can be utilized, no equipment development is required. The costs are estimated in Table 2.30. The cost range is $202,010 to $422,200.

Table 2.30: Development of Manufacturing Procedure for Low Strength Particle Board Waste Process

	Dollars
Scale-up studies	
Technical services*	3,360
Process line cost, 1,500/hr	12,000
Material cost	50
Total	15,410
Pilot run	
Technical services*	10,080
Process line cost, 1,500/hr	48,000
Material cost	600
Total	58,680
Start-up and adjustment to product needs	
Technical services*	6,720
Process line cost, 1,500/hr**	120,000
Material cost**	1,200
Total	127,920
Estimated cost	202,010

(continued)

Table 2.30: (continued)

$$\text{Probable cost} = \text{Estimated cost } (K_1)^{***}$$
$$= 202{,}010\ (2.09)$$
$$= 422{,}200$$

*Includes burden.
**Assume 75% of product marketable.
***K_1 has been discussed in General Considerations
section.

Source:　EPA 600/2-78-092

Application of the Product to the Market: In order to make this project feasible, the organic board will have to be promoted on its superior performance at a higher cost than sheetrock. This marketing should be accomplished through an existing organization with compatible product lines. Marketing is a controlled cost, but when performance and not cost is the sales feature, it can be expensive. An estimate of $250,000 is projected for this activity.

Product Acceptance: Since the product would have code approval and would be surface treated to the same appearance as existing structures, the superior properties would make the product easily acceptable. In summary, to get the product on the market a cost of $459,880 to $686,051 would be required. Before initiating such an activity, a very complete marketing analysis would be required to determine the additional cost that the market would sustain for a superior product to sheetrock. This cost would then have to be compared with the development costs involved to establish economic feasibility.

Lumber Substitute: The requirements for a product as a direct lumber substitute are: equivalent strength, equivalent nail and screw retention, dimensional stability, and workability with carpenter-type tools.

There have been a variety of commercial approaches to this concept such as U.S. Plywood's Novoply. These usually consist of fiber-oriented dense outer skins on either side of a low density core. The costs are not very competitive with ordinary lumber. The advantages of these materials over lumber are the utilization of waste and dimensional stability.

The only active work done in this study to determine the applicability of the waste process to a lumber substitute was to determine workability and screw and nail retention. All organic formulations considered were easily workable with conventional saws, drills, etc. Tests with straight nail pull indicated that the rice hull panel was inferior to the commercial panel and far below that of wood chip panels.

Costs — The cost of a 2" x 4" board from organic material would be $0.037 per foot for material and would retail for $0.120 per foot. This compares very well with the $0.15 to $0.20 per foot for conventional 2" x 4" lumber.

There would have to be more engineering development on fiber orientation or improved reinforcement before the material could be considered as a lumber replacement. The strength properties of the dense peanut shells and wood chips produced with this process are equivalent to that of pine lumber or Douglas fir. The material would be produced in a continuous press or extrusion system designed for shapes. The process would be the same as that shown in Figure 2.6 except the preformer, dryer, loading hoist, press, and unloading hoist would be redesigned for a continuous feed process. An estimate of the equipment cost based on the same 1967 base as that shown in Table 2.25 is presented in Table 2.31.

Table 2.31: Estimate of Continuous Shape Facility

	Dollars
Unloading and storage	120,000
Acid wash	75,000
Preforming into line	150,000
Press line, continuous	250,000
Finishing section	150,000
Auxiliary equipment	100,000
Total	845,000

Source: EPA 600/2-78-092

Then, based on the previously discussed data and inflation rate, a facility would cost approximately $4.5 million. The following analysis can be made for this process

Cost Analysis for Lumber Substitute

Assumed plant cost is $4.5 million.
Material cost is $0.055 per board foot.
Assumed sales price to retailer is 0.195 per board foot.
Generated difference is $0.14 per board foot.
Fixed operation costs, per year, are as follows:

Labor	420,000
Maintenance and operating supplies	275,000
Indirect costs	322,000
Depreciation	450,000
Total	$1,467,000

Per day costs = $5,642.

The break-even production rate would then be 5,642 board feet per day (generated difference $0.14 per board foot) to equal 40,300. This is sufficient lumber for 5 houses per day.

Assume full production is 500,000 board feet per day, then the profit is as follows: generated income, $500,000 (0.14) = $70,000; costs = $5,642; profit = $64,358. This would generate on a yearly basis an income of $16,733,000. Since the production equipment is yet to be designed, the total available output is questionable. However, assuming the product can be marketed on a direct competitive basis, the lumber substitute does appear to have promise.

The consideration involved in advancing this product from concept to market will be slightly more involved than the particle board operation. However, the same basic steps are involved.

Design and Qualification: Some improvement in strength and nail and screw retention will be required. A summary of cost estimates is presented in Table 2.32. The costs for this activity would range from $31,070 to $54,683.

Table 2.32: Design and Qualification Cost for Lumber Substitute

	Dollars
Technical services*	16,800
Required tests	
Mechanical properties	1,000
Flame spread	500
Smoke generation	300
Recommended tests	
Weathering	400
Materials	500
Press time	5,000
Tooling	5,000
Filing fees	570
Travel and support	1,000
Estimated cost	31,070

$$\text{Probable cost} = \text{estimated cost } (K_{11})$$
$$= 31,070 \ (1.76)$$
$$= 54,683$$

*Includes burden.

Source: EPA 600/2-78-092

Development of the Manufacturing Procedure: A press line must be developed to make this system economically viable. The details are summarized in Table 2.33. The development of the press system is a large unknown value with the limited information that is available. Also, this would require in all probability a new facility. Therefore, the cost for this activity would range from $3 to $6.3 million.

Table 2.33: Development of Manufacturing Procedures for Lumber Substitute

	Dollars
Process development	
Technical services*	43,680
Laboratory equipment	50,000
Material cost	500
Total	94,180
Scale-up studies	
Technical services*	43,680
Process line purchase	475,000
Material cost	1,000
Total	519,680
Pilot-run studies	
Technical services*	43,680
Additional line purchases	370,000
Process line operation (1,000/lb)	160,000
Material costs	5,000
Total	578,680
Start-up and adjustment to product need	
Technical services*	43,680
Additional equipment	1,660,000
Process line cost (1,000/hr)**	80,000
Material cost**	23,827
Total	1,807,507
Estimated total	3,000,047

$$\begin{aligned} \text{Probable cost} &= \text{estimated cost } (K_1) \\ &= 3{,}000{,}047 \ (2.09) \\ &= 6{,}270{,}098 \end{aligned}$$

*Includes burden.
**75% of product marketable.

Source: EPA 600/2-78-092

Application of Product to Market: Demonstratable proof of direct lumber substitution will be required. The marketing should be accomplished through an existing wood products distribution system. The cost can be regulated by the marketing plan, but a reasonable estimate of cost would be $125,000.

Product Acceptance: Trial projects with builders may require some subsidization to create acceptance. A cost of $250,000 may be a reasonable estimate.

In summary, to get this product on the market a cost of $3.4 to $6.7 million may be incurred. However, if the market can sustain a 500,000 board-feet-per-day production, this cost could be recovered in one year. This would be unlikely as the product would have to be introduced slowly into the market.

Fire Doors: There exists a major requirement in the developing building standards for fire doors which will perform in excess of 1 hour. A blank of 1½-inch thick rice hulls, peanut shells or wood chips produced from the waste process would perform for at least 2 hours and possibly 3 hours.

Costs — The molded blank could be machined by routine door equipment. The surface is of a wood appearance requiring no veneer. Hardware can be installed directly into the blank. A standard 3' x 6'8" door would have a material cost of $1.17 to $1.67, with a cost to the retailer of $2.44 to $3.49. The door industry pays $12 for a core which then has to have stiles, rails, crossbands, and veneer or plastic surfaces applied. If it is assumed that the particle board facility described was capable of handling 1½-inch blanks, then the following cost analysis can be made:

Cost Analysis for Fire Door:

A door utilizes 150 lb of material.
The material cost for a door is $1.67.
Assumed sales to retailer are the same as core sales, i.e., $12 per door. The generated difference is $10.33 per door.

The operational costs are $8,326 per day.

The break-even production rate would then be

$$\text{Doors per day} \quad = \quad \frac{\$8,326}{\$10.33} \quad = \quad 806.$$

Assume a production rate of 2,500 doors per day:

Generated sales = 25,825
Operation cost = 8,326
Profit, per day = $17,499

This would generate yearly sales of $4,549,740. It is concluded, therefore, that if a sufficient market is available for fire doors, the organic panels would make an excellent product for commercial development. (These figures were based on the manufacturers own data and must be presumed to be based on reasonably accurate assumptions. There is no way to verify.)

The activities required to take this product from concept to the market will involve those previously discussed. Since the particle board facility and this requirement are compatible, it will be assumed that the fire door is an addendum product to that of the board.

Design and Qualification: Consideration of hinge and latch attachment and fire resistance is required. The design would be based on the material selected for the particle board plant. A summary of cost estimates is presented in Table 2.34. The cost for this activity would range from $17,750 to $31,240.

Table 2.34: Design and Qualification for a Fire Door

	Dollars
Technical services*	10,080
Required test, ASTM-E-152	2,500
Materials	200
Press time	400
Tooling	3,000
Filing fees	570
Travel and support	1,000
Estimated cost	17,750

$$
\begin{aligned}
\text{Probable cost} &= \text{estimated cost } K_{II} \\
&= 17{,}750\ (1.76) \\
&= 31{,}240
\end{aligned}
$$

*Includes burden

Source: EPA 600/2-78-092

Development of the Manufacturing Procedure: This will be based on the assumption that particle board is already being produced. Therefore, the development will be based on the molding of 1½-inch to 1¾-inch blanks. These costs are summarized in Table 2.35. This activity will cost from $102,075 to $213,336, depending on complexities.

Table 2.35: Development of Manufacturing Procedures for Fire Doors

	Dollars
Scale-up studies	
Technical services*	6,720
Process line cost (1,500/hr)	12,000
Material cost	50
Total	18,770
Pilot run	
Technical services*	6,720
Process line cost (1,500/hr)	36,000
Material cost	500
Total	43,220

(continued)

Table 2.35: (continued)

	Dollars
Start-up and adjustment to product needs	
Technical services*	6,720
Process line cost (1,500/hr)**	30,000
Material cost**	3,365
Total	40,085
Estimated cost	102,075

$$
\begin{aligned}
\text{Probable cost} &= \text{estimated cost } K_I \\
&= 102{,}075\,(2.09) \\
&= 213{,}336
\end{aligned}
$$

*Includes burden.
**Assume 75% marketable.

Source: EPA 600/2-78-092

Application of Product to the Market: This step will be relatively simple since the door will have code approval and the price is extremely competitive and should also be accomplished through an existing wood products distributor. The marketing cost can be regulated and could be limited to $50,000.

Product Acceptance: Product acceptance should not be difficult as the resulting door will not appear different than present products. The expenses incurred will be of a standard nature associated with any product line.

In summary, to achieve a market with this fire door a cost of $169,825 to $294,576 will be incurred. This cost can easily be recovered in one year of fire door production.

Inorganic Matrix Products

There are a variety of products conceivable from inorganic materials. The ones evaluated in this program with the most promise are: fire-rated partition wall, floor/ceiling system, and fire-door core.

Also evaluated with minimal success were framing materials and ceiling panels. Other products which are derivatives of the partition wall are: interior wall panels, floor systems, ceiling systems, and roof systems. Each of these will be discussed in detail.

Fire-Rated Partition Wall: The first design concept for a partition wall panel is presented in Figure 2.8. Rice hull syntactic foam formulation RH-31 (Table 2.21) was selected for this study.

Figure 2.8: Section—Proposed Fire Wall

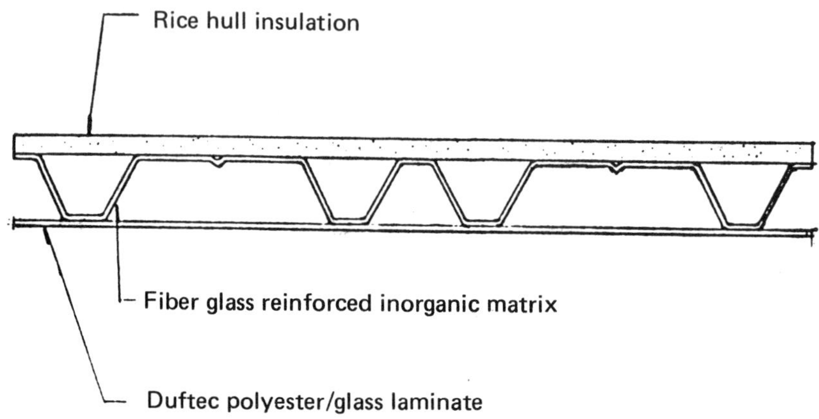

Source: EPA 600/2-78-092

Although fire does not penetrate through the rice hull surface, the back temperature gets as high as 380°F. The structural corrugation that carries the required load was designed and made from glass reinforced inorganic matrix to which the rice hull insulation is bonded, either directly when fabricated or with heat resistant epoxy adhesive.

This specimen was tested for flexure and found superior to MSC qualified structural wall. However, the fiber glass polyester inner skin softens and burns at the higher temperature. It was decided to construct an all-inorganic system.

Preparation and Testing of Inorganic Panel — The all-inorganic system utilizes RH-31 and is constructed as shown in Figure 2.9.

Preparation: The test specimen was made in two halves and then bonded together utilizing inorganic adhesive [63-97: 109 g $MgCl_2 \cdot 6H_2O$; 100 g MgO (Fast Thompson); 1 g Cab-O-Sil (M-5); and 6 g $\frac{1}{8}''$ glass fibers (K832)]. The panel halves were first formed in a mold utilizing a rice hull/plaster mix as follows:

	Grams
Rice hulls	100
90-minute casting plaster	300
$\frac{3}{4}''$ long glass fibers	5
Polyvinyl acetate adhesive (761 PVAC)	40
Fungicide (Busan 30)	0.5
Water	220

Figure 2.9:　Fire-Rated Partition Wall

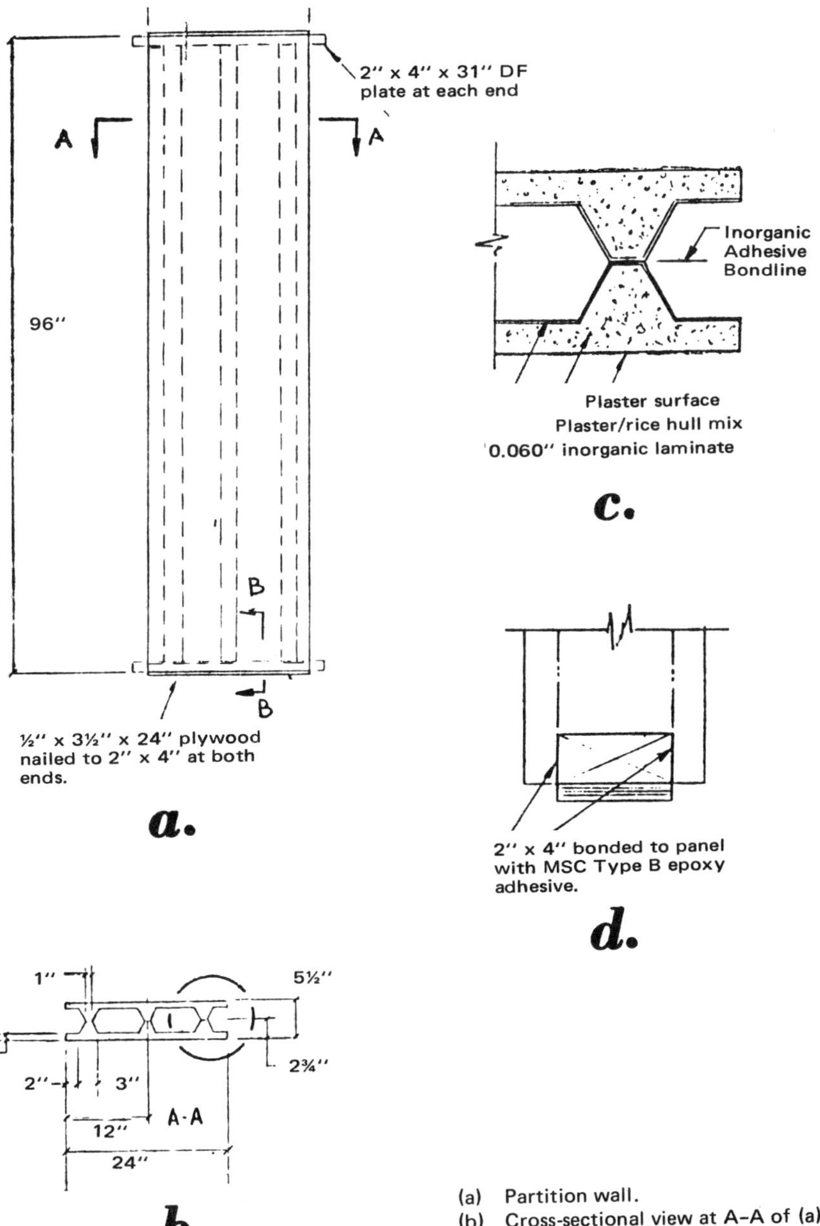

(a)　Partition wall.
(b)　Cross-sectional view at A–A of (a).
(c)　Detail of (b).
(d)　Cross-sectional view at B–B of (a).

Source:　EPA 600/2-78-092

An 0.060-inch thick inorganic laminate consisting of 1½-ounce glass mat which had been impregnated with an inorganic formulation containing 104 grams $MgCl_2 \cdot 6H_2O$ and 100 grams MgO (Fast Thompson) was then applied to each half. The exterior surfaces received a layer of plaster trowelled on approximately 0.060-inch thick.

Testing: Flexure Test — The flexure test (a nondestructive test) was administered first by adding one 40-lb concrete block to each load point at a time and observing deflections. A total of 10 blocks or 400 lb (equivalent of 25 lb/ft^2) was applied with uniform recorded deflections. The blocks were removed two at a time at five-minute intervals, to allow for any creep, and the resulting set measurements noted. This panel is much stiffer than a marketed MSC panel.

Axial Compression Test — The panel was taken to failure in the axial compression test, which was conducted per ASTM E-72 criteria. Loading was applied at 1,000 lb or 500 lb/ft intervals following a 400 lb/ft preload, after which all gauges were zeroed. Following each load application, the load was relaxed and the set readings noted.

Fire Test — Two modified E-119 fire tests were conducted on the panel shown in Figure 2.9. After three hours the fire began to penetrate through the surface of the face exposed to the fire.

Costs — A detailed cost analysis of this concept installed versus a standard wall installed is presented in Table 2.36.

Table 2.36: Cost Comparison of a Two-Hour Fire Wall

	$/ft^2
Waste-Wall Concept	
Glass and plaster	0.030
Rice hull foam (0.129 ft^3) (1.50)	0.194
Inorganic glass pan (2.79) (0.112)	0.312
Adhesive (0.079 lb) (0.30)	0.024
Material cost	0.560
Assembly labor, depreciation, etc.	0.159
Field installation labor	0.156
Total cost	0.875
Standard Wall	
2 Double-layers of ½" sheetrock	0.24
Clips and MSC hardware	0.06
2" x 4" boards, 2 (0.18)	0.36
Material cost	0.66

(continued)

Table 2.36: (continued)

	$/ft^2

	$/ft^2$
Labor, framing* 2 (0.30)	0.60
Dry wall sheathing* 4 (0.132)	0.53
Total cost	1.79

*Lee Saylor, Inc. construction costs.

Source: EPA 600/2-78-092

As can be seen, the installed cost of the waste system is 49% of the cost of a conventional system. This wall is over-designed and may be further optimized to reduce cost. The inorganic glass pan represents more than 50% of the material cost. The effect of this pan was determined on the strength of the panel. A panel was made, as shown in Figure 2.9, but without the fiber glass pan. This wall failed at 1,000 kp/ft load when the bond between the two halves failed.

The material is processed similarly to concrete. Therefore, continuous concrete panel production machinery should be applicable. The next consideration is the cost required to advance the product from concept to a market-accepted product. The cost for this is discussed below.

Design and Qualification: The design and qualification costs are summarized in Table 2.37. This activity will range from $14,430 to $25,397. However, the material and design is such that an estimate half-way between the two would be conservative.

Table 2.37: Design and Qualification Cost for the Fire Wall

	Dollars
Technical services*	3,360
Mechanical tests**	5,000
Fire test, E-119	2,500
Tunnel test, E-84***	800
Materials	200
Tooling	1,000
Filing fees	570
Travel and support	1,000
Estimated cost	14,430

(continued)

Table 2.37: (continued)

Dollars

Probable cost = estimated cost (K_{II})
                = 14,430 (1.76)
                = 25,397

*Includes burden.
**Axial compression, transverse loading,
   racking shear and impact tests.
***Smoke and flame tests.

Source: EPA 600/2-78-092

Development of Manufacturing Procedure: The plant facility, optimization and production of the panel to achieve reliability and minimum cost possible are involved here. This process will utilize standard concrete manufacturing equipment with some modification yet to be determined. The cost of scale-up studies, pilot runs, and production start with adjustments to product needs are estimated in Table 2.38. The estimated cost range is $79,600 to $144,076.

Table 2.38: Development of Manufacturing Procedure for Fire Wall

	Dollars
Scale-up studies	
Technical services*	6,720
Equipment cost ($150/hr)	6,000
Material cost	1,000
Total	13,720
Pilot run	
Technical services*	6,720
Equipment cost ($150/hr)	6,000
Material cost	3,000
Total	15,720
Start-up and adjustment to product needs	
Technical services*	13,440
Equipment cost ($150/hr)**	6,000
Material cost**	30,720
Total	50,160
Estimated cost	79,600

Probable cost = estimated cost (K_I)
                = 79,600 (1.81)
                = 144,076

*Includes burden.
**Assume 75% of product marketable.

Source: EPA 600/2-78-092

Application of the Product to the Market: The cost depends on the organization involved. This system will require an organization close to a manufacture of housing or housing elements. In all probability, the product would be incorporated into an existing system. A $75,000 cost should be a conservative estimate.

Product Acceptance: Ability to perform as a fire-rated structure is significant. Its appearance will be similar to that of any ordinary plastered wall. Therefore, acceptance will come through the builder and not the public. This will necessitate some trial projects and some subsidization may be required to create builder acceptance. A cost of $250,000 may be a reasonable estimate.

In summary, to get the fire wall on the market a cost of $419,030 to $494,473 will be incurred.

Floor/Ceiling System: The wall panel shown in Figure 2.9 was tested as a floor. The 8-foot panel was only loaded to 25 pounds per square foot, but the deflection is linear. Therefore, the deflection at 45 pounds per square foot would be 0.09 inch. The criterion for stiffness (according to the *HUD Criteria Guide*) is $\Delta = L/360$, or for 8 feet, $\Delta = 0.267$ inch. This panel is nearly 3 times as stiff as required, a 12-foot span floor/ceiling concept is still nearly twice as stiff.

In a two-hour fire test, the first 2 inches of panel can be assumed to be destroyed. At that time the panel is still capable of supporting a full 45 pounds per square foot live load plus the weight of the remaining structure. However, the three-hour fire test only destroyed the first half-inch of the surface, which makes the concept exceptionally strong and fire resistant.

Table 2.39 presents a cost comparison of this concept versus two standard floor/ceiling concepts. The waste concept is 62% of the cost of a standard wood construction and 59% of the cost of a concrete slab system.

There is a definite need for both the two-hour rated fire wall and floor/ceiling combination in construction. There is a special safety need in multifamily construction. It is proposed to design the wall as a standard $4' \times 8'$ panel with interlocking attachments designed to fit over standard $2'' \times 4''$ sill plates. The material can be cut with a standard carbide power saw which permits wall closeouts and adjustments for doors and windows. The panel will weigh less than 200 lb, which permits it to be handled by two men. It can also be prefinished in the factory. The joints can be filled in with inorganic matrix with a compatible texture.

It is proposed to design the floor/ceiling panel in standard 2-foot widths with varying lengths. These panels would be interlocking with end attachments designed for standard footings or floor beam construction and would weigh less than 200 lb, which permits handling by two men. The floor can be finished with an attractive hard-wearing ceramic surface and the ceiling side with a textured surface. Joints on both sides can be filled in with an inorganic matrix of a compatible texture. The same processing developed for the fire wall will be utilized for the floor ceiling. The cost to advance the product from concept to a market accepted product is discussed below.

Table 2.39: Cost Comparison of Two-Hour Fire-Rated Floor/Ceiling Panel

	$/ft^2

	$/ft^2$
Waste concept	
Glass and plaster	0.030
Rice hull foam (0.174 ft^3) (1.50)	0.261
Inorganic glass pan (2.79 ft^2) (0.112)	0.312
Adhesive (0.79 lb) (0.30)	0.024
Material cost	0.627
Assembly labor, depreciation, etc.	0.171
Field installation labor	0.208
Total cost	1.006
Standard wood construction*	
1 Double layer of ½" sheetrock	0.12
2 Boards 2" x 6" @ 0.27	0.54
1 Layer ½" plywood	0.30
Clips and miscellaneous hardware	0.06
Material cost	1.02
Labor	
Framing	0.250
Plywood sheathing	0.090
Dry wall sheathing, 2 (0.132)	0.264
Total cost	1.624
Standard concrete construction*	
Forms, including labor	0.027
Structural concrete, including labor	0.579
Rough finishes, including labor	0.190
Fire and acoustic insulation system,	
including labor	0.900
Total cost	1.696

*Lee Saylor, Inc. construction costs.

Source: EPA 600/2-78-092

Costs — Design and Qualification: The design work remaining is optimization.
Table 2.40 summarizes the qualification cost. This activity will cost from
$14,930 to $26,277.

Table 2.40: Design and Qualification Cost for Floor/Ceiling Systems

	Dollars
Technical services*	3,360
Mechanical tests**	3,000
Fire test, E-119	5,000
Tunnel test***	800
Materials	200
Tooling	1,000
Filing fees	570
Travel and support	1,000
Estimated cost	14,930

$$\text{Probable cost} = \text{estimated cost } (K_{11})$$
$$= 14,930 \ (1.76)$$
$$= 26,277$$

*Includes burden.
**Short-term and long-term beam bending.
***Smoke and flame.

Source: EPA 600/2-78-092

Development of Manufacturing Procedure: The procedure would be the same as the fire wall and Table 2.38 would apply. This results in a cost range of $79,600 to $144,076.

Application of the Product to Market and Product Acceptance: This would be similar to the fire wall. Therefore, a cost for these activities of $325,000 would be applicable.

In summary, the cost to get the floor/ceiling structure on the market will range from $419,530 to $495,353.

Fire-Door Core: The inorganic rice hull material has potential as a fire-door core. Core panels 1½-inch thick faced with standard wood veneer surfaces were fabricated and fire tested utilizing ASTM E-152 and E-119 test techniques. The formulation for the core is presented below with material costs:

	Dollars
Rice hulls, 3,000 g (0.019/lb)	0.126
Casting plaster, 9,000 g (0.022/lb)	0.436
Proprietary binder, 1,200 g (0.220/lb)	0.581
Water, 6,600 g	—
Busan, 30 g (2.750/lb)	0.182
Total	1.325

Note:　Dry weight = 29 lb; Volume = 0.74 ft^3
　　　　(2% waste); Cost = $0.0457/lb, $1.791/ft^3.

Costs — The commercial fire-door cores are now being sold to the door manufacturer for $12 per unit. These are 3' x 6'8" doors. There is a 7/8"-wide stile and rail around the door resulting in a core of 2.33 ft^3. The waste core could be sold to a door manufacturer for $8.71 per unit.

A commercial one-hour fire door and two waste doors were fire tested for comparison. The commercial door failed by burn-through in 78 minutes. The fire test was terminated after 140 minutes on the waste core with a thin inorganic glass facing under the veneer and 130 minutes for the waste core covered only with veneer. From these results it is apparent that the waste core is far superior, with an easily attainable two-hour fire rating.

The manufacturing system proposed is a modified plaster mixer with a continuous feed onto a conveyor of molds. The facility cost for a production rate of 480 per day should not exceed $50,000.

Design and Qualification: A formula selection and a test are required. The details are presented in Table 2.41. The cost will range from $9,080 to $15,981.

Table 2.41: Design and Qualification Cost for Fire-Door Core

	Dollars
Technical services*	3,360
ASTM E-152 fire test	4,000
Materials	50
Tooling	100
Filing fees	570
Travel and support	1,000
Estimated cost	9,080

$$\text{Probable cost} = \text{estimated cost } (K_{11})$$
$$= \$9,080 \,(1.76)$$
$$= \$15,981$$

*Includes burden.

Source: EPA 600/2-78-092

Development of the Manufacturing Procedure: The details are presented in Table 2.42. This cost will range from $82,753 to $149,782.

Application of the Product to the Market: The market for the cores are fire door manufacturers. The core design is common to all. Sales will be made directly to the manufacturer. The first step will be to select an interested manufacturer and supply him with a core. He will construct a door with the core and then together qualify the door. These costs are covered in Design and Qualification. Another $10,000 should be considered for market analysis for major product acceptance.

Table 2.42: Development of Manufacturing Procedures for Fire-Door Core

	Dollars
Pilot plant studies	
Technical services*	20,160
Equipment cost**	1,384
Material cost	1,086
Total cost	22,630
Start-up and adjustment to product needs	
Technical services*	20,160
Equipment cost (4.00/hr)***	1,038
Material cost***	38,925
Total cost	60,123
Estimated cost	82,753

$$\text{Probable cost} = \text{estimated cost } (K_I)$$
$$= \$82{,}753\ (1.81)$$
$$= \$149{,}782$$

*Includes burden.
**$50,000/5 yr = $4.00/hr.
***Assume 75% of product marketable.

Source: EPA 600/2-78-092

Product Acceptance: Since the initial production will be 150,000 units per year at least three door manufacturers will have to be qualified. One is already qualified, which leaves two more at a cost of $9,080 each. Assuming another $10,000 for marketing services, product acceptance will cost an estimated $28,160.

In summary, to get the fire-door core on the market, a cost of $129,993 to $203,923 will be required. If the $12 sales price is maintained and the waste core cost is $8.71, in one year the sale of 150,000 cores will return $493,500 over costs. This makes the core economically viable.

Lumber Substitute for Framing Material: Wood elements (2" x 4") may be used for window and door framing. These elements have to be warp-free in order to fit into the system. Formulation RH-54 (Table 2.19) is lightweight, nailable and fire resistant. One structural application for this formulation was intended to be window and door framing.

Preparation and Testing — The specimens were produced by incorporating the RH-54 into 0.050 inch Duftec channels. The form was the Duftec channel itself supported by a wooden box to maintain alignment. The wet mixture was poured into the form and allowed to set-up overnight. After this it was allowed to dry and was eventually removed from the mold. It was then secondarily bonded to the channel with MSC Type B epoxy.

A 51-inch wide window panel and a 73-inch wide sliding-glass door panel (minus frames and glazings) were constructed and then tested in a MSC axial compression apparatus. The window panel failed at a load of 752 pounds per linear foot, while the sliding-glass door panel failed at a load of 360 pounds per linear foot. Failure occurred when the supporting vertical legs failed in column buckling. The failing load for the corresponding qualified ICBO window and door panels is 1,800 pounds per linear foot for each.

Both specimens were tested to failure. The mode of failure in both cases was column buckling of the vertical rice hull filled Duftec channels at relatively low load levels (1,600 pounds axial load on the column for the window and 1,100 pounds axial load on the column for the sliding-glass door).

The material cost of a 2" x 4" board of RH-54 would be $0.10 per foot, resulting in a $0.32 per foot retail cost, which is approximately twice that for commercial lumber. Since the product exhibits no significant properties, exhibits no dimensional stability, no further consideration is warranted.

Ceiling Panels: Rice hull formulation RH-21 (Table 2.19) was selected for ceiling panel product development. The design concept used a skin of gypsum plaster which was cast into a mold. A glass surfacing mat (10 mils) was laid on as reinforcement and a retainer for the rice hulls. The mix was immediately applied and all dried together; if the plaster skin was already hard, the total material could be dried in a microwave oven in a matter of minutes. The panel was subjected to a $1600°F$ propane torch test. The comparative results with commercial products are presented in Table 2.43. The waste product performed much better than the commercial products.

Costs — There are at least 10 major manufacturers of ceiling tiles and panels offering collectively at least 239 various styles and specialty products. The product sale price ranges from $0.15 to $0.39 per square foot. Certain specialty panels range from $0.45 to $9.00 per square foot. Panels that generate no smoke sell from $0.185 to $0.455 per square foot. The only price available on a 0 flame spread product is $0.20 to $0.30 per square foot but these generate smoke. No price is available on a 0 flame spread 0 smoke product. The only such product offered is an aluminum-clad vinyl-coated gypsum or mineral board offered by Acoustiflex. The weights of the panels range from 0.75 to 2.38 pounds per square foot.

The ceiling panel market appears to be a very specialist-oriented one and a competitive one. The market area for this product would probably be in the fire-rated application. The waste ceiling would possibly provide an additional half-hour to one hour to any ceiling designs on the market. However, due to the fact that this product would be in the upper cost range and many acceptable products are already on the market, no further consideration is recommended.

Table 2.43: Comparative Propane Torch Test for Ceiling Panels

	Test Formulation	Armstrong Fashiontone	Celotex Safetone	Celotex Protectone	Owens-Corning Fissure
Panel thickness, inch	0.560	0.595	0.556	0.582	0.580
Time to reach 380°F, min/sec	6/30	2/45	2/45	3/45	1/15
Equilibrium temp, °F	1180	not tested	not tested	1430	1430
Time to achieve equilibrium temp, min	25	not tested	not tested	7.5	3
Flame	none	surface flash	surface flash	surface flash	—
Smoke	none	some	some	some	some
Appearance	severe cracking	char	char	slight cracking, char	char
Cost, $/ft^2	0.102	—	—	—	—
Sale price, $/ft^2	0.328	0.169	0.165	0.195	0.160

Source: EPA 600/2-78-092

Product Derivatives from the Partition Wall: There are a variety of products that can be produced from the facility utilized to produce the fire-rated partition wall or floor/ceiling system. These products are less demanding functionally and, therefore, conventional solutions can be resolved at a cost that makes the waste product less attractive although viable. All of the products below can be produced as prefinished components and all are fire resistant, non-smoke generating products.

Floor System — This is a variation of the floor/ceiling concept without the ceiling panel. The cost is 53% of standard wood construction and 74% of a concrete slab.

Interior Wall Panel — This is a variation of the two-hour fire wall. The center rib is removed and the surfaces reduced to $3/8$" thickness. The cost is 76% of that of a standard 2" x 4" stud dry-wall construction.

Roof System — The roof panel requires an impermeable seal as required by any standard roof. It is a variation of the floor concept with shorter length stiffness. The cost is 69% of that of a standard wood construction.

Ceiling System — This is a self-supporting ceiling system. The cost of the system is 69% of a standard 2" x 4" dry-wall ceiling construction.

SUMMARY

It is clear from the above discussion of products and costs that marketable building materials could be manufactured using waste materials. Satisfactory products could be made using both inorganic and organic systems. Often structural properties of the formulations were superior to existing commercial products. The economic analyses performed indicate that several products would be competitive at the marketplace—notably fire-retardant materials containing rice hulls (as either matrix or reinforcement).

REFERENCES

Reinforcements

Anderson, A.B., Wong, A. and Wu, K., "Utilization of White Fir Bark in Particle Board." *Forest Products Journal* 24(1).

Anonymous, *Cultural and Harvesting Methods for Kenaf Production,* U.S. Department of Agriculture Research Report No. 113.

Anonymous, "How Sewage and Solid Wastes Can Be Recycled into Useful Products," *Research Trends,* pp 54–58 (Autumn 1971).

Chow, P., "New Uses Found for Discarded Christmas Trees," *Illinois Research* 15(3) (Summer 1973).

Clark, T.F., et al, "A Search for New Fiber Crops," *The Journal of Technical Association of the Pulp and Paper Industry* 50(11) (November 1967).

Cox, F.B. and Geymayer, H.G., *Expedient Reinforcement for Concrete for Use in Southeast Asia,* U.S. Army Corps of Engineers, Technical Report C-69-3 #1, Vicksburg, Mississippi.

Cox, F.B. and McDonald, J.E., *Expedient Reinforcement for Concrete for Use in Southeast Asia,* U.S. Army Corps of Engineers, Technical Report C-69-3 #3, Vicksburg Mississippi.

Currier, R.A., *An Assessment of Current Bark Utilization Opportunities,* Department of Forest Products, Oregon State University.

Currier, R.A. and Lehmann, W.F., *Bark as an Ingredient in Molded Items, Particle Boards, Adhesive and Other Products,* Department of Forest Products, Oregon State University.

Fan, LT., Retsloff, D.G. and Vanderpool, W.O., "Solid Waste—Plastic Composites: Physical Properties and Feasibility for Production," *Environmental Science and Technology,* 6(13) pp 1085–1091 (December 1972).

Gloria, H.F., "Bagasse Structural Board—Our Hope?," *Sugarland,* (June-July 1972).

Grover, R.R. and Barbour, J.F., *Industrial Utilization of Solid Waste—Economic and Engineering Analysis of a Straw-Particle Board Plant,* Department of Agricultural Chemistry, Oregon State University.

Chow, P., Walters, C.S. and Guiher, J.K., "Specific Gravity, Bulk Density and Screen Analysis of Midwestern Plant Fiber Residues," *Forest Products Journal* 23(2).

Henn, J.J. and Peters, F.A., *Cost Evaluation of a Metal and Mineral Recovery Process for Treating Municipal Incinerator Residues,* U.S. Department of Interior, I.C. 8533.

Hough, J.H. and Barr, H.T., *Possible Uses for Waste Rice Hulls in Building Materials and Other Products,* Bulletin No. 507, Agricultural Experiment Station, Louisiana State University and A & M College.

Kenahan, C.B. and Flint, E.P., *Bureau of Mines Research Programs on Recycling and Disposal of Mineral, and Energy Based Solid Wastes,* U.S. Department of Interior, I.C. 8529.

Kenahan, C.B. and Kaplan, R.S., *Bureau of Mines Research Programs on Recycling and Disposal of Mineral, Metal, and Energy Based Wastes,* U.S. Department of Interior, I.C. 8595.

Lockhart, R.J. and Bartz, S.A., "Development of Carbon Products from Lignin (Paper Mill) Wastes," *Proceedings of the Third Mineral Waste Symposium* (1974).

Miller, D.J., "Molding Characteristics of Some Mixtures of Douglas Fir Bark and Phenolic Resin," *Forest Products Journal* 22(9).

Sullivan, P.M., Stranczyk, M.H. and Spendlove, M.J., *Resource Recovery from Raw Urban Refuse,* U.S. Department of Interior, R.I. 7760.

Van Vliet, A.C., *Converting Bark into Opportunities,* Oregon State University, Department of Forest Products, (personal communication).

Walters, C.S., *Utilization of Plant-Fiber Residues,* University of Illinois, College of Agriculture, (personal communication).

Fillers

Abrahams, J.H. Jr., "Recycling Container Glass," *Proceedings of the Third Mineral Waste Symposium* (1974).

Anonymous, "Refuse Glass Aggregate in Portland Cement Concrete Waste Glass as an Ingredient in Lightweight Concrete," *Proceedings of the Third Mineral Waste Symposium* (1974).

Anonymous, *Solid Waste as Fuel for Power Plants,* Horner and Shifrin Inc., pp 220–316.

Anonymous, *Utilization of Mining and Mill Wastes,* U.S. Bureau of Mines, Contract No. H0190397, IITRI Project No. G6027.

Anonymous, *Utilization of Phosphate Slimes,* International Minerals and Chemical Corporation, EPA Project 14050 EPV.

Covey, J.N. and Farber, J.H., "Ash Utilization—Views on a Growth Industry," *Proceedings of the Third Mineral Waste Symposium* (1974).

Cox, J.L., "Phosphate Wastes," (International Minerals and Chemical Corporation), First Mineral Waste Utilization Symposium, 1972.

Dean, K.C., Chindgren, C.J. and Peterson, L., "Recovery of Values from Shredded Urban Refuse," *Proceedings of the Third Mineral Waste Symposium* (1974).

Davis, R.L., Hansen, P.G. and Kekar, S.C., "Extrusion—A Means of Recycling Waste Plastic and Glass," *Proceedings of the Third Mineral Waste Symposium* (1974).

Faber, J.H., "Fly Ash Utilization—Problem and Prospects," (U.S. Bureau of Mines), First Mineral Waste Utilization Symposium, 1972.

Gouivens, P.R., "Utilization of Foundry Waste By-Products," First Mineral Waste Utilization Symposium, 1972.

Grubbs, M.R. and Luey, K.H., *Recovering Plastics from Urban Refuse by Electrodynamics Techniques,* College Park Metallurgy, College Park, Maryland; Research Center, U.S. Bureau of Mines, Solid Waste Research Program TPR 63 (December 1972).

Hansen, P.G. and Davis, R.L., *Utilization of High-Pressure Forming for Converting Waste Glass into Usable Structural Materials,* Department of Mechanical Engineering, University of Missouri, Rolla-Contract GO 100158 (SWD-27), U.S. Bureau of Mines.

Hecht, N.L., "Application of Silicate Waste from Paper Processing," *Proceedings of the Third Mineral Waste Symposium* (1974).

Hough, J.H. and Barr, H.T., *Possible Uses for Waste Rice Hulls in Building Materials and Other Products,* Bulletin No. 507, Agricultural Experiment Station, Louisiana State University and A & M College.

Pincus, A.G., "Wastes from Processing of Aluminum Ores," (IITRI), First Mineral Waste Utilization Symposium, 1972.

Shotts, R.O. and Cox, R.M., *Feasibility of Utilizing Waste Glass as a Component for Lightweight Structural Building Products,* U.S. Bureau of Mines, Contract G0100S9 (SWD-28), College of Engineering, University of Alabama, BER Report 140–119.

Sullivan, G.D., "Coal Wastes," American Mining Congress, First Mineral Waste Utilization Symposium, 1972.

Sullivan, P.M. and Stanczyk, M.H., *Economics of Recycling Metals and Minerals from Urban Refuse,* U.S. Bureau of Mines, Solid Waste Research Program, Technical Progress Report 33 (April 1971).

Vasan, S., "Utilization of Florida Phosphate Slimes," *Proceedings of Third Mineral Waste Symposium* (1974).

Matrices

Anonymous, "Industrially Significant Organic Chemicals Part 7: Lignin Sulfonic Acids (Na and K Salts)," *Chemical Engineering* (June 24, 1974).

Barbour, J.F. and Grover, R.R., *The Chemical Conversion of Solid Waste to Useful Products,* Department of Agricultural Chemistry, Oregon State University (personal communication).

Hough, J.H. and Barr, H.T., *Possible Uses for Waste Rice Hulls in Building Materials and Other Products,* Bulletin No. 507, Agricultural Experiment Station, Louisiana State University and A & M College.

Nee, C.I. and Hsich, W.C., "Furfural from Bagasse," *Proceedings Int. Soc. Sugar Cane Tech. 13th Cong.,* pp 1881–1890 (1970).

Parker, H.W., "Fuels and Petrochemicals from Agricultural Waste," 76th National AICHE Meeting (March 1974).

Weakley, F.B. and Roth, W.B., "Mill Evaluation of Dialdehyde. Starch-Protein Glue for Hardwood Plywood Manufacture," *Forest Products Journal* 23(7) (July 1973).

Wellons, J.P. and Krohmer, R.L., "Self-Bonding in Bark Composites," *Wood Science* 6(2) (October 1973).

Production and Evaluation of Waste-Derived Building Components

Information in this chapter is based on *A Study of the Feasibility of Utilizing Solid Wastes for Building Materials, Phases III and IV Summary Reports,* EPA Report, 600/2-78-111, May 1978 prepared by Material Systems Corporation for the U.S. Environmental Protection Agency (Municipal Environmental Research Laboratory, Cincinnati, OH).

Material Systems Corporation and the Solid and Hazardous Waste Research Division of the Municipal Environmental Research Laboratory at Cincinnati, Ohio have performed a joint study investigating the applicability of waste materials for residential and commercial construction.

Research reported in the previous chapter (Phases I and II of this study) demonstrated the potential technical and economic feasibility of utilizing waste materials for building construction. It is apparent that there exist product possibilities from waste materials. Production and qualifications (Phases III and IV) of waste-derived building materials which were developed in Phase II of the study will be discussed in this chapter.

ORGANIC MATRIX PRODUCTS

A two-step process of "in-situ" formulation of furfural from wastes such as wood, peanut hulls, rice hulls, and cotton stock was described in the previous chapter. It was discovered that materials containing cellulose and pentosans when treated with acid, yield a binder during the process of molding. The acid treatment is very simple. A 3 to 7% solution of hydrochloric, phosphoric, or p-toluene sulfonic acid is used depending on the waste involved. The first step is to soak the material in the acid solution for 30 minutes and then dry it in an oven at 50° to 60°C. The second step is to transfer the material to a cold mold and cure it under pressure for 2 to 10 minutes. This concept appeared to be a feasible application to the production of particle board. The results of work with 4" x 6" specimens supported this. However, when a limited quantity of 30" x 30" panels were made, scale-up problems became apparent but were considered solvable.

Processing Conditions

The effort was directed to the development of processing conditions, which would permit the fabrication of 48" x 48" panels that could be qualified as exterior structural particle board. The basic conditions to be resolved were as follows:

      (1) Type and percent of acid absorbed by material
      (2) Moisture content
      (3) Time under pressure
      (4) Press temperature
      (5) Pressure technique
      (6) Post cure
      (7) Preheat
      (8) Particle size

Peanut hulls and wood waste, which provide the most resinous binder by in situ formation, were selected for this study.

Type and Percent of Acid Absorbed by the Material: Peanut Hull Waste — Two acids were considered for use with peanut hull waste: p-toluene sulfonic acid and phosphoric acid. There are no appreciable differences in properties and tests indicate that a 4 to 6% acid absorption by the hulls is the minimum acceptable for either with peanut hulls. The cost of phosphoric acid is $0.18 per pound and the cost of p-toluene sulfonic is $0.25 per pound. Therefore phosphoric acid was used in all peanut hull waste scale-up studies.

To acid-soak large quantities of peanut hulls, it was necessary to abandon laboratory methods which soaked the hulls in a 3% solution of acid in water for 15 minutes followed by draining. Later, a washing machine and clothes dryer were effectively used. Bags were sewn with fine polyester mesh fabric and hulls put into these for soaking and centrifuging. Without these bags, the vents in the dryer were rapidly plugged, drying efficiency drastically reduced, and there was also a considerable loss of material. It was obvious that the centrifugation of the soaked peanut hulls would remove much more of the phosphoric acid solution used to treat the hulls, thus leaving behind less acid in the hulls. The properties of the product were greatly affected by the amount of phosphoric acid in the hulls.

The amount of acid in the hulls when drained by gravity in the lab method on small quantities vs that of the centrifuged material was determined by soaking hulls in acid using both methods. The results of this test are presented in Table 3.1. It can be seen from these data that the ratio of hulls to absorbed acid is much greater with the spin process than with the laboratory soak process. The moisture content was lowered by centrifugation and this was advantageous because of more rapid drying with lower energy consumption.

Table 3.1: Composition by Percent Weight of Peanut Hulls-Phosphoric Acid Mixture

Method	Hulls (%)	Acid* (%)	Water (%)	Hulls/Acid
Lab Process				
Test #1	20.7	2.3	77.0	9.0
Test #2	23.1	2.2	74.7	10.5
Test #3	24.9	2.2	72.9	11.3
Spin and dry after 3% solution of 75% acid in water	43.1	1.66	55.2	26.0
Spin and dry after 7% solution of 75% acid in water	44.4	3.64	52.0	12.2

*100% concentrate

Source: EPA 600/2-78-111

The reuse of drained acid solution with added fresh acid solution resulted in a considerable cost savings compared to the lab scale method where the drained acid was discarded. Titration results are presented in Table 3.2.

After three applications, the acid soaking solution was made strongly alkaline with sodium hydroxide solution and this produced an amine-like order which caused indicator paper to show a pH of 9 for the vapors above the solution. It appears that peanut hulls contain a basic material which removes hydrogen ion by neutralization but permits reuse up to three times.

Table 3.2: Titration Studies of Phosphoric Acid Soak Solutions with Reuse Theoretical Molarity = 0.224

Item	0-Use	1-Use	2-Uses	3-Uses
H_1^+ (pH 5.75), M	0.215	0.161	0.115	0.062
H_2^+ (pH 8.6), M	0.213	0.218	0.220	0.194
Amount of 1st hydrogen used, %	0	25	47	71
Amount of 2nd hydrogen used, %	0	0	0	0

Source: EPA 600/2-78-111

The soaking time was reduced from 15 minutes or longer to 5 minutes. This was determined by soaking peanut hulls in 3% acid solution for 5 minutes and 800 minutes (16 hours). The initial ratio of H_1^+/H_2^+ was 0.98. After 5 minutes the ratio was 0.785 and after 800 minutes it was 0.79, indicating no further change after 5 minutes.

Two large-scale mixes were made to produce material for use in full scale process studies at Washington State University. The solution used was 8 gallons of a 7% solution of 75% phosphoric acid in water for 8.82 pounds of hulls. The acid utilization is presented in Table 3.3. These samples were further dried removing more of the acid and solution. It can be seen from Table 3.4 that acceptable 12" x 15" panels can be made with a 4% acid content. For further discussion see the section on full scale production studies.

Table 3.3: Acid Used in Large-Scale Mixer

Peanut Hulls, lb	75% Phosphoric Acid, lb	Percent of Acid*
1,000	73.51	5.5
1,300	117.62	6.8

*Based on weight of peanut hulls, calculated as 100% phosphoric acid.

Source: EPA 600/2-78-111

Wood Waste — The wood wastes from Ponderosa Pine, Southern Hard Pine, and Douglas Fir were evaluated with different percentages of acid absorption and with both phosphoric acid and p-toluene sulfonic acid. Ponderosa Pine does not provide an acceptable product with this system. Hard Pine provided better results. The best results were obtained with Douglas Fir and p-toluene sulfonic acid.

A series of 12" x 15" panels were made to more closely approximate full scale production with 0.35% and 1.78% acid absorption. The 0.35% yielded too little resinous binder and the 1.78% generated too much. Combining the two materials in quantities of 60 to 67% of 1.78% absorption and 33 to 40% of 0.35% absorption, yielded potentially acceptable results. These data are shown in Table 3.5.

Because of the relatively long time required to produce acid treated particles with the soak-dry method, and the limited time available on the Washington State University presses, it was decided to use the Washington State University spray equipment to make acid treated particles.

The acid was sprayed onto the wood chips using 20 grams of 25% p-toluene sulfonic acid in water, per pound of wood. A small amount of insoluble impurity (presumably sulfone) had to be filtered out of the solution to protect the spray nozzles against stoppage. This resulted in a material with an acid absorption content of 1.05%. The results are shown in Table 3.6.

**Table 3.4: Medium-Sized Peanut Hull Panels Made with Phosphoric Acid
(12" x 15")**

| | | Moisture WSU Method (%) | | ....Molding Conditions....... | | | |
Sample	Acid (g/100 g of chips)		Platen Temp (°F)	Pressure (psi)	Pressure Relief Cycle (min)	Time Under Pressure (min)
46-1	3.98	5.5	375	1,000	None	7
46-2	3.98	5.5	375	1,000	5	10
46-3	3.98	5.5	375	1,000	5, 10 Blew	15
46-4	3.98	5.5	340	1,000	5	10
46-5	3.98	5.5	390	1,000	5	10
46-6	3.98	5.5	390	1,000	5, 10	15

| | | | | ....Properties of Panel................ | | | |
| | Charge Size | Thickness | Density | Internal Bond IB | .. Flexure .. | | |
Sample	(g)	(inch)	(lb/ft^3)	(psi)	MOR (psi)	MOE (10^6 psi)	Notes
46-1	1,900	—					Blown
46-2	1,900	0.542	65	164	2,087	0.470	OK
46-3	1,900	—					Blown
46-4	1,900	0.525	65	195	2,150	0.487	OK
46-5	1,800	0.525	64	147	2,112	0.466	OK
46-6	1,800	0.545	64	183	2,132	0.492	Blown

Source: EPA 600/2-78-111

Moisture Content: Peanut Hull Waste — Only limited variation on the effect of
moisture content was evaluated for peanut hull waste. No real effect is discern-
ible. For the purpose of the large scale work a moisture content between 5 and
6% was selected. This was similar to that now used in the industry and was considered to be the most reliable.

Wood Waste — The results from limited studies on the effect of moisture on
wood waste for 4" x 6" panels show no real trend. However, when tests were
conducted on larger panels (12" x 15") increasing the water content from 1.5
to 5.5% assisted the processing of 0.35% acid absorbed mixture and a mixture
of 0.35% and 1.78% acid absorbed material with 3.8% moisture was better
(see Table 3.5). Table 3.6 presents the results of a study on an acid content
similar to the mix in Table 3.5 but with a 7.8% moisture content which achieves
similar results. This indicates that moisture content has an effect on processing
although of less importance than the other parameters.

Table 3.5: Longview Douglas Fir (on 20 Mesh) Treated with p-Toluene Sulfonic Acid (12" x 15" x 0.5")

| | | Moisture | | | | | | | | | | | Internal | . Flexure . | | |
| | Acid | WSU | Platen | | Pressure Relief | Time Under | Time to Relieve | Charge | | | | Bond | | | MOE | |
Sample	(g/100 g of chips)	Method (%)	Temp. ($^\circ$F)	Pressure (psi)	Cycle (min)	Pressure (min)	Pressure (min)	Size (g)	Thickness (inch)	Density (lb/ft^3)	IB (psi)	MOR (psi)	(x 10^6 psi)	Notes
10	0.35	1.5	390	750–1,500	7	12	0	1,800	0.5	—	—	—	—	Blown
11	0.35	1.5	390	1,100–1,500	7	12	0	1,800	—	—	—	—	—	Blown
12	0.35	1.5	390	1,100	7	12	0	1,600	—	—	—	—	—	Blown
13	0.35	5.5	390	1,100	7	12	0	1,600	—	61	—	—	—	Crumbly
14	1.78	3.0	300	1,000	None	5	0	1,700	0.470	70	—	—	—	Blown
20	1.78	3.0	300	1,000	None	7	1	1,800	—	—	—	—	—	Blown
22	1.78	3.0	300	1,000	None	7	0	1,800	—	—	—	—	—	Blown
15	75%–1.78 25%–0.35	3.6	310	1,000	None	6	0	1,700	0.505	65	—	—	—	Blown
16	75%–1.78 25%–0.35	3.6	310	750	None	8	1	1,700	0.502	64	—	—	—	Blown
17	67%–1.78 33%–0.35	3.8	300	750	14 blew	15	3	1,900	—	—	—	—	—	Blown
18	67%–1.78 33%–0.35	3.8	300	1,000	None	8	2	1,800	0.491	70	—	—	—	Blown
19	67%–1.78 33%–0.35	3.8	300	1,000	None	10	2	1,800	0.504	68	22	1,516	0.594	OK
21	60%–1.78 40%–0.35	4.0	300	1,100	None	7	0	1,800	0.508	68	14	2,096	0.783	Blown

Source: EPA 600/2-78-111

Table 3.6: Longview Douglas Fir (+20 Mesh) Treated by p-Toluene Sulfonic Acid Spray Method (12" x 15" x 0.5")

		Moisture	. . . . . . Molding Conditions.			
	Acid	WSU	Platen		Pressure Relief	Time Under
	(g/100 g	Method	Temp	Pressure	Cycle	Pressure
Sample	of chips)	(%)	(°F)	(psi)	(min)	(min)
40	1.046	7.8	325	1,100	None	8
41	1.046	7.8	325	1,100	5	10
42	1.046	7.8	340	1,100	5	10
43	1.046	7.8	340	1,100	6	10

| | . . . . Properties of Panel. . . . . | | | | . . . Flexure. . . | | |
| | Time to Relieve Pressure | Charge Size | Thickness | Density | MOR | MOE (x 10^6 | |
Sample	(min)	(g)	(inch)	(lb/ft^3)	(psi)	psi)	Notes
40	0	1,800	0.519	68	—	—	Blown
41	1	1,800	—	—	—	—	OK
42	1	1,800	0.492	68	2,402	0.781	Blown
43	1	1,800	0.512	65	2,144	0.685	Blown

Source: EPA 600/2-78-111

Time Under Pressure: Peanut Hull Waste — The effect of molding time on properties for a 375°F and a 500 psi cure with a material moisture content of 13% and 9% was studied at molding times of 1 to 15 min. There is a definite relationship between press cure time and density and a relationship between density and strength retention with water pickup. Longer press cure times can be expected to produce more resin. Increased resin decreases voids which reduces water pick-up that effects strength loss. There is a point where further generation of resin becomes self-defeating because the chemical reactions forming the resinous material will eventually lead to excessive shrinkage and eventual cracking of the laminate. From this study, it can be concluded that a minimum of 5 minutes press time is required at a cure temperature of 375°F to generate sufficient resin for satisfactory properties.

If the generation of resin is a function of time and temperature, it can be theorized that shorter times with higher temperatures will produce equal results to longer times and lower temperatures. Temperatures up to 450°F were evaluated with shorter times. The results are presented in Table 3.7. As can be seen, times less than 5 minutes show a marked decrease in initial properties as well as resistance to water.

Wood Waste — The work on peanut hulls was applicable to wood waste. The effects of variations of time under pressure are presented for Douglas Fir in

Table 3.7: Effect of High Press Temperatures and Shorter Press Times on Properties of Peanut Hull Waste Panels

Pressure – 500 psi   Moisture Content – 3%

Press Temp °F	Press Time (minutes)	% Weight Gain after Water Soak		Flexural Strength, psi after Water Soak		
		2hrs	24hrs	0 hrs	2 hrs	24 hrs
410	5	10	40	1672	1279	191
410	5	11	35	1600	1263	274
410	5	9	18	1502	1100	988
425	5	12	14	1403	1184	1052
425	5	11	20	1764	813	883
425	5	17	44	1330	826	184
450	5	All attempts to make panels resulted in serious blowing.				
410	3	*	*	670	*	*
410	3	*	*	537	*	*
425	3	*	*	937	*	*
425	3	*	*	1303	*	*
410	2	*	*	504	*	*
410	2	*	*	596	*	*
425	2	*	*	1104	*	*
425	2	*	*	1117	*	*
425	1	*	*	380	*	*
425	1	*	*	307	*	*
450	1	*	*	740	*	*
450	1	*	*	809	*	*
450	1	*	*	285	*	*
450	1	*	*	224	*	*
450	1	*	*	989	*	*
450	1	*	*	85	*	*
450	1	8	22	–	–	63

*These specimens fell apart after 2-hr water soak.

Source: EPA 600/2-78-111

Tables 3.5 and 3.6. Cure times of 5 minutes appear to be minimum; times between 5 and 10 minutes are optimum.

Press Temperature: Peanut Hull Waste — Some effects of varying temperatures on the material properties are presented in Tables 3.4 and 3.7. The possibility of a panel blowing increases with temperature. The temperature range that consistently provided dense, structurally sound panels was 350° to 400°F. The theory that increased temperature reduces press time was proven ineffective in the previous section. Therefore, 375°F was chosen as the starting point for full scale studies.

Wood Waste — The fact that wood generates more volatiles than peanut hulls results in more possibilities for blowing. Therefore, lower temperatures were evaluated. Tables 3.5 and 3.6 present data for Douglas Fir. The temperature range that consistently provided dense and structurally sound panels was 300° to 350°F.

Pressure Technique: Peanut Hull Waste — For the purpose of this discussion a pressure relief cycle is defined as rapid release, at a predetermined time, of the pressure applied to the material. The press platens are slightly opened to allow the vapor build-up in the material to be released. The pressure is then reapplied and maintained until the press is completely closed.

"Decompression time" is a gradual reduction of the final pressure to 0 psi over a predetermined time after the press time selected was complete. For a 4" x 6" panel and for pressure over 500 psi, the pressure relief cycle improves the properties of the product. This is particularly true where multiple cycles are used. However, the fabrication of the larger panels showed less tendency for blowing without pressure relief. It appears that a decompression of slightly over one minute will materially improve the product.

Wood Waste — The wood waste small panels have less effective pressure relief cycles than peanut hull panels. The fabrication of the larger panels showed that one pressure relief cycle appears to reduce blowing considerably especially when the release occurs two-thirds through the press time. As in peanut hull waste, a decompression time of slightly over one minute improves the product.

Effects of Postcure: The postcure studies were conducted on peanut hull waste. The primary purpose was to determine if the properties of short press time products could be improved. The first effort was an attempt to improve the properties of a 1 minute cure at 450°F. The results are presented in Table 3.8. There was minimal improvement in flexural strength with postcure (Table 3.7) but the resistance to water was improved. The effects of postcure were then determined on a more conventional processing procedure.

Table 3.8: Effect of Postcuring Conditions on Peanut Shell Properties

Press molded 1 minute at 450°F

Specimen	Post Cure Conditions	Wt., grams hrs, H_2O soak 0	24 hrs	Flexural Strength hrs, H_2O soak 0	24 hrs
26-2	1 hr/275°F	*	*	853	
27-1	2 hr/275°F	*	*	659	
28-1	16hr/300°F	*	*	468	
28-2	16hr/300°F	31.9	50.6		113
28-3	16hr/300°F	30.6	49.0		101

* Specimens failed during 2-hr. soak.

Source: EPA 600/2-78-111

Test panels were fabricated under identical conditions but subjected to various postcure and precure conditions, such as using peanut hulls of two different moisture contents. The pressing conditions of 5 minutes, 500 psi at $375°$F were selected because there was a sharper increase in strength beyond 5 minutes which potentially made postcure effects more noticeable, either better or worse. Table 3.9 data on small panels shows changes in dimensions, weight and density for various postcures.

Table 3.9: Effect of Postcure on Peanut Hull Panels

Moisture Content = 9%; Processed – 5 mins @ 500 psi @ $375°$F

Postcure Conditions	No.	Dimensions, cm			Volume cm^3	Weight grams	Density g/cm^3
		W	T	L			
None (Control)	1	10.2	0.81	15.2	125.1	116.9	0.96
	2	10.2	0.85	15.3	132.7	116.6	0.88
	3	10.2	0.82	15.2	127.1	115.0	0.90
	4	10.2	0.92	15.2	142.6	117.5	0.82
	5	10.2	0.84	15.2	130.2	117.7	0.90
	6	10.2	0.74	15.2	114.7	120.0	1.05
30 mins/$400°$F	2	10.1	0.76	15.0	115.1	98.2	0.85
2 hrs/$375°$F	3	10.0	0.81	15.0	121.5	94.5	0.78
16 hrs/$325°$F	4	10.1	0.88	15.1	134.2	105.5	0.79
2 hrs /$375°$ + 1hr/$425°$	5	9.8	0.76	14.7	109.5	89.3	0.82
16 hrs/$325°$ + 1hr/$375°$	6	9.9	0.69	14.8	101.1	97.3	0.96

Source: EPA 600/2-78-111

Postcure of the panels indicated definite shrinkage in dimensions, resulting in volume, weight and density changes. Thickness was most sensitive to change; weight exhibited greater changes than volume or density. There seemed to be no correlation in these data. The weight loss is important because this is now considerably greater than the moisture content of the treated hulls prior to processing. This indicates that water is evolved by a dehydration reaction, probably from a polymerization reaction during pressing.

All six panels were next cut into flexural specimens. Five were used for water soaking with one serving as control. Postcure resulted in a definite decrease in percentage weight, volume and density gained on water exposure. The percentage flexural strength loss after 24-hour water immersion was decreased under all postcuring conditions. Strength increases of over 200% are not realistic and are probably due to a faulty control specimen providing a low flexural strength level.

The above procedure was repeated except that the panels were press cured for only 3 minutes at $375°$F and then postcured.

The same effects were found, again with postcuring causing further decrease in weight, dimensions and density. It appeared that the 3 minute cure resulted in smaller decreases in volume than panels cured for 5 minutes, both being cured at 375°F, while the change in density was larger for the 3 minute cure. This phenomenon is reasonable only if weight changes are about the same for either cure and this appears to be the case. Overall, however, there appears to be no improvement in properties that would justify a postcure in a production process.

Effects of Preheat: This study was conducted with peanut hull waste only. There are several important reasons why the use of preheated, treated peanut hulls is of interest: They can go directly from drying ovens to the press and this would save energy, and permit faster heat-up to desired temperature; they can be used to preadvance the resin to remove a part of the condensation volatiles, thus minimizing blowing tendencies; and they achieve more rapid resin flow to improve binder action, thus also minimizing blowing.

After treatment with acid, the peanut hulls were dried to 9% and 3% moisture content and immediately put into sealed containers. Panels were prepared by taking sufficient, 130 grams of peanut hulls, preheating 15 minutes at 400°F, immediately transferring to a preheated mold and pressing.

Data for peanut hulls with 9% moisture are presented in Table 3.10 for various press schedules on material preheated 15 minutes at 400°F.

Table 3.10:   Use of Preheated Peanut Hulls Molded at Various Press Cycles (Effect of Water Exposure on Properties)

Press Cycle	% Weight Change Water Soak		% Density Change Water Soak		Flexural Strength psi Water Soak		
	2 hr	24 hr	2hr	24 hr	0hr.	2hr.	24hr
15 mins/375°F	3.8	7.4	0	+2.7	2043	2230	1484
10 mins/375°F	5.3	17.4	2.8	+12.1	1894	1109	458
5 mins/375°F	11.8	39.4	5.8	+14.3	1745	585	76
2 mins/375°F	48.8	66.7	23.6	-3.5	762	27	0
1 min/375°F	33.4	51.1	15.3	-1.0	578	34	0

Source: EPA 600/2-78-111

As seen in the table with press times decreasing, changes in volume and weight vary inversely while strength varies directly with press time regardless of water soaked or not. The abovementioned tests were repeated but using treated peanut hulls having a 3% moisture content. Again these same trends were found. The best overall performance resulted with the 15 minute cure on material containing 3% moisture before preheat. The data also verified previous results that indicated a minimum press time of 5 minutes at 375°F. Overall however, the use of a preheat to improve a particle board made from peanut hulls is apparently effective with longer press cures and is not attractive commercially except for use in very humid or damp environments.

Particle Size: Peanut Hull Waste — The effects of particle size became of interest after the first large scale production. Evidence indicated that a high concentration of fine particles can cause blowing because of the following:

> Fine particles block the escape route of water vapor and volatiles between larger particles; and

> Fine particles can react more rapidly and produce more resinous binder in situ and this can then undergo reaction to a higher degree for a given time period, than can coarse particles.

In blown panels, especially those that exploded, it was noticed that dark areas were formed away from edges, where higher degrees of resin formulation had taken place. These dark areas were always found where panels exploded and where there were considerably more fine particles present. Consistent with this is a cracking phenomenon. Such behavior occurs with formulation of excess resin and subsequently more extensive reaction giving off more water (increasing internal pressure) and also causing excessive shrinkage leading to cracking. Shrinkage is rarely seen in 4" x 6" panels.

It was decided to eliminate any material that would pass through a –32 to –42 Taylor screen from consideration. Also it was decided to mix all material thoroughly in order to insure a random particle size.

Wood Waste — The initial work on Douglas Fir was on a hammer milled material where the particle sizes ranged from –6 to 14 mesh. The final work was done with commercial wood. As with the peanut hull waste, the large particles provided a better product.

Full Size Panel Production

Peanut Hull Waste: The panels fabricated at the Washington State University's facility were 50" x 50" x 0.50" thick and 12" x 15" x 0.50" thick. The 50" x 50" panels were molded in an oil heated press and the 12" x 15" panels in an electrically heated press. Stops were used to control final board thickness.

The mat was formed by hand in a deckle box, on a sheet of Mylar placed on an aluminum caul plate. A heavy board was placed on the mat in the deckle box with the frame and board removed. The mat was covered on top by Mylar film, and an aluminum caul plate. The entire assembly, except for the particle board base, was slid into the press and pressure applied. For the small panels, a single steel caul plate was used in the bottom of the mat without Mylar film. A steel wear plate mounted on the bottom of the top press plate was in contact with the top of the mat during pressing. No sticking was encountered without Mylar.

All boards, except one, that remained intact were tested for modulus of rupture (MOR) which is also called flexural strength, and internal bonding (IB) according to ASTM-D-1037 "Standard Methods of Evaluating the Properties of

Wood Base Fiber and Particle Panel Materials." Modulus of elasticity (MOE) was also determined in some. Figure 3.1 shows the test specimen cut up pattern of the intact panels evaluated. Portions of some of the "blown" panels were also treated. The results of the pressing operations are given in Table 3.11 for large panels.

The processing variables study, described above, gave excellent indication of problems and approximate processing requirements. This work was conducted with small specimens. Fabrication of panels whose areas and volumes were 78 and 312 times greater, respectively, needed some changes in moisture content. Rather than use moisture contents of 7 to 13% the first material was dried to about 6% as used for wood particles in the particle board industry. Temperatures, pressures and press times were as determined on small panels except that a decompression time of 3 minutes was used for the large panels.

A wide variation in physical and mechanical properties was found. Three panels were good and eight exploded during decompression, all boards had blisters or severe shrinkage cracks. Portions of the blown panels, such as in No. 2, that remained intact had rather high internal bond values and the best modulus of rupture value of all the large panels. All the blowing problems occurred during pressure release after the press cycle.

The blowing phenomenon is caused by excessive vapor pressure in the panel during the press cycle. This vapor pressure emanates from water and/or other volatile materials. Water can come from that already present in the peanut hulls after processing or from the resinous binder being formed in situ from pentoses in a cyclodehydration reaction in which 36% of the pentose molecule is evolved as water. This is a large amount to be given off and occurs during the press cycle under elevated temperatures. To give some idea of potential internal vapor pressure (due to water) during press cure, the following table was taken from the *Handbook of Chemistry and Physics,* "Steam Tables":

Temp, °F	Pressure, psi
200	11.5
250	29.8
300	67.0
350	134.6
375	184.3
400	247.2

To determine relative steam pressures generated during cure, thermocouples were embedded into the mat and temperature recorded during cure. The resulting temperatures are shown in Figure 3.2. It is obvious that vapor pressure within the board easily exceeds that of the internal bond strength of the panels. This is particularly so in a hot panel and even more so in this study where the resin matrix is thermoplastic at this temperature. Commercial particle board is at high and low moisture contents in the hulls. Blowing with a high (8.5%) moisture content is understandable but blowing with a 4.2% moisture content is

Figure 3.1: Test Specimen Cut-Up Diagram

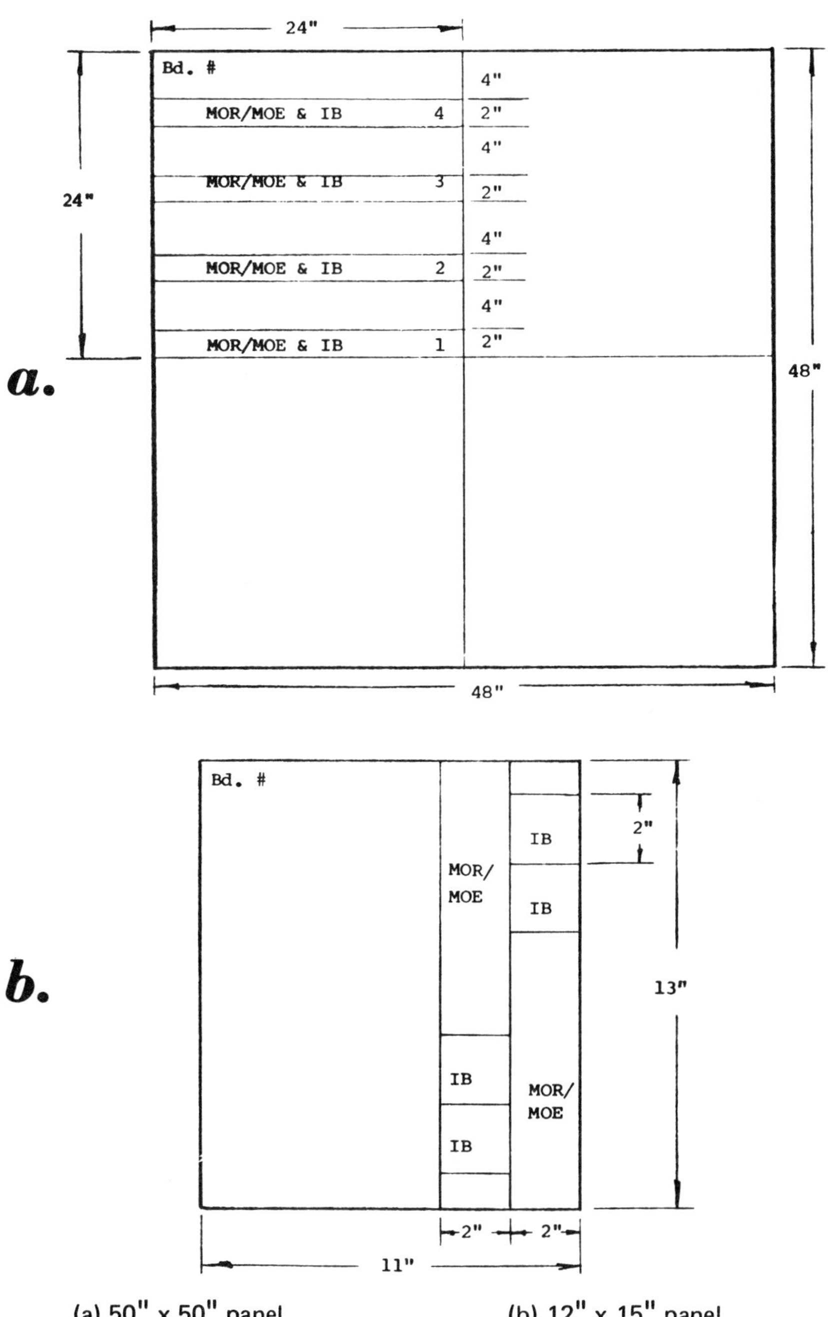

(a) 50" x 50" panel   (b) 12" x 15" panel

Source: EPA 600/2-78-111

Table 3.11: Pressing Conditions and Averaging Physical Properties of the 50" x 50" Panels

Board No.	Furnish MC (%)	Weight Furnish Used, lbs	Press Temp (^{o}F)	Press Time (min)	Press Pressure psi	Comments
1	5.5	60	375	5+3 *	500	Did not reach stops, good board
2	8.5	51	375	5+3	500	Reached stops board blew @ loops
3	4.8	51	375	5+3	500	Reached stops good board
4	5.9	51	375	5+3	500	Board blew
5	4.6	47	375	5+3	500	Board blew at 100 psi
6	4.6	47 +	375	7+3	500	Reached stops, board blew
7	4.2	47	375	5+3	700	Reached stops, board blew @ 40 psi
8 ‡	5.5	47	375	5+3	500	Board blew (blistered)
9	5.7	42 #	375	5+3	500	Reached stops, board blew
10	6.8	42	375	5+3	500	Reached stops, board blew
11	5.9	42	375	5+3	500	Reached stops, good board

Board No.	Internal Bond		Modulus of Rupture and Modulus of Elasticity		
	SG	PSI	SG	MOR (psi)	MOE (psi x 10^{6})
1	0.96	49	1.02	710	–
2	1.06	193	1.03	1550	–
3	0.91	146	–	–	–
4	1.10	–	–	–	–
5	–	–	–	–	–
6	–	–	–	–	–
7 *	–	–	–	–	–
8	0.98	128	0.96	1260	–
9	0.89	14	–	–	–
10	0.87	103	0.86	900	0.236
11	0.88	101	0.89	940	0.567

* Five minutes under pressure, three minutes for decompression.
+ Thermocouple study. Put down 23.5 lb hulls, put in Thermocouples and and added remaining 23.5 lb of hulls.
‡ Five minutes under pressure, three minutes for decompression.
# Thirty-two material screened out.

Source: EPA 600/2-78-111

unusual to say the least. One explanation is that low moisture content made for more difficult resin flow due to insufficient plasticizing action.

In the blown panels, especially those that exploded, it was noticed that dark areas were formed away from edges, where higher degrees of resin formation had taken place. The dark areas were always found where panels exploded and where there were always considerably more fine particles present. Evidence presented in the section on Particle Size indicated that fine particles are also instrumental in blowing and cracking. In the blown panels described there cracks 0.75" wide and surrounded by dark areas were always present.

Figure 3.2: Internal Panel Temperature

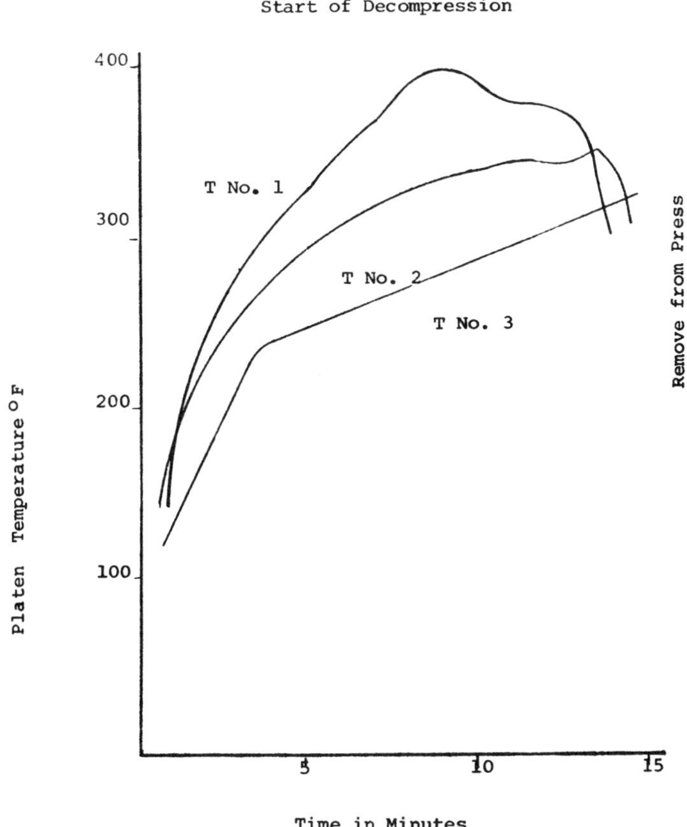

Source: EPA 600/2-78-111

Such behavior is consistent with formation of excess resin and subsequently more extensive reaction giving off more water (increasing internal pressure) and also causing excessive shrinkage leading to cracking. This meant that another, and unknown variable, was operative during the first 9 panels and could be the reason why panel No. 8 was unsuccessful even though it was a duplicate of No. 1 in all other respects. The processed material was not mixed or randomized as is normal procedure. Consequently there could be major variations in particle size distribution in the various drums. Once this parameter appeared to be a factor, examination of individual drums revealed large differences in the amount of fines in various drums.

The curves in Figure 3.2 show that the peripheral regions of the panel never exceeded 300°F at the end of the press cycle. Since volatiles can escape more readily near edges of panels, the cooling effect is greater and the absence of insulation around the panel permits greater heat loss to the environment. The shape of curve 3 shows no sudden drop in temperature as in curves 1 and 2. This suggests that the sudden drop in temperature is caused by the sudden evolution of vapors (cooling) as occurs just prior to blowing (increased hissing noise heard prior to explosions). All this suggests the use of a "hotter" acid system to permit resin formation occurring at lower temperatures to permit more strength development in the periphery while also reducing the steam pressure in the panel.

Figure 3.3:   Cut Up Diagram of Board Made with Urea-Formaldehyde Resin (Peanut Hull Furnish)

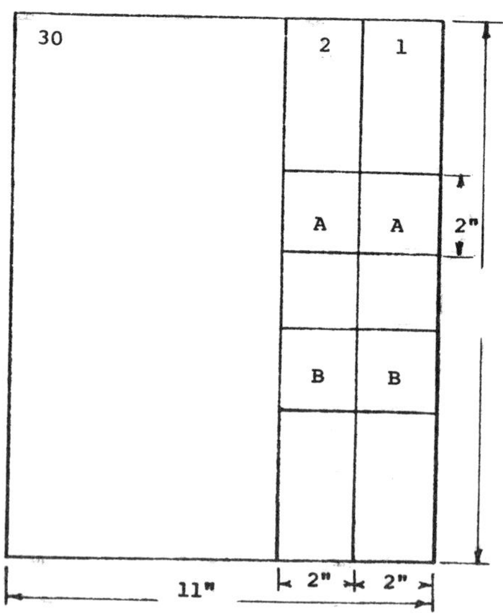

Source: EPA 600/2-78-111

There was concern that peanut hull waste composites would not meet the 2,400 psi modulus of rupture (flexure) requirement for structural qualification because of the lack of reinforcement with the slenderness ratio of a fiber. Therefore, on the next full-scale test it was decided to make a peanut hull panel conventionally with a urea resin to determine if the reinforcement theory was correct. The results of this evaluation are presented in Table 3.12 (Figure 3.3).

The peanut hull furnish was prepared at Material Systems Corporation (see section on Type and Percent of Acid Absorbed by the Material — Peanut Hull Waste and Table 3.3). The furnish was post dried to between 1.5 and 8% moisture content and screened to all –20 material. The work at Washington State University was started with 4" x 6" panels, Table 3.4 to develop the previously discussed process parameters. The next step was to fabricate 12" x 15" panels to further refine the process.

For the purposes of this discussion a pressure relief cycle or a "bump cycle" can be defined as rapid release, at a predetermined time, of the pressure applied to the mat. The press platens were slightly opened to allow the vapor build-up in the mat to be released. The pressure was then reapplied and maintained until the press was completely closed. "Decompression time" is a gradual reduction of the final pressure to 0 psi over a predetermined time, after the press time selected was complete.

Table 3.12:   Evaluation of Peanut Hull Board Made with Urea-Formaldehyde Resin

MOR/MOE

Spec No.	SG	MOR (psi)	MOE (psi x 10^6)
1	0.81	1100	0.270
2	0.81	1148	0.278

INTERNAL BOND

Spec No.	SG	PSI
1-A	0.81	115
1-B	0.81	122
2-A	0.81	122
2-B	0.81	122

Source: EPA 600/2-78-111

The closing pressure for each board was selected before pressing. This pressure was reached within 0.5 minutes after pressing was begun. Once the target pressure was obtained an additional 100 psi was added and the pump turned off.

Table 3.13: Board-Making Conditions for Peanut Hull Furnish

Board No.	Weight Formed	MC (%)	Temp (°F)	Time (min)	PSI	Thickness in.	Density	Board Conditions
Run 1 - 0.5 x 12 x 15" Boards								
1	1900g	5.5	375	7	1000	-	-	Blown, no bump
2	1900g	5.5	375	10	1000	-	-	Blown, bump at 5 min, did not reach stop
3	1900g	5.5	375	15	1000	-	-	Blown, bump at 5 & 10 min, pop at 10 min
4	1900g	5.5	390	10	1000	-	-	Blown, bump at 5 min, close at 7 min
5	1800g	5.5	390	10	1000	-	-	Blown, bump at 5 min, close at 6 min
6	1800g	5.5	390	15	1000	-	-	Blown, bump at 5 & 10 min, close at 5.5 min
Run 2 - 0.5 x 50 x 50" Boards								
7	55 lbs	5.5	390	10	1000	0.55	-	Blown, bump at 3 & 7 min, blow at 7 min
8	55 lbs	5.5	390	10	1000	-	-	Blown, bump at 2 & 5 min, blow at 5 min
9	55 lbs	5.5	375	10	1000	0.45	1.01	Blown at 100 psi, bump at 3 min, hold open for 2 min, back to pressure at 5 min
Run 5 - 0.5 x 50 x 50" Boards								
25	51 lbs	5.7	375	9	800	0.47	1.09	Blown, close at 7 min
26	51 lbs	5.7	375	4	1200	0.56	.92	Intact/blister, close at 3.5 min
27	51 lbs	5.7	375	5	1200	0.53	1.07	Intact/blown, close at 3.5 min
31	51 lbs	5.7	375	5	1200	0.50	1.03	Blown, close at 3.5 min
32	51 lbs	5.7	375	4.5	1200	0.55	0.98	Blown, close at 3 min
33	51 lbs	5.7	375	4	1200	0.56	0.93	Intact, close at 3 min
34	51 lbs	5.7	375	4	1200	0.57	0.89	Intact/blister, close at 3 min.
35	51 lbs	5.7	375	4	1200	0.55	0.93	Blown, close at 3 min
36	51 lbs	5.7	375	4	1200	0.51	1.01	Intact/blister, close at 3 min.
37	51 lbs	5.7	375	4	1200	0.53	0.94	Blown, close at 3 min
38	51 lbs	5.7	375	4	1200	0.52	1.01	Intact/blister, close at 3 min
39	51 lbs	5.7	375	4	1200	0.56	0.92	Blown, close at 3 min
Run 7- 0.25 x 50 x 50" Boards								
44	25.5 lbs	5.7	375	3.5	1200	0.24	-	Blow at 300 psi, close at 1.5 min
45	25.5 lbs	5.7	355	3.5	1200	0.33	0.84	Intact/blister, warp, close at 1.5 min
46	25.5 lbs	5.7	355	3.5	1200	0.28	0.97	Intact/blister, warp, close at 1.75 min
47	25.5 lbs	5.7	355	3.5	1200	0.32	0.82	Intact/warp, close at 2 min.

Source: EPA 600/2-78-111

As compression of the mat continued the pressure decreased. This pressure drop was allowed to reach 100 psi lower than the target pressure. At this point the pump was started and the pressure returned to the 100 psi above the target and the procedure repeated. Once the press was closed (on stops) the pressure was reduced to about 200 psi in approximately 3 minutes and this pressure than held for any remaining time.

Board making data are presented in Tables 3.13 and 3.14 for the peanut hull furnish. The tables are divided into runs depending on the board size made.

Table 3.13 covering the hammer milled peanut hulls, shows a trend from run to run towards pressing conditions that are quite close to what might be desired for making successful boards. Runs 5 and 7 indicate that conditions are straddling the borderline between blown and intact boards. More investigation should be carried out to determine exactly what the optimum condition would be. Table 3.14 presents the processing parameters for a peanut hull waste panel fabricated with conventional processing techniques.

Table 3.14:   Board-Making Conditions for Peanut Hull Furnish with Urea Resin

Run 10 - 0.5 x 12 x 15 in. boards treated peanut hulls with 6% urea resin added
(Board pressed at a SG of 0.72)

Board Number	Weight Formed	MC (%)	Temp ($^{\circ}$F)	Time (min)	PSI	Closing Time (min)	Board Condition
28	1200g	7.3	325	5	500	1	Intact
29	1200g	7.3	325	5	500	1	Intact
30	1200g	7.3	325	5	500	1	Blown

Source: EPA 600/2-78-111

Table 3.15 presents the results of the tests for modulus of rupture, modulus of elasticity, and internal bond according to the American Society for Testing and Materials Standard D-1037, "Standard Methods of Evaluating the Properties of Wood-Base Fiber and Particle Panel Materials" on board #27 from run 5. The dimensions of the board are illustrated in Figure 3.3.

These results indicate superior properties to that of a conventional process (Table 3.12) with peanut hull waste. It is believed that the reinforcing theory holds. Although the economics (discussed in the section Economics) is acceptable, the strengths are less than the required 2,400 psi modulus of rupture. This makes the board acceptable for nonstructural applications but not qualifiable under structural codes.

Wood Waste: The Douglas Fir wood waste was treated with p-toluene sulfonic

Table 3.15: Physical Test Results for Board 27 (Peanut Hull Furnish)

Spec No.	SG	MOR/MOE MOR (psi)	MOE $(\text{psi} \times 10^6)$
1-1	0.97	1427	--
1-2	0.96	1351	0.397
1-3	--	--	--
2-1	0.89	597	0.166
2-2	0.01	1329	0.373
2-3	0.98	1410	0.363
3-1	0.93	918	0.277
3-2	1.06	1433	0.404
3-3	--	--	--

Spec No.	Internal Bond SG	PSI
1-1A	0.92	59
1-1B	1.00	105
1-2A	0.99	158
1-2B	1.00	155
1-3A	0.99	156
1-3B	1.00	152
2-1A	0.88	44
2-1B	0.87	37
2-2A	1.04	169
2-2B	1.03	197
2-3A	0.96	163
2-3B	1.01	177
301A	0.89	44
3-1B	0.93	53
3-2A	1.04	179
3-2B	1.05	204
3-3A	1.05	223
3-3B	1.08	238

Source: EPA 600/2-78-111

acid in a commercial blender. The furnish was dried to between 1.5 and 8% moisture content and screened to remove all –20 mesh particles. The initial work was done on 4" x 6" panels. The processing information developed was used to produce 12" x 15" panels. This data is presented in Tables 3.5 and 3.6.

The material was formed into a mat and pressed, as described for peanut hull waste in the preceding section. Variations that were tried included three binder treatments, combinations of binder treatments, a range of moisture contents from 1.5 to 7.8%, press temperatures of 300° to 390°F, press times of six to fourteen minutes, bump and no-bump cycles and 0 to 2.5 minutes of decompression time.

Table 3.16: Board-Making Conditions for Douglas Fir Furnish

Board Number	Weight Formed	MC (%)	Temp (°F)	Time (min)	PSI	Thickness	Density	Decompression Time	Comments
Run 9 - 0.5 x 50 x 50 in. boards									
55	51 lbs	4.4	335	9.5	1200	0.39	0.93	1.25	Blown, no bump, close at 8.5 min
56	51 lbs	4.4	335	10	1200	0.55	0.98	1.25	Blown, bump at 5 min, close at 8.5 min
57	51 lbs	4.4	335	10	1200	0.54	1.01	1.25	Blown, bump at 8.5 min, close at 8 min
58	51 lbs	4.4	335	9	1200	0.55	0.97	4.00	Blown, no bump, press to Back to stops and take out pressure for 30 sec.
59	51 lbs	4.4	335	9	1200	0.57	0.97	1.25	Intact, bump at 5.5 min, close at 9 min
60	51 lbs	4.4	335	9	1200	0.57	0.96	1.25	Intact, bump at 5.5 min, close at 9 min.
61	49 lbs	4.4	335	9	1200	0.54	0.98	1.25	Blown, bump at 5.5 min, close at 9 min
62	49 lbs	4.4	335	9	1200	0.59	0.89	1.25	Intact, bump at 5.5 min, close at 9 min
63	49 lbs	4.4	335	9	1200	0.58	0.91	1.25	Intact, bump at 5.5 min, close at 9 min
64	49 lbs	4.4	335	9	1200	0.58	0.91	1.25	Intact, bump at 5.5 min, close at 9 min
65	49 lbs	4.4	335	9	1200	0.59	0.91	1.25	Intact, bump at 5.5 min, close at 9 min
66	49 lbs	4.4	335	9	1200	0.61	0.87	1.25	Intact, bump at 5.5 min, close at 9 min

Source: EPA 600/2-78-111

By the end of Run 9, the proper conditions for pressing were being approached. Only one of the final eight 0.5" x 50" x 50" boards blew. The cause of this blow is not known as it was pressed under the same conditions as the others. Run 9 is shown in Table 3.16.

Twelve 0.5" x 50" x 50" boards were made in the ninth run. The only variations between boards were the press time, bump cycle, and the amount of furnish used. The last nine boards were made with only one blown panel resulting under the following conditions: Binder Treatment 69-48-3, 51 and 40 pounds of furnish to form the board, 4.4% moisture content, 335°F press temperature, nine minute press time, 1,200 psi closing pressure, a bump cycle of 5.5 minutes and 1.25 decompression period. The cause of the blow is not known, but apparently the conditions were again in the borderline category.

Table 3.17 presents the results of the tests for modulus of rupture, modulus of elasticity, and internal bond according to the American Society for Testing and Materials Standard D-1037, "Standard Methods of Evaluating the Properties of Wood-Base Fiber and Particle Panel Materials" for board 66 of Run 9. Cut-up diagram of the board appears in Figure 3.4.

Table 3.17: Physical Test Results for Board 66 (Douglas Fir Furnish)

Spec No.	SG	MOR	MOE ($psi \times 10^6$)
1-1	0.84	1080	0.257
1-2	0.84	880	0.222
1-3	0.83	990	0.245
2-1	0.95	1830	0.455
2-2	1.00	2430	0.607
2-3	0.99	1970	0.564
3-1	0.96	1900	0.532
3-2	1.00	2130	0.582
3-3	1.00	2270	0.590

· **Internal Bond** ·

Spec No.	SG	PSI	Spec No.	SG	PSI	Spec No.	SG	PSI
1-1A	0.82	28	2-1A	0.97	84	3-1A	0.96	90
1-1B	0.87	42	2-1B	0.97	88	3-1B	0.98	96
1-2A	0.84	32	2-2A	1.02	99	3-2A	1.02	95
1-2B	0.83	32	2-2B	1.06	107	3-2B	0.99	94
1-3A	0.82	33	2-3A	0.98	86	3-3A	1.00	106
1-3B	0.82	36	2-3B	1.00	87	3-3B	1.02	105

Source: EPA 600/2-78-111

Figure 3.4: Cut-Up Diagram for Board 66 (Douglas Fir Furnish)

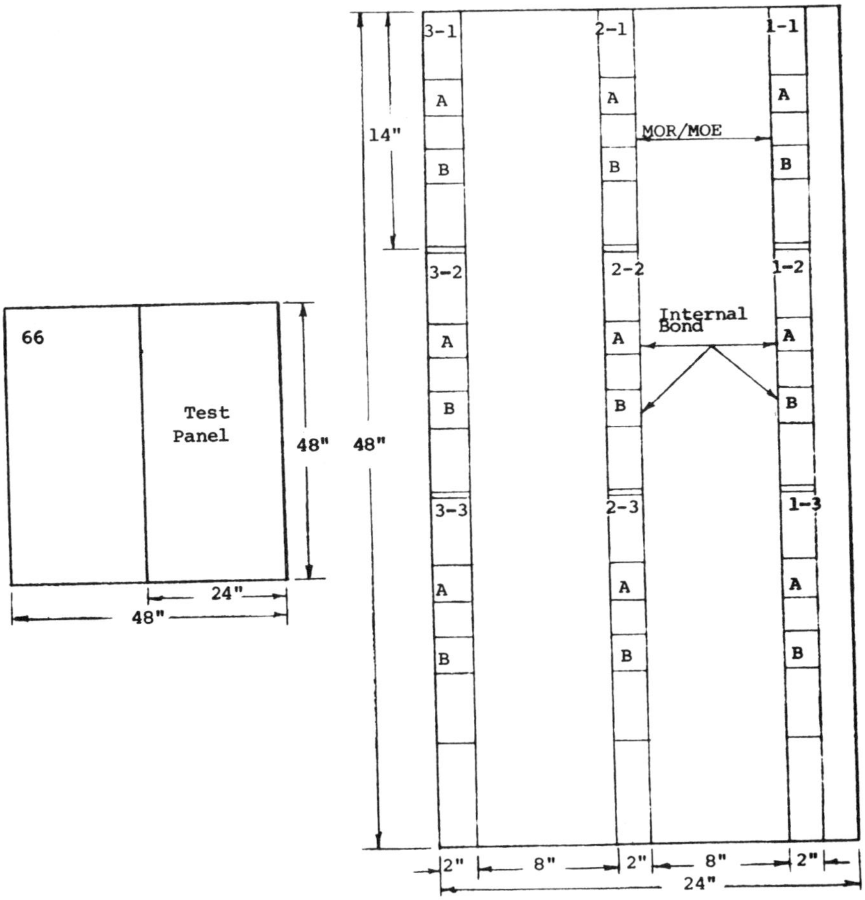

Source: EPA 600/2-78-111

The results show that the material can qualify structurally but will require additional full-scale studies to develop product reliability.The economics show that this process is equivalent to that of commercial board. Since there exists neither a cost advantage nor a structural advantage, the product was not pursued through qualification.

Recommended Processes

Peanut Hull Waste: Although further full-scale development would be required to productize this material, the following is presented as a starting point.

(a) Screen the material to eliminate all particles –20 mesh.
(b) Use a commercial blender and mix with the hulls a solution of water with 7% by weight by phosphoric acid (75% strength). Use 8 gallons of solution for 8.82 pounds of hulls. Mix for 5 minutes.
(c) Place the mix in a dryer, remove and save the solution for reuse. Dry to 5.7% moisture content which will result in a 3.98% acid content.
(d) Place in a preheated 355°F press.
(e) Mold at 1,200 psi for 3.5 to 4 minutes depending on thickness.
(f) Close press within 2 minutes.
(g) Use a 1.25 minute decompression time.

Wood Waste: Douglas Fir can be produced with the following procedure.

(a) Screen the material to eliminate all particles –20 mesh.
(b) Spray the wood particles with a solution of water containing 2.5 to 2.7% p-toluene sulfonic acid technical grade.
(c) Place the mix in a dryer, remove and save the solution for reuse. Dry to 4.4% moisture content which will result in a 1.05% acid absorption.
(d) Place in a preheated 335°F press.
(e) Mold at 1,200 psi for 9 minutes.
(f) Use a pressure relief cycle, "bump", at 5.5 minutes.
(g) Use full 9 minutes to close press.
(h) Use a 1.25 minute decompression time.

Economics

Economic factors will be discussed first and then applied. This analysis is based on the references listed at the end of this chapter.

Capital Investment: The cost of a particleboard plant in 1975 dollars is approximately $3.2 million plus $135,000 per million square feet of annual capacity. This cost is estimated to be accurate within 10% of the estimate two thirds of the time.

Primitive plants of less than 100 million square foot capacity cost considerably less than the estimate given above, probably from $1 million for a 3 million square foot plant to $3 to $4 million for a 10 million square foot plant. The cost can vary a great deal depending on sophistication, precise process, and whether new or used equipment is purchased.

The waste process will require five to eight times as much drying capacity as conventional plants, an amount proportional to the increase in water content of the wood to be dried. It will also require centrifuging to reduce the water content.

The corrosive nature of the waste process may also require extensive use of stainless steel or fiber glass in storage tanks, dryers, presses, blenders and materials handling equipment. This requirement may cause a dramatic increase in the capital cost of a plant.

Labor: The number of workers required per shift in a particle board plant can be calculated by starting with a base number of 21 and adding one worker per 8,000,000 square feet of annual capacity. Small plants are much more labor intensive than large ones.

Labor costs vary slightly with square feet and tonnage of board produced. This report will assume constant labor costs per 1,000 square feet of board produced of $23.22.

Power: Power is directly related to tonnage of board produced and averages 250 kWh per 1,000 sq. ft. of ¾" 45# particle board. Power is used primarily in refining (flaking, chipping, blending, and drying) and in pressing. Power cost assumed is $0.011 per kWh.

Heat: Conventional Particle Board Process — Heat is directly related to tonnage produced and averages 1,650,000 Btu (1,500 cu. ft. of natural gas) per 1,000 sq. ft. of ¾", 45# conventional particle board. This includes 770,000 (47%) Btu consumed in drying and 880,000 (53%) Btu consumed in pressing.

Waste Particle Board Process — In the waste particle board process, the incoming wood at between 50 and 150% moisture is dried to 5%. It is then pressed at 350°F where the moisture content is reduced to 2%.

The following is the composition of 1,000 square feet of 45 pound per cubic foot density, ¾ inch thick particle board made by the waste process.

Material	Raw Material Required (lb)	Part by Weight	Finished Board, (lb)
Wood	3,000	100	2,605
Binder	180	6	156
Water	1,500–4,500	2	52

The heat required in the waste process at 80% efficiency based on moisture is:

Moisture (%)	Total Btu	Drying Btu, (%)	Pressing Btu, (%)
15	1,420,000	740,000 (52)	680,000 (48)
50	2,890,000	2,210,000 (75)	680,000 (25)
100	5,000,000	4,320,000 (86)	680,000 (14)
150	7,100,000	6,420,000 (90)	680,000 (10)

For purposes of this study, gas will be presumed to cost $0.50/100 cu. ft. and the conventional process to utilize wood at 15% moisture (planer shavings) while the waste process used wood at 100% moisture (planer shavings soaked in acid bath and spun dry) or estimated 50% moisture (spray technique).

The calculation of heat required does not include the heat needed to remove humidity from the air coming into the dryers. Industry sources estimate that a conventional particle board plant will use twice as much heat on a humid day as on a normal day. Since the conventional process uses about 47% of its Btu requirements to dry the incoming wood while a plant using the waste process and wood at 100% moisture uses 86% of its Btu requirement to dry the wood, humid days would increase the Btu requirements of a waste plant to 285% of normal compared to 200% for a conventional plant.

Also not included in the Btu calculations are extra heat requirements to cause the water to be released from the acid in the waste process, or the effect of exotherm during pressing. These factors are believed to have a small impact on total Btu requirements.

Overhead: The following are overhead costs for a 60 million square foot plant per year:

Salaries:	
Plant manager	33,000
Plant supervisor	24,000
Technical director	20,000
Bookkeeper	16,000
Clerk/typist (2)	24,000
Shipping clerk	16,000
Insurance	50,000
Property taxes	90,000
Office expenses	80,000
	353,000
Overhead per 1,000 square feet	$5.88

Cost Analysis for Peanut Hull Waste Particle Board: The minimum density of acceptable particle board from peanut hull waste is 55 pounds per cubic foot. This is the density used in this cost analysis. In this study the soak and dry process was used to treat the peanut shells. It was possible to recover all but 5.8% of the acid in one case and 6.8% in the other (Table 3.3).

Further drying reduced the acid absorption content to 4%. It is reasonable to assume that this extra 2% could be recovered also with a controlled process. It is also reasonable to assume that the spray process would work with peanut hulls as well as with wood waste. Therefore, an acid absorption value of 4% is used in the following cost analysis. In addition the spray process reduces the moisture content to be removed from the wood resulting in lower fuel costs.

Table 3.18 lists the material and costs with the following assumptions. All boards considered are of 55 lb/ft^3 density and ¾" thickness. 15% of the scrap is reprocessed. The conventional boards contain urea or phenolic resin (8%) and wood which are assumed to cost 10.5, 27 and 0.4¢/lb, respectively. The cost of peanut hulls and phosphoric acid in the waste process board is estimated at 0.75 and 18¢/lb, respectively; 4% of phosphoric acid is utilized.

Table 3.18: Materials and Costs for Peanut Hull Waste Particle Board

	. . . . Conventional.		. . . .Waste Process	
	55# Urea	55# Phenolic	. . . . . . 55#	
. . . . Material Used, lb/1,000 ft^2				
Wood	3,667	3,667	Peanut Hulls	3,667
Binder	293	293	Acid	147
Wax	37	37		
	3,997	3,997		3,814
. . . . Material Cost, $/1,000 ft^2				
Wood	15.03	15.03	Peanut Hulls	27.50
Binder	30.77	79.11	Acid	26.46
Wax	1.85	1.85		
	47.65	95.99		53.96
. . . . .Reprocessing Costs of Scrap*, $/1,000 ft^2				
Wood	—	—	Peanut Hulls	—
Binder	30.77	79.11	Acid	—
Wax	1.85	1.85		
	32.62	80.96		0
. . . . .Material Cost of Finished Board**, $/1,000 ft^2				
Primary Run, 85%	40.50	81.59		45.86
Scrap Rerun, 15%	4.89	12.14		
	45.39	93.73		45.86

. . . . Total Manufacturing Costs***, $/1,000 ft^2				
	. . . . Conventional.		. . .Waste Process 55# . .	
Item	55# Urea	55# Phenolic	Soak Test	Spray Test
Variable Costs				
Materials	45.39	93.73	45.86	45.86
Power	3.36	3.36	3.36	3.36
Fuel	0.92	0.92	2.77	1.60

(continued)

Table 3.18: (continued)

| | . . . . Total Manufacturing Costs***, \$/1,000 ft^2 . . . . | | | |
| | . . . . Conventional . . . . . | | . . . . Waste Process . . . . | |
Item	55# Urea	55# Phenolic	Soak Test	Spray Test
Labor	23.22	23.22	23.22	23.22
Maintenance and Supplies	2.44	2.44	2.44	2.44
	75.33	123.67	77.65	76.48
Fixed Costs				
Overhead	5.88	5.88	5.88	5.88
Depreciation	18.83	18.83	18.83	18.83
	24.71	24.71	24.71	24.71
Total Costs	100.04	148.38	102.36	101.19

*If no additional resin or wax is needed to reprocess waste scrap and
    normal amounts are required to reprocess conventional scrap.
**If 15% of the board produced is scrap.
***In a 60,000,000 square foot particle board plant.

Source: EPA 600/2-78-111

Conclusions — From this analysis it is apparent that no economic advantage over conventional wood particle board exists with peanut hulls. However, in the event that large supplies of the waste exists, it could be an advantageous method for waste utilization.

Cost Analysis for Wood Waste Particle Board: The minimum density of acceptable particle board from wood waste is 55 lb/ft^3 also. The spray technique for treating the wood waste was demonstrated to be acceptable. The p-toluenesulfonic acid is used at an absorption content of 1.05% of the wood weight. All other acids can be removed. Materials and costs are listed in Table 3.19 with the following assumptions.

All boards considered are of 55 lb/ft^3 density and ¾" thickness. 15% of the scrap is reprocessed. The conventional boards as earlier, are assumed to contain 8% of phenolic and/or urea resin and wood estimated at 27, 10.5 and 0.4¢/lb, respectively. The waste process board contains 1.05% of p-toluene sulfonic acid which is estimated at 23¢/lb.

In Table 3.19 materials and costs for the wood waste particle board process are again compared to materials and costs for a conventional 55 lb/ft^3 particle board manufacturing process. The latter values were repeated from Table 3.18 for easier comparison.

Table 3.19: Materials and Costs for Wood Waste Particle Board

	. . . . . Conventional		. . .Waste Process . . .	
	55# Urea	55# Phenolic	. . . . . .55#	
. . . . .Material Used, lb/1,000 ft^2				
Wood	3,667	3,667	Wood Waste	3,667
Binder	293	293	Acid	39
Wax	37	37		
	3,997	3,997		3,706
. . . . .Material Cost, $/1,000 ft^2				
Wood	15.03	15.03	Wood Waste	15.03
Binder	30.77	79.11	Acid	8.97
Wax	1.85	1.85		
	47.65	95.99		24.00
. . . . Reprocessing Costs of Scrap*, $/1,000 ft^2				
Wood	—	—	Wood Waste	—
Binder	30.77	79.11	Acid	—
Wax	1.85	1.85		
	32.62	80.96		0

	. . . . .Conventional.		. . . .Waste Process . . . .
. . . . .Material Cost of Finished Board**, $/1,000 ft^2			
	55# Urea	55# Phenolic	55#
Primary Run, 85%	40.50	81.59	20.40
Scrap Rerun, 15%	4.89	12.14	—
	45.39	93.73	20.40

. . . . Total Manufacturing Costs***, $/1,000 ft^2 . . . .

Item			
Variable Costs			
Materials	45.39	93.73	20.40
Power	3.36	3.36	3.36
Fuel	0.92	0.92	1.60
Labor	23.22	23.22	41.80
Maintenance and Supplies	2.44	2.44	2.44
	75.33	123.67	69.60
Fixed Costs			
Overhead	5.88	5.88	5.88
Depreciation	18.83	18.83	18.83
	24.71	24.71	24.71
Total Cost	100.04	148.38	94.31

*If no additional resin or wax is needed to reprocess waste scrap and normal amounts are required to reprocess conventional scrap.
**If 15% of the board produced is scrap.
***In a 60,000,000 square foot particle board plant.

Source: EPA 600/2-78-111

The time to process the panel is 9 minutes rather than 5 minutes used conventionally. This labor cost could be reduced by using a press with more openings but this would increase capital cost and depreciation cost.

This product has limited economic advantages and is limited to a minimum density board of 55 lb/ft^3 in a market where the major sales are with 45 lb/ft^3. The effort on this program was not sufficient to develop full processing parameters. Although the limitations are known, not all of the potentials have yet been established.

Conclusions and Recommendations

Peanut Hull Waste: The resulting product is limited to a minimum weight of 55 lb/ft^3 and without the benefit of some fibrous reinforcement will not be able to achieve a modulus of rupture of 2,400 psi. However, values of 1,400 psi to 2,100 psi (see Tables 3.4 and 3.15) are respectable. The economics of the product are marginal based on the present price of peanut hulls. This price would change dramatically if there were large surplus quantities of hulls which required disposal. In the United States peanut hulls have many uses and are a marketable waste. However, in many of the developing nations peanuts are major crops with oil as the primary product. It is these nations which could make use of this product.

Wood Waste: This product is limited to a minimum weight of 55 lb/ft^3 also. A modulus of rupture value in excess of 2,400 psi was achieved (Table 3.17) although not consistently. The product has some economic advantage. This advantage could be increased by judicious process development work. This program demonstrated a process that can make 50" x 50" board somewhat consistently (see Run 9, Table 3.16). However, additional process development is required on full-scale equipment to define

    (a)   Particle size and distribution
    (b)   Pressures, and
    (c)   Pressure relief and decompression cycles.

INORGANIC MATRIX PRODUCTS

The Phase II study developed two classes of inorganic materials. One was an inorganic matrix foam using rice hulls. The other was a dense inorganic matrix reinforced with wood waste and/or rice hulls as a lumber substitute. The rice hull foam could be produced from a variety of formulations. Within the denser range products suitable for structural walls, floors, ceilings, and combination floor-ceilings could be produced with a possible two or three hour fire rating. On the opposite end of the density scale, a rice hull foam could be produced which could be used as a core for a fire door.

Full scale products developed on the basis of data discussed in the previous chapter will be discussed and evaluated here.

Wall System

Material Selection: The rice hull foam formulation selected for qualification is presented in Table 3.20.

Table 3.20: Rice Hull Foam Formulation

Constituent	Amount, lb
Water	100
Rice hulls	57
Untreated glass fibers	3.4
MSC additive	5
Plaster	343
Busan 30	0.6

Source EPA 600/2-78-111

The MSC additive improves the water resistance of the material. Once the material has cured, the moisture content stabilizes at 10%. Then the weight and cost distribution of the foam is as shown in Table 3.21.

Table 3.21: Cured Weight and Cost Distribution

Constituent	Cured Weight, lb	Cost/lb	Total Cost
Water	46	—	—
Rice hulls	57	$0.62*	$3.534
Untreated glass fiber	3.4	0.40	1.360
MSC additive	5	0.432	2.160
Plaster	343	0.0252*	8.644
Busan 30	0.6	2.75	1.6500
Total	455	0.038	17.348

*Price delivered to factory.

Source: EPA 600/2-78-111

This formulation was selected for its properties and resistance to water. The effects of water on the strength retention of rice hull foam were studied by constructing a panel and cutting it into 144 compression blocks, 1" x 1" x 2" in size. Thirty-six of the blocks were uncoated. The remaining blocks had their exterior surfaces coated with one of the following three materials: Swimming Pool Paint produced by Zynolite Products Corporation; Lytron 621 produced by Monsanto; and W-102 produced by Wetco Chemicals.

The uncoated samples performed as well or better than the coated ones. The major reduction in strength when tested wet occurs the first day. After that, over a month's period of submersion, there is very little change. In all cases there appeared to be even a slight regain in wet strength. W-102 coating appears to have an adverse effect. Up to one week submersion there appears to be a 100% regain in strength on all but W-102 coated samples, when the material dries out. After one month submersion strength retention upon drying out appears to be between 82 and 97%.

Figure 3.5 compares the uncoated samples' strength retention against the strength retention of Douglas Fir, a common building material.

Figure 3.5: Percent Strength Comparison of Rice Hull/Inorganic and Wood

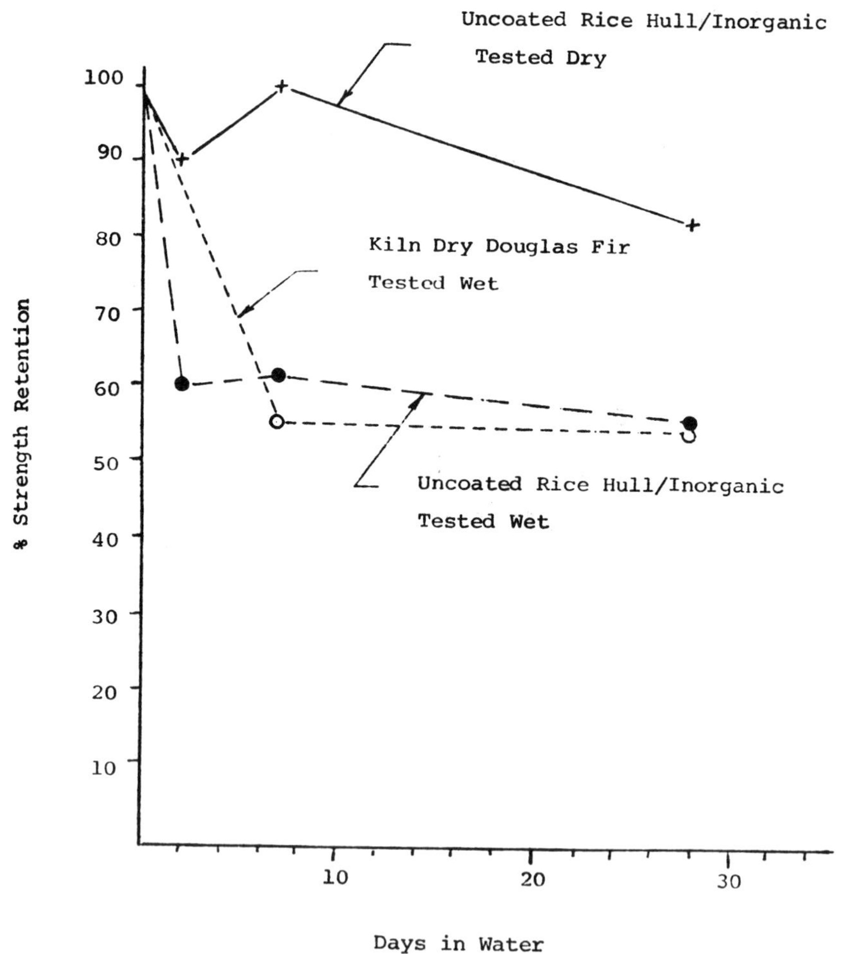

Source: EPA 600/2-78-111

The average wet compression load after 30 days submersion is slightly over 300 psi. The area of a linear foot of wall as now designed is 15.5 square inches. Thus the wall, wet after 30 days submersion, will support up to 4,650 pounds per linear foot. A typical maximum wall design load would range from 800 to 1,200 pounds per linear foot. Therefore, this wall would provide the required Factor of Safety of 3 with some additional margin.

The mechanical properties of the foam were evaluated by Testing Engineers of San Diego. The mean results are summarized in Table 3.22.

Table 3.22: Mechanical Properties of Rice Hull Foam

	psi
Compression Strength	952
Tensile Strength	54
Modulus of Rupture	165
Shear Strength	1,361

Source: EPA 600/2-78-111

The first sample population for compression testing was too small for a foam material and had to be retested with a larger population. The test scatter is a result of the size of the specimen which is small compared to the variation in porosity distribution from the rice hulls. The tensile value appears low and in all reality would be much higher if evaluated in a four foot wide specimen rather than one with a one inch cross section. However, 54 psi is adequate when the maximum wall tensile load probable for a house is 115 pounds per linear foot. The wall cross section 15.5 square inches would result in a tensile stress of 7.4 psi providing a safety factory of 3 with considerable to spare.

Design Selection: The full scale walls described in the previous chapter utilized a molded shape bonded at the center line with an inorganic adhesive. These panels always failed in the center borderline, the point of maximum shear. Therefore, an attempt was made here to produce a monolithic wall having a thickness of 3½ inches.

The mold was made in such a way that inserts were used to form the ribs and void space and these were removed by slowly forcing out the inserts. Despite the generous use of wax, as a parting agent, it was not possible to remove the inserts without damage to the final structure. The design was then changed to produce elements as shown in Figure 3.6. The internal dimension of 3½ inches was chosen for compatibility with conventional construction. These panels could be extruded or cast continuously by machine. The length selected for

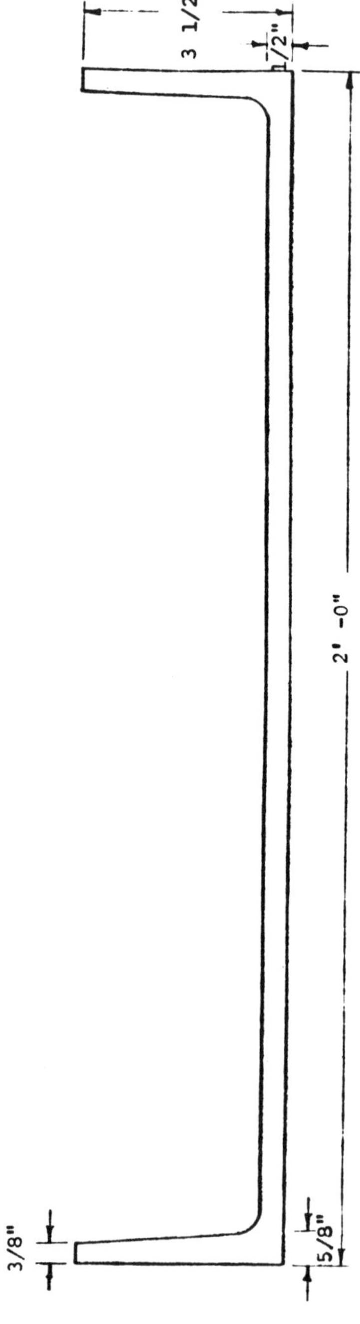

Figure 3.6: Cross Section of Wall Material

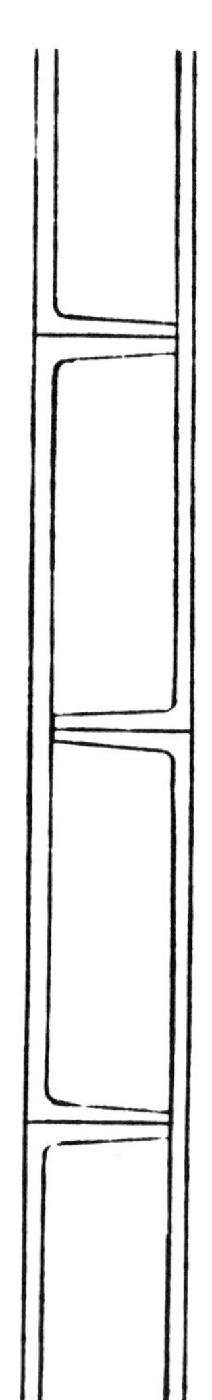

Figure 3.7: Assembly of Wall Material into a Panel

Source: EPA 600/2-78-111

this study was 8 feet. The elements for this study were cast and bonded together to form the wall as shown in Figure 3.7.

Compression Strength of Wall: The first compression test conducted to verify this design was on a two foot wide by four foot long specimen. This resulted in a failure load of 6,000 pounds per linear foot. This was then followed by three full scale qualification tests on four foot wide by eight foot long panels. A diagram of the compression test set up is shown in Figure 3.8. A representative of Testing Engineers-San Diego witnessed the fabrication and bonding of all panel components.

The sample panels were tested at Material Systems Corporation's plant, Escondido, California. The compressive load was applied by means of a hydraulic system recently calibrated by Testing Engineers-San Diego. The test set-up was as described in ASTM E-72-74.

Lateral buckling of the panel was measured at mid-height by 0.01 inch taut wire deflectometers on each panel edge. Axial compression of the specimen under load was measured by means of 0.001 inch steel rod compressometers on each of the four corners of the panel. The panel was preloaded to approximately 400 pounds prior to setting deflection gauges. The loading was then applied in increments of approximately 600 pounds in test SD31-1226 and 900 pounds in test SD31-2043 until failure occurred. After each loading increment the load was returned to zero and set measurements were made.

Figure 3.9 presents the relationship of load to deflection and permanent set. Sample SD31-1226 was the first full scale panel produced and tested. Samples SD31-2043 were panels produced in a simulated production run and were selected at random. It is believed that these later panels represented a better quality product and this is the reason for a stiffer product and one with less permanent set.

In either case, the wall is considerably stiffer than other qualified systems and exhibits less permanent set. The qualifiable design allowable is the ultimate divided by a factor of safety of 3 multiplied by the width of the panel.

> Panel SD31-1226: 31,800/(3 x 4) = 2,650 lb/ft
> Panel #1 (SD31-2043): 30,000/(3 x 4) = 2,500 lb/ft
> Panel #2 (SD31-2043): 28,000/(3 x 4) = 2,333 lb/ft

The test curve indicates that the panel was within its elastic limit. Therefore, the certified allowable will probably be 2,333 pounds per foot which is approximately twice that of a stud wall.

Racking Shear Strength of Walls Bonded with Adhesive: These tests are also required for structural wall qualifications. A 48" x 96" panel was fabricated per Figure 3.10 for a racking shear test. Because of the low tensile strength of the material it was decided to incorporate a 0.040" thick fiber glass strip at the

Figure 3.8: Material Systems Corp. Panel Axial Compression Test Set-Up

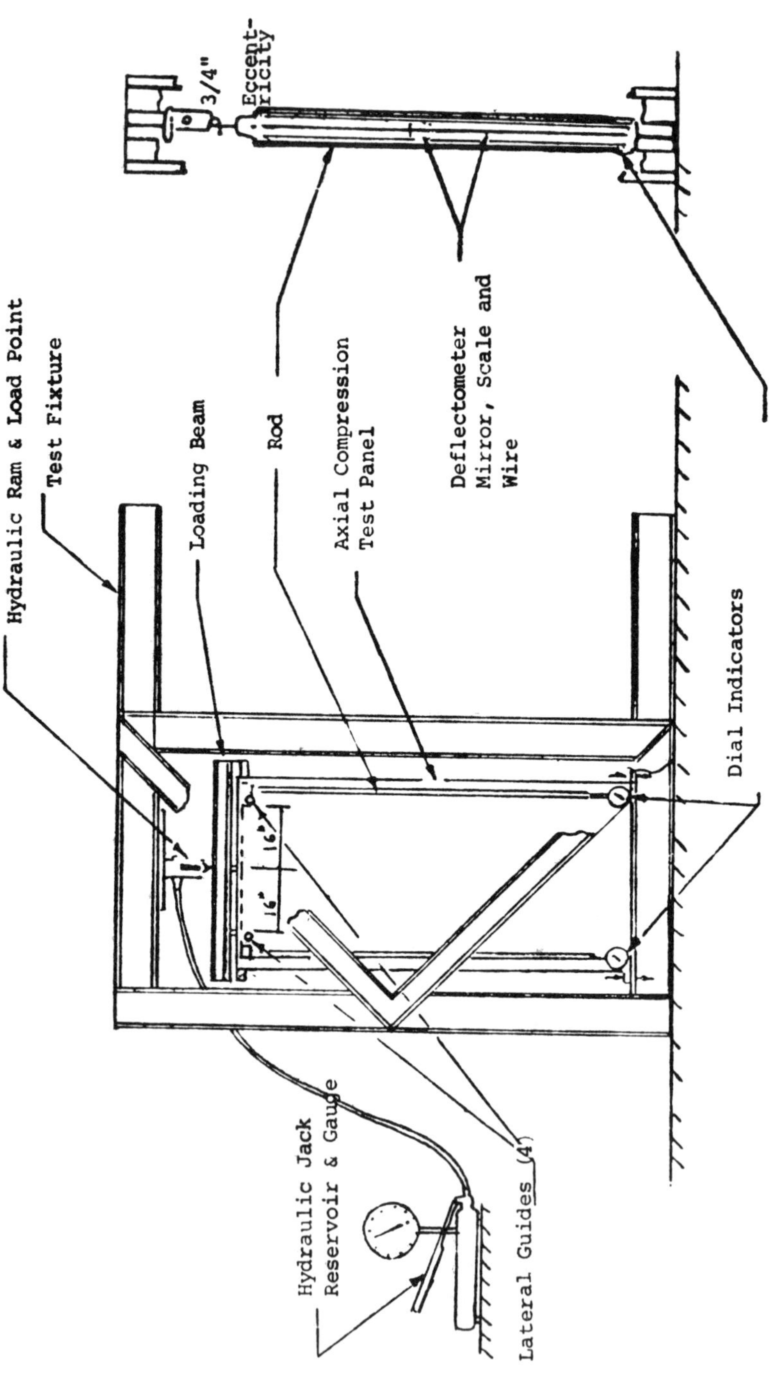

Source: EPA 600/2-78-111

**Figure 3.9: Compression Load vs Deflection and Permanent Set for a
4 ft x 8 ft Rice Hull Foam Fire Wall**

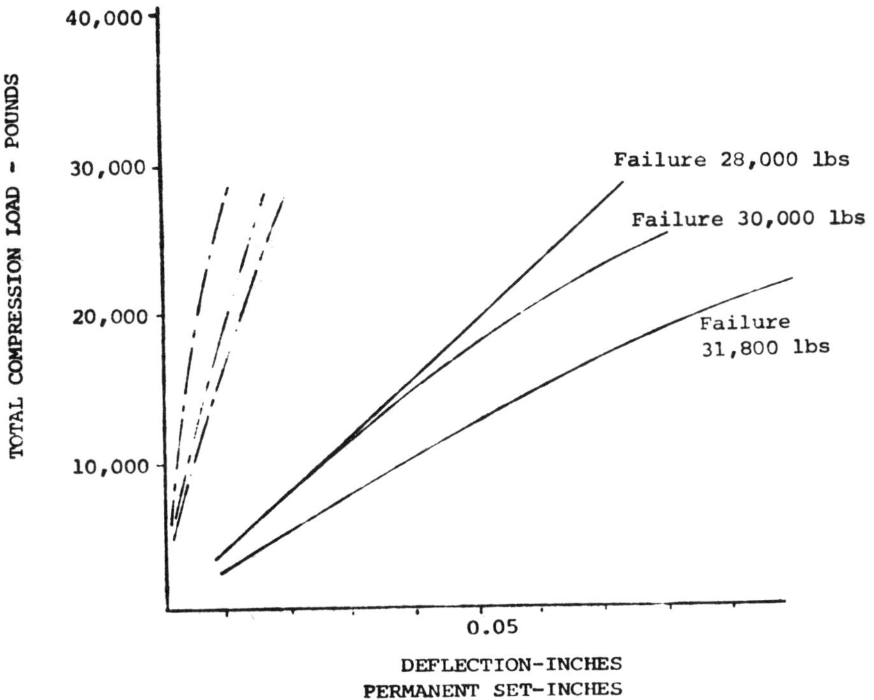

Figure 3.10: Wall Specimen

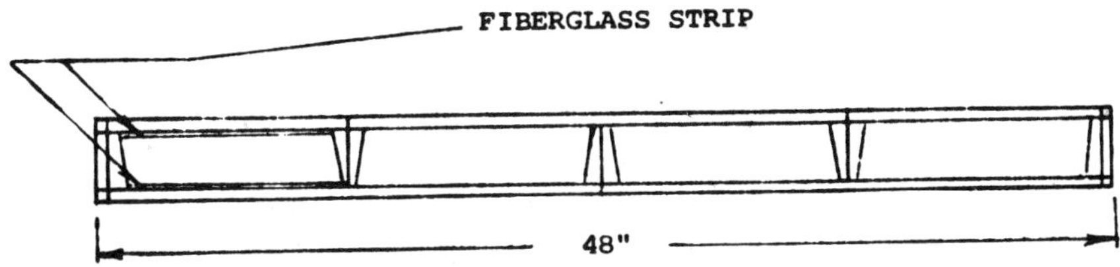

Source: EPA 600/2-78-111

lower bottom corner to assist in transferring tension at that point. The upper
and lower sill plates are 2" x 4" lumber bonded with epoxy to the panel.

The panel was tested and the results of this test are shown in Figure 3.11. The
deflection under load shows that this panel is considerably stiffer than an ICBO
approved panel. Also the failure load is approximately four times higher than
that of the approved panel.

Figure 3.11: Racking Shear Test on Panel Without Reinforcement

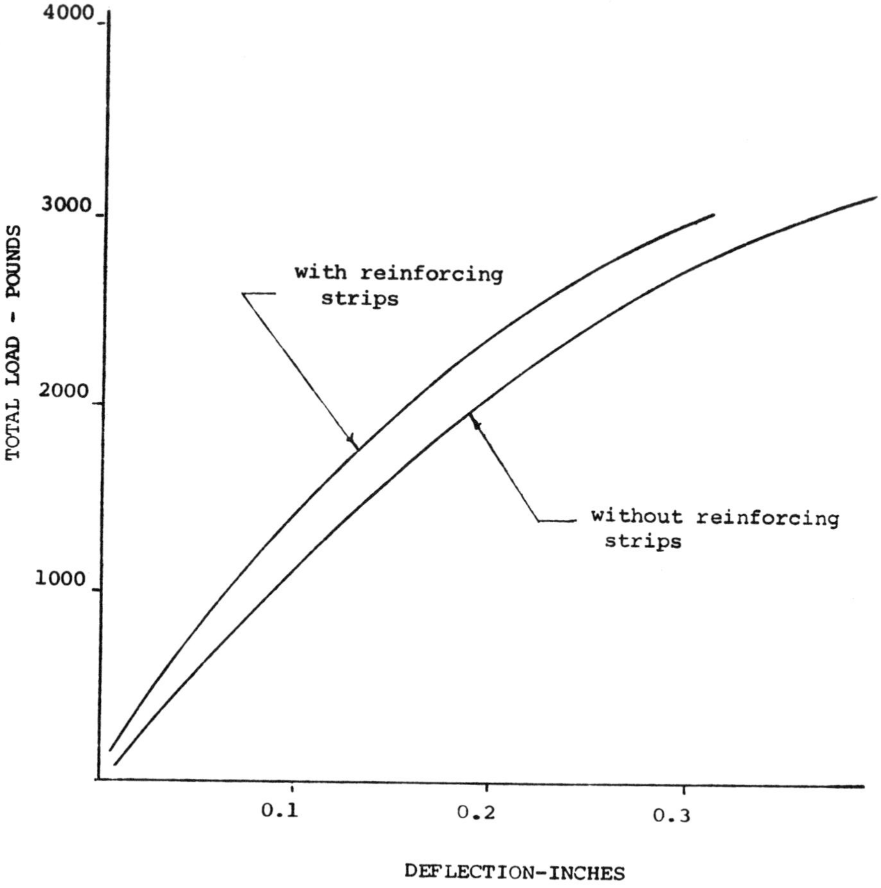

Source: EPA 600/2-78-111

The allowable racking shear load is the lower of the load that creates one-eighth inch lateral deflection or the failure load divided by a factor of safety of 3. In this case both values are the same, 450 pounds per foot for a four foot wide panel. The failure of this panel was one of pure theoretical shear in which a shear crack formed diagonally across the panel. These test results were sufficiently high to encourage a repeat test without the strips.

A panel was again fabricated per Figure 3.10 without reinforcing strips and tested in racking shear. The results are presented in Figure 3.11. Although this panel provided results slightly lower (failure 48,000 pounds compared to 54,000 pounds and one-eighth inch deflection at 14,000 pounds rather than 18,000 pounds) the design values are still higher than that generally found in a

48 inch wide shear panel. Failure started with a slight crack in the lower tension corner which was reinforced with the fiber glass strip in the previous tests.

Based on the above results three more panels were fabricated under Testing Engineers'-San Diego observation per Figure 3.10 without reinforcement for testing under racking shear by them in the Material Systems Corporation's facility.

The racking shear loading was applied by means of a hydraulic system recently calibrated by Testing Engineers-San Diego. The panels were mounted in a test frame and deflection measured as outlined in ASTM E72-74.

Preloads of approximately 400 pounds were applied to the racking shear panels and dial gauges reset prior to testing. The loading was then applied to the racking shear test panels in 200 pound increments until failure occurred. After each increment of loading the load was returned to zero and set measurements were made.

Figure 3.12 presents the relationship of side load to deflection and permanent set. The qualifiable allowables are established on the lower of the values derived from ultimate load or at one-eighth inch deflection. These are discussed below.

Ultimate Load Basis — The ultimate load has to be divided by a factor of safety of 3 times the width of the panel to achieve a design allowable load per foot.

Panel #1:   3,000 pounds/(3 x 4) = 250 pounds/foot
Panel #2:   2,800 pounds/(3 x 4) = 233 pounds/foot
Panel #3:   3,000 pounds/(3 x 4) = 250 pounds/foot

Load at One-Eighth Deflection — The load at one-eighth inch deflection can also be used as the allowable provided it does not exceed that of the above.

Panel #1:   1,150 pounds/4 = 288 pounds/foot
Panel #2:   1,300 pounds/4 = 325 pounds/foot
Panel #3:   1,350 pounds/4 = 338 pounds/foot

The calibrated equipment was limited to a force of 3,000 pounds which was not sufficient to fail two of the three qualification panels. However, the failure of one panel at 2,800 pounds would offset any higher loads developed by the two other panels.

The load allowable that will be certified by ICBO will probably be 233 pounds per foot. The load can be raised by repeat testing of three more panels assuming that these three all fail in a close and similar pattern. However, the 233 pounds per foot is a very acceptable load when compared to standard constructed four foot wide walls.

The allowable based on deflection for panel #3 was close to that established by earlier tests. However, the other two values were 25 to 60 pounds per foot lower.

Figure 3.12:　Racking Shear Load vs Deflection and Permanent Set

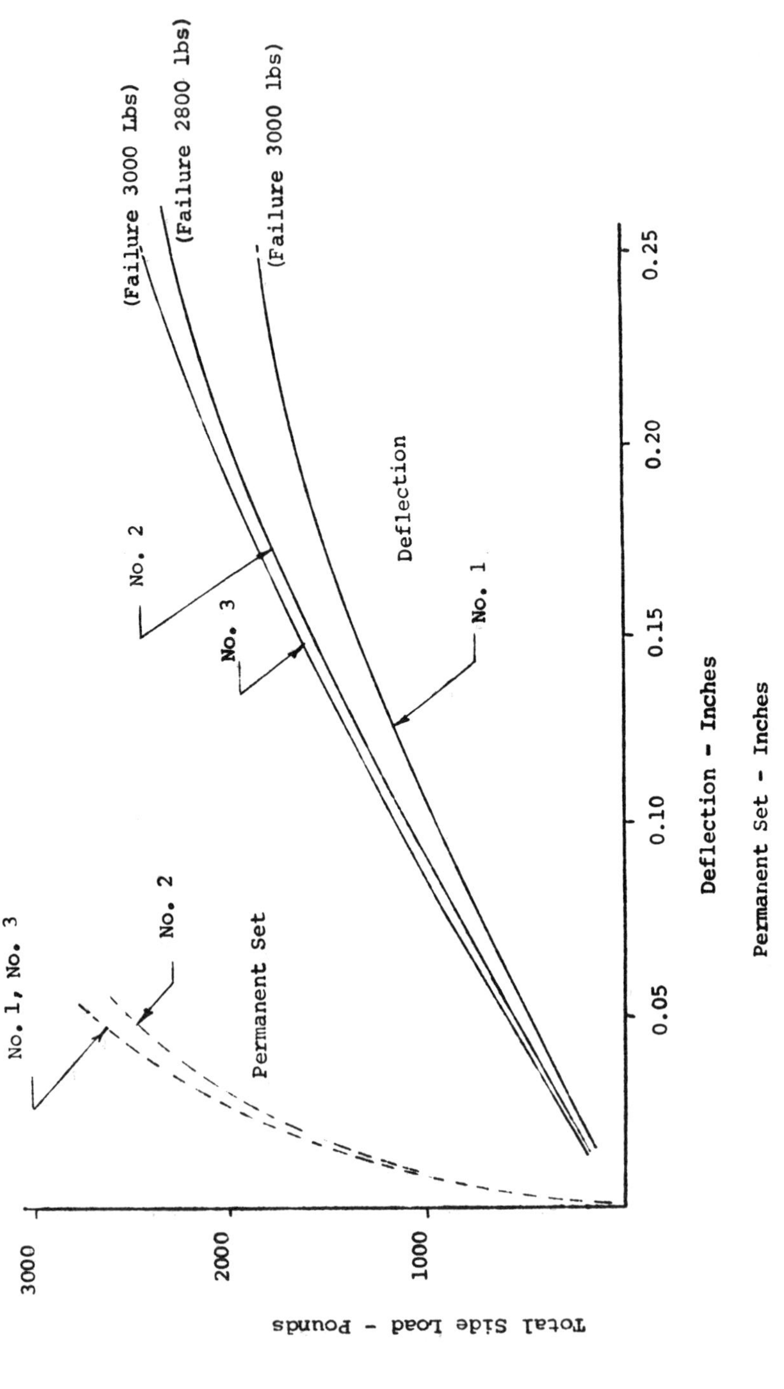

Source:　EPA 600/2-78-111

The allowable load based on ultimate failure at 2,800 pounds (233 lb/foot) is lower than that determined by earlier tests. However, the earlier tests developed a crack at 3,000 pounds but still supported loads up to 4,800 pounds. This would indicate that the safest criteria would be to accept the 2,800 pounds as the limit.

Impact Load Test of Walls: These panels were fabricated per Figure 3.10. Three panels were tested utilizing the testing techniques described in ASTM E-72 with the test specimen mounted horizontally. Three specimens rather than six (as indicated in ASTM E-72) were tested since construction of these panels is such that interior and exterior faces are the same.

Each test was conducted as follows: Initial drop of the 60 pound sand bag was made from a height of 6" above the geometric center of upper panel face. Subsequent drops were made from increasing increments of 6" until the panel being tested exhibited visual evidence of failure. Deflection readings were made after each one-half foot increment of drop. Set readings were made after each one-foot increment of drop.

Results − Panel No. 1: Maximum deflection was 0.65 inch and maximum set 1.85 inches. Failure was in the form of complete fracture through the panel section at a drop height of 2.5 feet.

Panel No. 2: Maximum deflection was 0.60 inch and maximum set 1.32 inches. Complete fracture through the panel section (at about mid-span) occurred at a drop height of 2.0 feet.

Panel No. 3: Maximum deflection 0.58 inch and maximum set 1.27 inches. Failure occurred at a drop height of 2.0 feet.

Fire Rating: Elements were produced for two 8' x 12' wide walls. These elements were assembled into panels, and mounted into test frames. The endurance panel was instrumented with nine thermocouples. It was placed in front of a furnace and loaded in compression to 1,000 pounds per linear foot by hydraulic jacks. After 1 hour and fifty minutes of fire endurance testing per ASTM E-119, the panel lost ability to support load and the upper right hand thermocouple exceeded 250°F above ambient. This high temperature was caused by a crack in the back panel caused by the buckling in the upper right corner. The unexposed surface was otherwise intact. This premature buckling was caused by the inadequacies of the bond of the stiffeners to the back surface.

Since the endurance panel did not achieve two hours it was decided to attempt to qualify the wall for one hour by conducting a one hour rating hose stream test on the remaining panel.

During this test, the wall assembly, 8 feet high and 12 feet wide, is exposed to fire for half an hour in accordance with the procedures specified in ASTM E-13 test methods. At the end of the 30 minutes, the temperature in the furnace reaches over 1500°F. One surface of the wall panel is directly exposed to this temperature. At the same time the wall is under a constant axial compression load of 100 pounds per linear foot.

The wall assembly is then removed from the furnace and subjected immediately to high pressure water spray, simulating fire hose exposure in real fire, for 1 minute. The water must not penetrate through the panel for the wall to be acceptable for 1 hour fire rating. In addition, at the end of the hose stream test, the axial compression load is increased to twice the required design load. The wall must not fail under the increased load.

The rice hull/inorganic matrix wall assembly successfully passed the entire test and thereby qualified for a 1-hour structural fire rating with an allowable design load of 1,000 lb/ft.

Wall Thermal Characteristics: The test equipment used was the calorimeter shown in Figure 3.13, a Leeds-Northrup Speed-O-Max W recorder with 24 thermocouple probe readout, Shimadzu Model R-101 with 2 junction differential iron constant thermocouple, Adjust-A-Volt 230 volt variable auto transformer connected to 4 black body heaters, and iron-Constantan thermocouples.

Tests were run with a uniform input to the heating elements and this was measured and monitored by a thermocouple placed on the hot face of the test specimen while the flow, of differential, was measured by an intermediate thermocouple in the center and another on the back side. The test was allowed to run for an 8-hour period where temperatures were marked at hourly intervals on the hour.

At the end of this period a hot side temperature of $250°F$ was often reached and it is felt that this should be regarded as the extreme. The use of the differential thermocouple involved placing one junction on the hot side and the other on the cold side. The only other probe necessary was one adjacent on the hot side for obtaining an absolute temperature with the Leeds-Northrup equipment. The "U" value is computed by measuring the heat flow across the specimen for a given period. This resulted in an "U" factor of 0.073 Btu/(hr) (ft^2) ($°F$) or an R of 13.7 for a waste panel as shown in Figure 3.7 without additional insulation.

Wall Manufacturing Technique: The configuration evaluated, Figure 3.6, was selected for the purpose of ease of production. This simple shape permits either casting or extrusion. Casting was selected for economy reasons. Experimentation with percentage of water was conducted to determine the effect of a dry viscous mix on strength as against a wet liquid mix. The ultimate strength was unaffected, only the drying time was greater with more water. The minimum amount of water required to react the plaster is prescribed in Table 3.20. The 90 minute plaster was used in this study to permit sufficient time for manual casting. Even with this plaster the part was handleable in 15 to 20 minutes. Limited experiments would indicate that normal plaster would permit handling in 20 to 5 minutes. This then opens two attractive possibilities for production.

Figure 3.13: Calorimeter

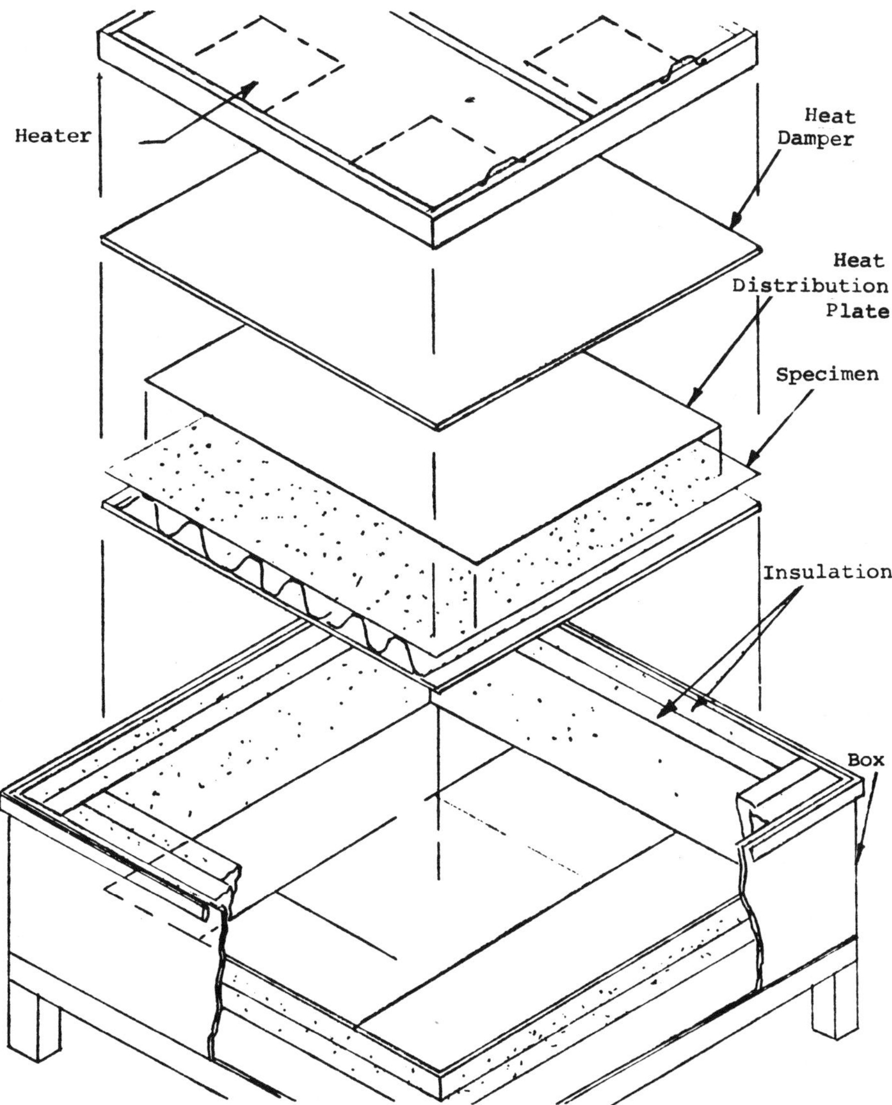

Source: EPA 600/2-78-111

The first and most readily available approach would be the utilization of the continuous concrete beam casting system. There are a multiplicity of these systems available and in use in the United States and elsewhere in the world. Any system that casts concrete can cast rice hull foam. The part should be cast on a tool with the tool surface textured to the desired surface characteristics of the part. This would eliminate the need for exterior finishing. The prototype production was done this way in order to control the critical dimension of the leg to the interior bond surface. This dimension can be controlled in a continuous casting process by a sizing roller following the cast into the mold. The primary advantage of this process is that no machinery needs to be developed. The only development costs would be the tooling and a limited process scale-up study.

In this process the exterior coating of magnesium oxychloride can be applied to the mold surface just prior to that of the rice hull foam. This permits dimensional stability as both cure at the same time.

The second approach would be extrusion of the material. A dry mix would be forced through dies to form the shape onto a conveyor belt running at the same speed as the extrusion. The material would be cut and trimmed while still damp. The advantage of this process would be to accelerate production in a smaller environment. This requires that the coating be applied separately from the extrusion which is accomplished by first applying a thin seal coat without sand. This seals the surface and then the sand coat is applied. This approach reduces distortion. The disadvantage is that the equipment and process have to be developed.

Once the elements shown in Figure 3.6 are available, the walls are assembled as shown in Figure 3.7. The recommended construction approach would be to stand the elements on one side of the wall onto the sill plate, nail the exterior skin to the sill plate and use the inorganic adhesive to bond the flanges of the element together. This would be followed by erecting the elements on the opposite side against the one completed and bonding the flanges and the two elements together as shown in Figure 3.7.

Wall Panel Application and Economics: The waste panel is a load-carrying wall. It has a two-hour fire rating which makes it an excellent partition wall for multiple family units. Table 3.23 presents the cost of such a partition wall installed. In order to provide the full two hours each exposed surface must be coated with magnesium oxychloride. This material acts as a weather seal also although not required for this application. The cost of this material per square foot per surface is $0.111 as presented in Table 3.24. This makes a total cost installed of $0.922 per square foot. A conventional two-hour, fire-rated wall costs nearly twice that — a cost of $1.802 per square foot (see Table 3.25 for details).

The waste wall panel can also be used as an interior panel. Although load supporting ability and fire protection are not usually required, the availability

Table 3.23: Cost of Waste Product Two-Hour, Fire-Rated Partition Wall

Item	Material Cost	Labor Cost	Total Cost
Rice Hull Foam 9.656 lbs/ft^2 ($0.038/lb)	$0.367	$0.076 *	$0.433
Glass Strands in Cap 0.031 lbs/ft^2 ($0.35/lb)	.011	Included above	.011
Adhesive 0.5 lb/ft^2 (0.103)	.052	Included above	.052

Assemble on Site:
  Four Sections (32 ft^2)
  Put in Place   16 min
  Apply Adhesive 8 min
  24 min $\frac{11.52/hr}{60}$ 32 ft^2
		.144 +	.144

Seal and Finish Joints	.020	.030 ‡	.050
Cost per ft^2 #	.450	.250	.700

* Estimate includes factory overhead, depreciation and labor and is based on MSC continuous production technology.

+ Estimate made from observing demonstration model construction.

‡ Estimate from Current Construction Costs, 1976 - Lee Saylor, Inc.

Weather seal and upper and lower plates not included.

Table 3.24: Magnesium Oxychloride Coating Cost/Square Foot

Item	Weight, lbs	Cost/lb	Cost
$MgCl_2 \cdot 6H_2O$	0.36	$0.071	$0.026
MgO	.36	.135	.049
Sand	.36	.010	.036
Cost/ft^2	-	-	.111

Table 3.25: Cost of a Conventional Two-Hour, Fire-Rated Partition*

Item	Material Cost	Labor Cost	Total Cost
Double Stud Wall @ 16" O.C.	$0.146	$0.236	$0.382
Two Layers 1/2 in Fire X Sht. Rock Both Sides	.680	.680	1.360
Nails, Clips, and Misc. Hardware	.060	-	.060
Cost/ft^2 +	.886	.916	1.802

* Current Construction Costs, 1976 - Lee Saylor, Inc.

+ Upper and lower plates not included.

Source: EPA 600/2-78-111

of it is an added safety measure. The cost of the waste wall, $0.700 per square foot installed, is very competitive with the conventional interior wall cost of $0.76 per square foot. Table 3.26 has details.

The waste wall panel can also be effectively used as an exterior wall. Although the load support is required, generally a one-half hour fire rating is considered adequate. A two-hour fire rating is definitely a positive safety factor. The exterior wall would utilize a cost of magnesium oxychloride on the weather exposed surface to act as a weather seal. This would result in a waste exterior wall cost of $0.811 per square foot. The conventional low cost exterior wall with one-half hour fire rating would cost nearly 40% more or $1.137 per square foot installed (Table 3.27).

Table 3.26: Cost of a Conventional Interior Wall* (½ Hour Fire Rating)

Item	Material Cost	Labor Cost	Total Cost
Stud Wall @ 16" O.C.	$0.073	$0.118	$0.191
One Layer of 1/2 in Sheet Rock on either side	.220	.320	.540
Nails, Clips, and Misc. Hardware	.030	-	.030
Cost/ft^2 $^+$	.323	.438	.761

* Current Construction Costs, 1976 - Lee Saylor, Inc.

$^+$ Upper and lower plates not included.

Table 3.27: Cost of a Conventional Exterior Wall* (½ Hour Fire Rating)

Item	Material Cost	Labor Cost	Total Cost
Stud Wall @ 16" O.C.	$0.073	$0.118	$0.191
One Layer of 1/2 Inch Sheet Rock one side	.110	.160	.270
One Layer of Exterior Plywood one side	.142	.244	.386
Textured Coating	.180	.080	.260
Nails, Clips, and Misc. Hardware	.030	-	.030
	.535	.602	1.137

* Current Construction Costs, 1976 - Lee Saylor, Inc.

Source: EPA 600/2-78-111

Transverse Load Tests: Three 48" x 96" wall panels were tested in transverse loading in accordance with ASTM E-72 test methods. Results of the tests are presented in Figure 3.14. As indicated by these load vs deflection curves, the wall panels are sufficiently stiff that ultimate load, rather than the deflection criterion, determines the allowable design loads. (The deflection criterion of L/180 would permit a maximum deflection of 0.53", but all three panels failed at less than half that value.)

The average failure load of 32.67 lb/ft^2 will result in an allowable transverse load of 10.89 lb/ft^2 based on a safety factor of 3. This is not sufficient to satisfy the minimum wind load requirements of 15 lb/ft^2 specified by the Uniform Building Code.

In order to improve the transverse load (bending) resistance of the walls, additional reinforcement would be required near the surface to increase tensile strength of the outer layers in bending. Reinforcing fibers or fabrics could be incorporated in a surface coating. The need for a surface coating, which would provide moisture protection, will be discussed in the section on the long-term weather exposure tests.

Figure 3.14:   Transverse Load vs Deflection Curves for Rice Hull/Inorganic Matrix Wall Panels

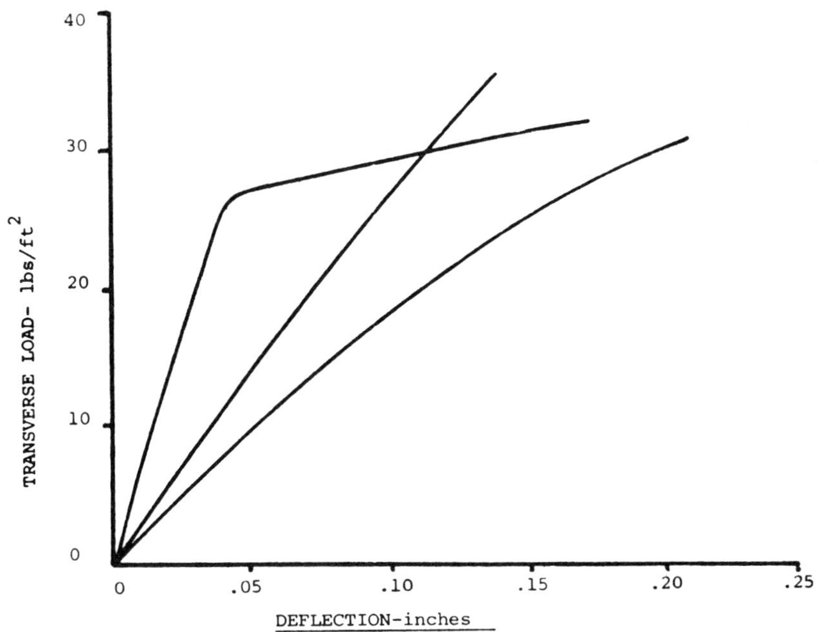

Source: EPA 600/2-78-111

Racking Shear Strength of Nailed Walls: Three 48" x 96" wall panels were tested in accordance with ASTM E-72 test methods. Results of the test are shown in Figure 3.15. From the corrected load-vs-deflection curves, the allowable racking shear load is determined based on the deflection or ultimate criterion, as specified by ICBO.

Figure 3.15: Racking Shear Load vs Deflection Curves for Rice Hull/Inorganic Matrix Wall Panels Nailed to Top and Bottom Plates

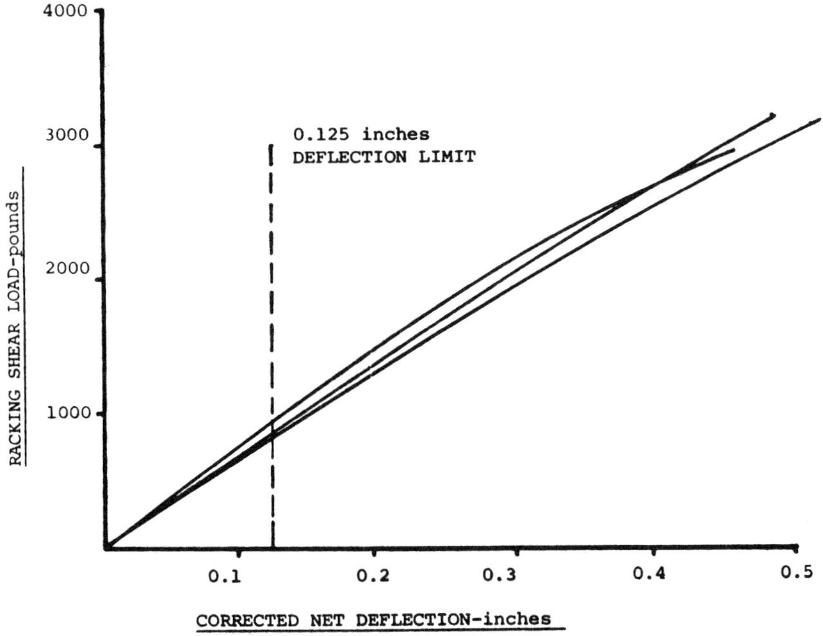

Source: EPA 600/2-78-111

Ultimate Load Criterion: The allowable loads for the three panels are

$$\text{Panel \#1:} \quad \frac{3{,}250 \text{ lb}}{4 \text{ ft} \times 3} = 270.83 \text{ lb/ft}$$

$$\text{Panel \#2:} \quad \frac{3{,}250 \text{ lb}}{4 \text{ ft} \times 3} = 270.83 \text{ lb/ft}$$

$$\text{Panel \#3:} \quad \frac{3{,}000 \text{ lb}}{4 \text{ ft} \times 3} = 250.00 \text{ lb/ft}$$

Average allowable load = 263.89 lb/ft

Deflection Criterion — The allowable design load based on the deflection criterion is the average of the loads obtained at 0.125 inch deflection.

>   Panel #1: 800 lb/4 ft = 200 lb/ft
>
>   Panel #2: 800 lb/4 ft = 200 lb/ft
>
>   Panel #3: 920 lb/4 ft = 230 lb/ft
>
>   Average allowable load = 210 lb/ft

Since the allowable load based on the deflection criterion results in the lower value, it will govern design and would be the value approved by ICBO.

Long-Term Weathering Exposure Tests: Tests were devised, exposing typical wall panels to the following conditions.

> (a) continuous axial compression load of 250 lb/ft, normal outdoor ambient exposure (Escondido, Calif.)
>
> (b) continuous axial compression load of 250 lb/ft, continuous rain soak exposure (simulated by continuous water film running over one exterior surface)
>
> (c) no load; repeated 24-hr cyclic exposure of one face to:
>
>   6 hours at $-20°F$
>   6 hours warm up to $120°F$
>   6 hours at $+120°F$, with 1 hour water spray
>   at beginning and at end
>   6 hours cool down to $-20°F$

Tests (a) and (b) were performed in specially constructed loading fixtures at MSC's Escondido facility; Test (c) was performed in MSC's cyclic environmental chamber.

Visual observations of wall panels in tests (a) and (b) indicated severe surface cracking of all specimens. In the case of the water-soaked panels, the surface of the wall degraded to a point at which it could be easily punctured by the push of a finger.

The axial and lateral deflection of the continuously loaded specimens were recorded. (Deflection history curves for two rain-soaked panels are presented in Figure 3.16.) Deflection was substantial in the first 30 days but appeared to level off after that. This would indicate that most of the water-caused degradation occurs during the first month. Of course, the deflection could be caused by warping due to the asymmetrical water exposure; if so, once the wet face was completely saturated, the warping would stabilize.

There was no measurable deflection of the panels exposed to the outdoor environment in Escondido.

One rain-soaked wall panel was removed for testing after 30 days and one after

Figure 3.16: Axial and Lateral Deflection of Rice Hull/Inorganic Matrix Wall Panels During Long-Term Rain Soak Exposure, Under Constant Axial Load of 250 lb/ft

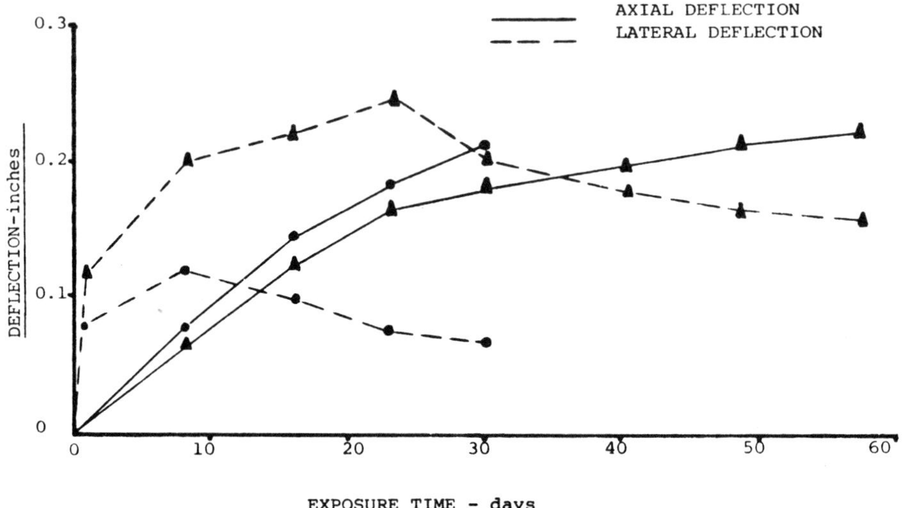

Source: EPA 600/2-78-111

60 days of exposure. The walls were tested in axial compression following a 30-day dry-out period. Test results (presented in Figure 3.17) show a drastic reduction in both stiffness and ultimate strength after 30 days of exposure. The wall exposed for 2 months shows some further reduction in stiffness, but the failure load was actually slightly higher than that of the 30-day specimen.

The difference between the 30- and 60-day results is not considered significant; it is apparent that most of the degradation takes place in the first 30 days of exposure to rain.

The two wall panels in the cyclic environment chamber were exposed for about 4 months to the repeated test cycle (c); the chamber then was shut down and the panels left in the chamber for 30 days to dry out. Visual inspection of the exposed face of the panels indicated that the surface cracks were similar to those of the rain-soaked panels.

One of these panels was tested in axial compression (test results are shown in Figure 3.17). This wall retained more of its original stiffness and strength than the rain-soaked walls, indicating that water has the most severe damaging effect on the rice hull/inorganic matrix composite.

One of the wall panels under continuous load in the outdoor environment for 5 months was also tested in axial compression. This wall failed at 26,400 lb,

Figure 3.17:   Axial Compression Load vs Deflection Curves for 4' x 8' Rice Hull/Inorganic Matrix Wall Panels After Various Long-Term Exposures

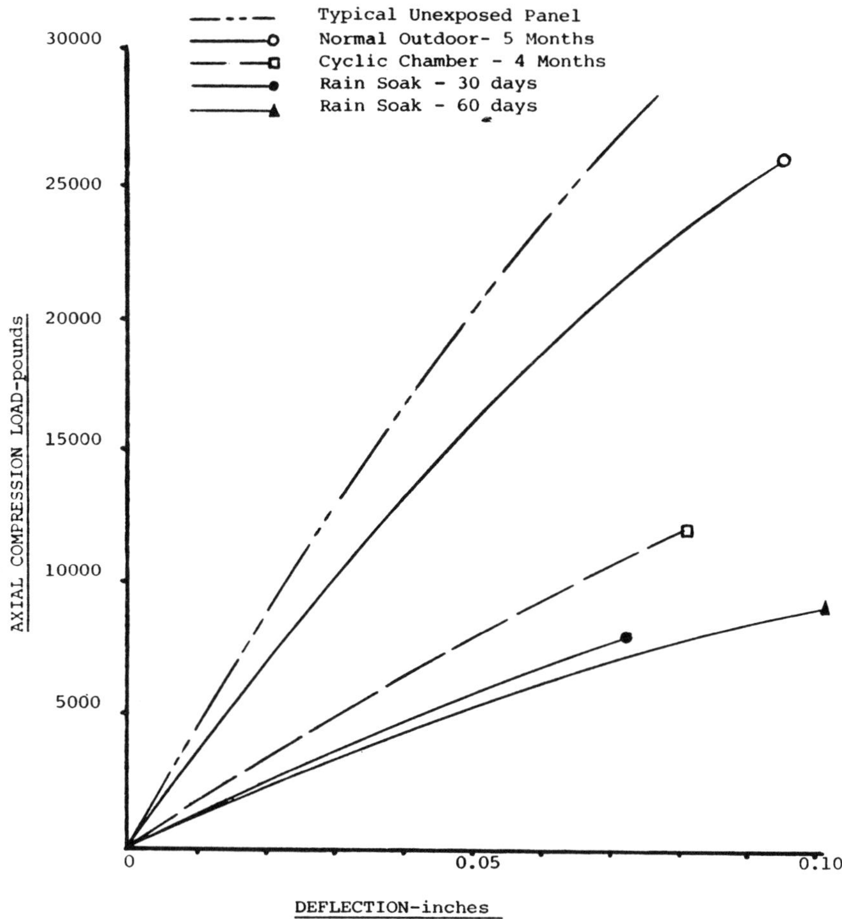

Source: EPA 600/2-78-111

which is only a 12% reduction from the typical initial strength of unexposed panels. This panel was severely cracked on the surface in a fashion similar to the rain-soaked walls, but the material remained hard. The deflection curve shown in Figure 3.17 indicated that this panel retained most of its original stiffness.

The results of the long-term exposure tests clearly indicate that the rice hull-inorganic matrix material of the walls tested is very sensitive to water damage. If these materials are to be used as building components, they must be protected from prolonged exposure to water. It is therefore recommended that future work should explore the development of surface coatings which will

    (a) provide moisture protection and thereby prevent the degradation of the rice hull/inorganic matrix composite;

    (b) reinforce the exterior surface of the panels against stress cracking and thereby increase the tensile strength of the facings, which will in turn improve the lateral load resistance (flexural strength) of the wall panels.

Roof and Ceiling System

Material Selection: The rice hull foam used for the wall was selected (Table 3.20) as the best of the formulation presented. Also from a manufacturing approach, it is desirable to maintain the same formulation for as many products as possible.

Design Selection: The design of the wall was selected for economy. No other configurations were evaluated because each configuration would require a new tool and a complete series of full-scale tests.

Flexural Strength of Roof and Ceiling System: Although the tensile strength of the material is low, it was decided to fabricate the first test specimen similar to the wall without any additional reinforcement. The specimen was built as illustrated in Figure 3.18 and was tested in bending as shown in Figure 3.19 with pin-ended supports. Concrete blocks were placed uniformly on the surface. Blocks were used from the same production batch and weighed $25\pm\frac{1}{4}$ pounds each. The design load for roofs is 20 lb/ft^2 and for floors 40 lb/ft^2. The major design criterion is that deflection does not exceed the span divided by 360 when at design load. Maximum permissible deflection for an 80 foot span is then 0.267 inch.

The first panel tested failed in lower skin tension at 28.4 lb/ft^2 with a maximum deflection of 0.170 inch. The results are shown in Figure 3.20.

From the results of this test, it was decided to reinforce the lower skin with one layer of one-half inch square mesh hardware cloth (Hail Screen). This improved the strength of the panel considerably. The panel failed at a load of 105 lb/ft^2. The deflection at 20 lb/ft^2 was 0.055 inch and at 40 lb/ft^2 0.108 inch, both considerably less than the allowed 0.267 inches. This would indicate that a reduction in cross-section or an increase in span length would be acceptable.

Long-Term Loading on Roof Panel: The next aspect to be considered for a floor or ceiling system is the effects of long-term loading on the panel. The panel was loaded at a level of 21.9 pounds per square foot. The panel was supported on blocks as shown in Figure 3.21 to more closely simulate the end conditions

Figure 3.18:   Floor and Ceiling Specimen

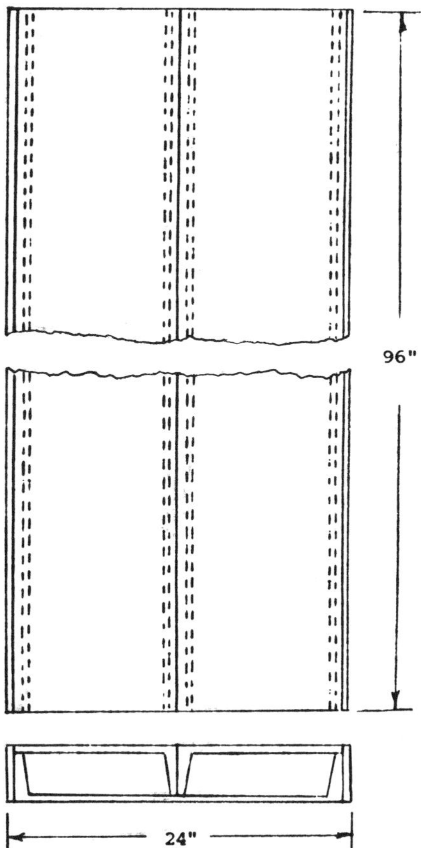

Figure 3.19:   Beam-Bending Test

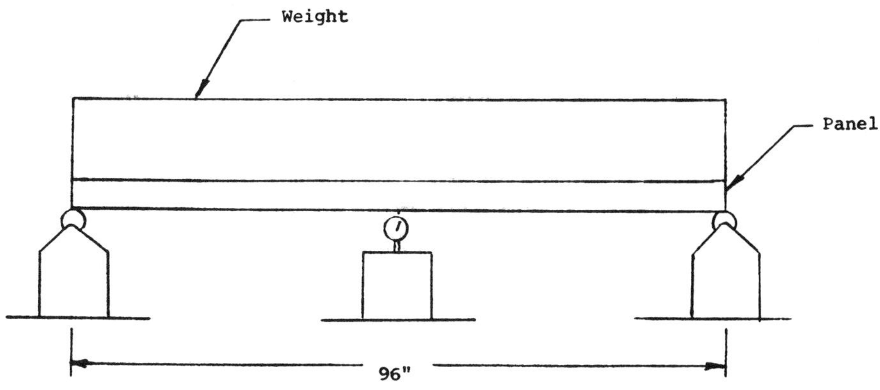

Source: EPA 600/2-78-111

that exist in a housing system. The beam maintained this loading over a period of 68 days with readings taken as indicated in Figure 3.22. The 20 lb/ft^2 loading condition for a roof is a combination of loads that may occur in a specific region. These include combinations of wind and snow. The 21.9 lb/ft^2 loading for a period of 68 days is a rather severe evaluation.

Figure 3.20: Beam-Bending vs Deflection

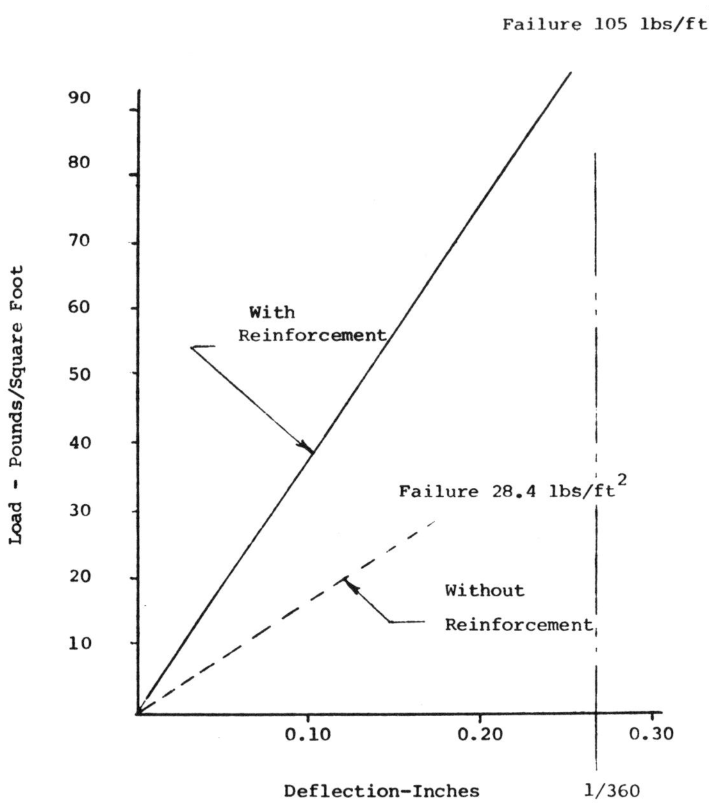

Figure 3.21: Beam-Bending Test (Long-Term Loading)

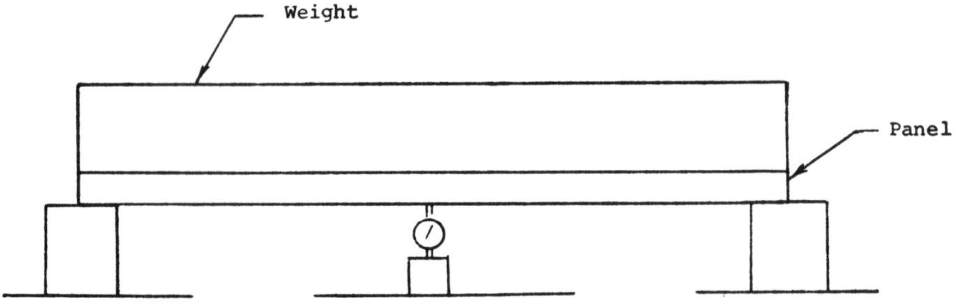

Source: EPA 600/2-78-111

Figure 3.22: Long-Term Loading Test: Uniformly Loaded 21.9 lb/ft^2 Beam Bending Dry

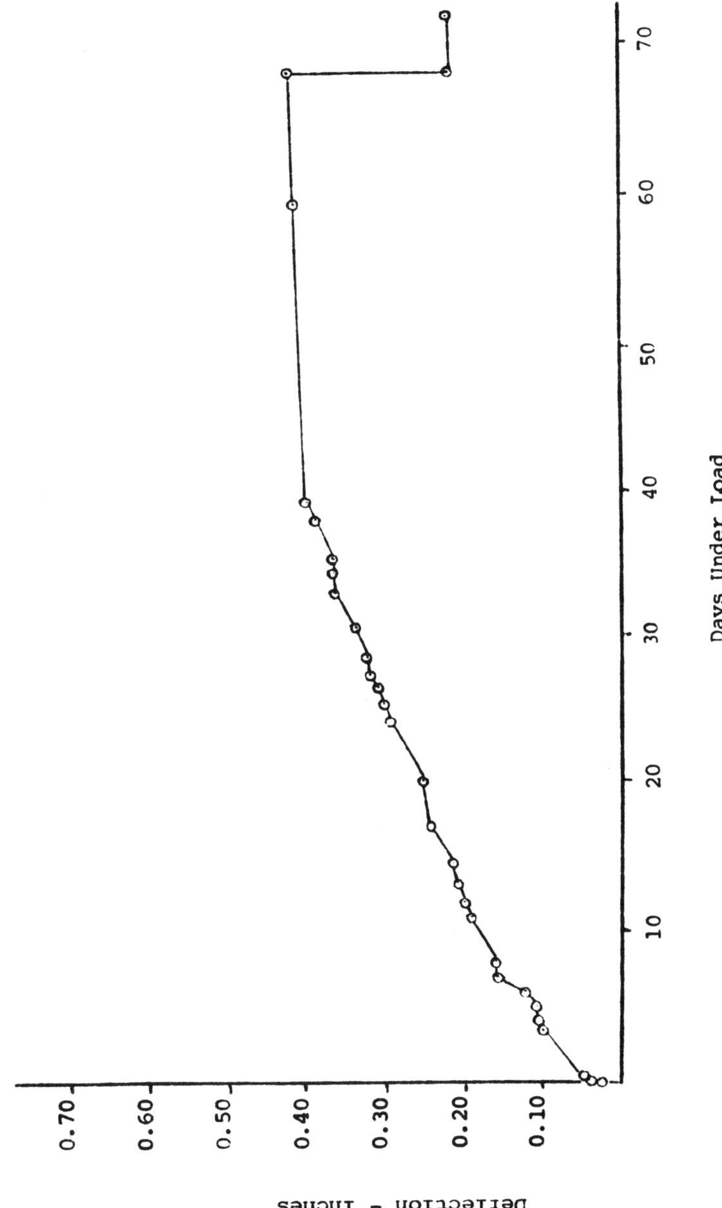

Source: EPA 600/2-78-111

The primary purpose here was to determine the creep characteristics of the material. As can be seen from Figure 3.22, the deformation rate was as follows:

Days	Inch/Day
0-6	0.020
6-39	0.007
39-68	0.002

The rate came close to leveling out after 39 days.

Removal of the load indicated an initial set of 0.220 inch. After a period of 6 days there were no changes.

The results of this study indicate that this panel would be acceptable in nonsnow climates where the maximum load is intermittent. However, in a snow climate additional reinforcement would be required.

Effects of Water on Long-Term Loading: An equivalent test was performed with the loaded panel subjected to a complete inundation of running water. The panel was tested as produced without surface coats. The bond deteriorated losing the beam effect and placing the lower skin in pure tension causing failure in 24 hours. This has resulted in a study of the effect of water on the waste product's bond.

This long-term test was severe but was designed to provide a rapid evaluation of the suitability of the waste materials for structures. A load level of 10 to 13 pounds per square foot would be more realistic and the rate of water flow should be sharply reduced.

A review of the joints of the previous specimen tested under running water indicated a failure of the substrate below the inorganic adhesive. It was felt that an epoxy adhesive would penetrate the substrate further and provide a better joint.

A panel was then manufactured with epoxy bonded joints and again without surface coating. A load of 10.9 lb/ft^2 was determined to be more near a realistic loading. Figure 3.23 shows the results of this test to date. The panel showed a decrease in deflection rate after four days. At the end of 5 days the water was turned off and the panel unloaded to determine the extent of permanent deformation. After 4 days of no load or water the permanent deflection appeared to be 0.283 inch. However, the panel was still damp and more recovery may have been possible.

The specimen was reloaded and the running water started. The slope of the deflection curve the second time appears to be slightly more than that of the first time.

After three days, the load was removed and the water turned off. The panel did

Figure 3.23: Uniformly Loaded 10.0 lb/ft^2 Beam

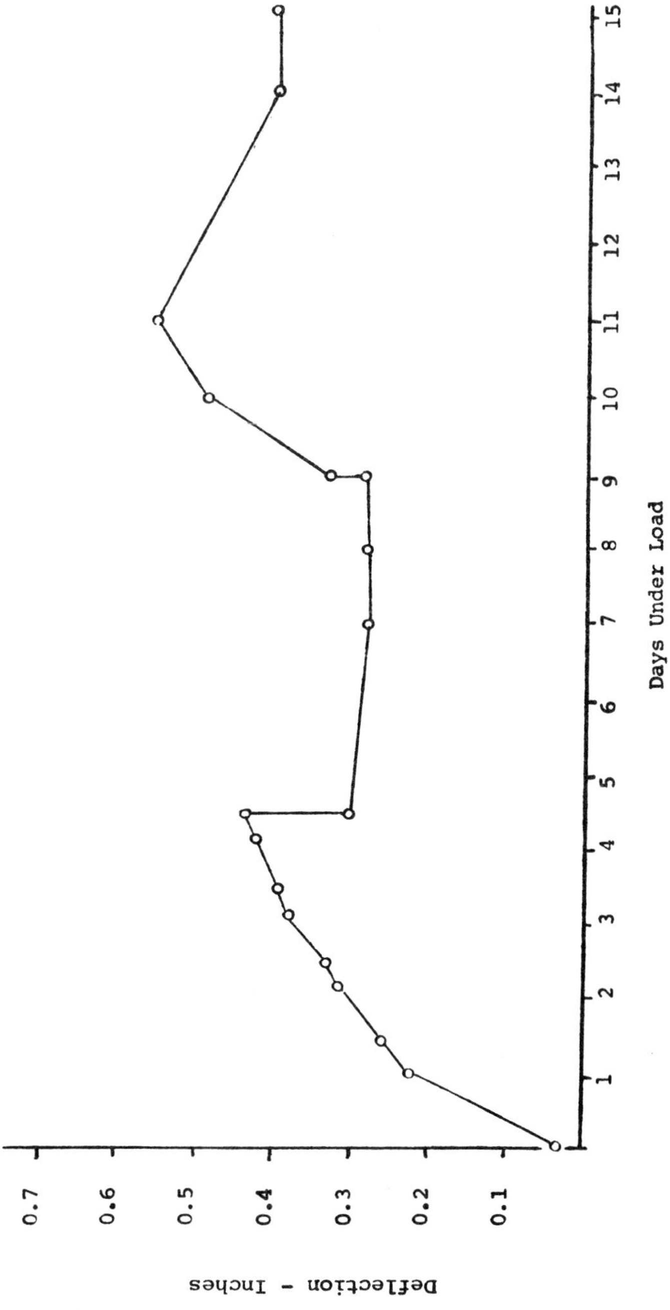

Source: EPA 600/2-78-111

not recover this time immediately. After three days, it recovered to a deformation of 0.40 inch and then stabilized with no further recovery.

Surface coatings would assist the material appreciably and further studies should be conducted on the protection of these panels from running water.

Roof Panel Manufacturing Technique: The techniques recommended for the wall would be applicable for the roof panel. The reinforcing is an additional complication. If an extrusion process is used, the reinforcement would have to be inserted in advance of the die. The hardware cloth is provided in rolls which permit ease of feeding. If metal lath is used, it is rigid and would have to be pre-cut to length and inserted incrementally into the dies.

If a casting process is used, the reinforcement would be installed into the mold prior to the casting of the rice hull foam.

Roof Panel Product Application and Economics: The major application explored here was for a load supporting roof with the lower surface used as the ceiling. The assembly technique would be to install all the lower reinforced sections on the roof first. Then the upper nonreinforced sections would be bonded to the lower reinforced section creating a structure similar to that shown in Figure 3.7.

The economics of the waste roof panel as a roof/ceiling combination are presented in Table 3.28. This compares favorably with the cost of conventional construction presented in Table 3.29.

The waste roof panel, if used as a ceiling would use only the lower elements, Figure 3.6, bonded together. Since there are no loads involved other than dead load, no reinforcement would be required in the elements. The economics of such a waste system are presented in Table 3.30. This compares favorably with the cost of conventional construction presented in Table 3.31.

Recommendations and Conclusions: The rice hull foam creates an acceptable roof-ceiling combination system, as well as an acceptable ceiling system. The major concern is the effects of long-term loading with and without water on the product. As can be seen in Figure 3.24, the panel under a short duration load is more than adequate when the tension side is reinforced. However, the same panel loaded under a typical 21.9 lb/ft^2 roof load showed considerable creep for the first 6 days and then showed a tendency to stabilize although not completely. A loading condition of this magnitude for such a long period is highly improbable. However, the creep characteristics of the material in tension have been indicated.

Running a similar long-term loading with the addition of running water over the sample indicated further concern. It is doubtful that water would be running over an unprotected panel for five days but the test does indicate some sensitivity to the effects of water.

Table 3.28: Cost of Waste Product Roof-Ceiling Panel with Hardware Cloth and Metal Lath Reinforcement

Item	Material Cost	Labor Cost	Total Cost
A. Hardware Cloth Reinforcement:			
Rice Hull Foam 9.656 lbs/ft^2 ($0.038/lb)	$0.367	$0.076 [*]	$0.443
Glass Strands in Cap 0.31 lbs/ft^2 ($0.35/lb)	.011	Included above	.011
Hardware Cloth 0.5 ft^2 ($0.1783/ft^2)	.089	Included above	.089
Adhesive 0.5 lb/ft^2 (0.103)	.052	Included above	.052
Assemble Four Sections (32 ft^2) on Site			
Put in Place 16 min			
Apply Adhesive 8 min			
24 min $\frac{11.52/hr}{60}$ 32 sqft^2	–	.144 [+]	.144
Seal and Finish Joints [‡]	.020	.030	.050
Cost/ft^2	.539	.250	.789
B. Metal Lath Reinforcement:			
A Above without Reinforcement	.450	.250	.700
Lath Reinforcement 0.5 ft^2 ($0.14/ft^2)	.007	–	.007
Cost/ft^2	.457	.250	.707

[*] Estimate includes factory overhead, depreciation, and labor and is based on MSC continuous production technology.

[+] Estimate made from observing demonstration model construction.

[‡] Weather seal not included.

Table 3.29: Cost of Conventional Roof-Ceiling System

Item	Material Cost [*]	Labor Cost [*]	Total Cost [*]
2 x 4 Joists	$0.126	$0.188	$0.314
Plywood Exterior	.142	.149	.291
Sheet Rock, Hang, Tape & Texture	.120	.160	.280
Cost/ft^2 [+]	.388	.497	.885

[*] Estimates from Current Construction Costs, 1976 – Lee Saylor, Inc.

[+] Weather seal not included.

Source: EPA 600/2-78-111

Table 3.30: Cost of Waste Product Ceiling Panel

Item	Material Cost	Labor Cost	Total Cost
Rice Hull Foam 4.828 lbs/ft^2 ($0.038/lb)	$0.183	$0.038 [*]	$0.221
Glass Strands in Cap 0.016 lb/ft^2 ($0.35/lb)	.006	Included above	.006
Adhesive 0.25 lb/ft^2 ($0.103)	.026	–	.026
Assemble Four Sections (32 ft^2) on Site			
Put in Place 16 min			
Apply Adhesive 8 min			
24 min $\frac{11.52/hr}{60}$ 32 ft^2	–	.144 [+]	.144
Finish Joints	.010	.015 [‡]	.025
Cost/ft^2	.225	.197	.422

[*] Estimate includes factory overhead, depreciation, and labor and is based on MSC continuous production technology.

[+] Estimate made from observing demonstration model construction.

[‡] Estimate from Current Construction Costs, 1976 - Lee Saylor, Inc.

Table 3.31: Cost of Conventional Ceiling System

Item	Material Cost [*]	Labor Cost [*]	Total Cost [*]
2 x 4 Joists	$0.126	$0.188	$0.314
Sheet Rock, Hang, Tape & Texture	.120	.160	.280
	.246	.348	.594

[*] Estimates from Current Construction Costs, 1976 - Lee Saylor, Inc.

Figure 3.24: Elements for a Floor Panel

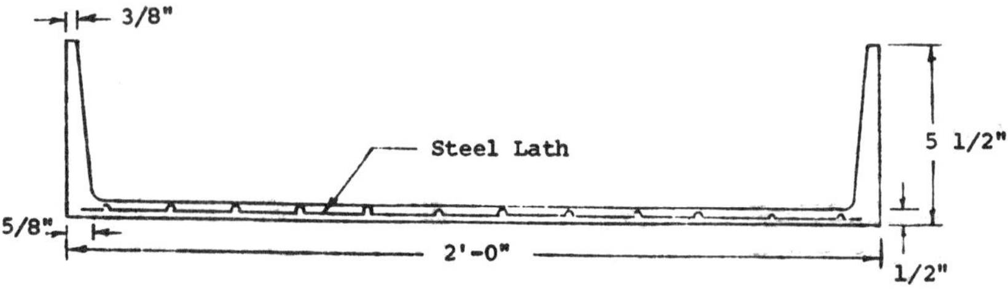

Source: EPA 600/2-78-111

The waste panel can be used for a roof-ceiling combination system. However, it should use the steel lath reinforcement rather than the hardware cloth. It is not only less expensive but will provide more stiffness. In addition, it is suggested that reinforcement be incorporated into the compression side as well as the tension side. This would reduce the potential for creep. A weather seal such as a composition roof cover, a built up roof cover, or any conventional weather seal system should be applied to the exposed surface of the panel. The ceiling system can be used as is for a nonloaded system.

Floor System

Material Selection: The same rice hull foam used for the wall and roof was selected (see Table 3.20).

Design Selection: The design selected was the one selected for the roof.

Flexural Strength of Floor Panel: The tests run for the roof were load extended to include floor requirements. Figure 3.20 shows that the floor is more than adequate for short duration 40 lb/ft^2 floor loads. Under these loading conditions an even longer floor span could be considered.

Long-Term Floor Panel Loading: The long-term loading effects of the panel used as a floor can be evaluated from Figure 3.22. This test definitely indicates a problem with the present design. It is therefore proposed to increase the element depth to 5½" to provide additional stiffness. This will increase the stiffness by a factor of 2.4 and reduce the tensile load on the elements surface by 1.6. It is also proposed that metal lath reinforcement be placed in both surfaces. For details see Figure 3.24.

This additional stiffness and reduction in tensile stress should improve the long-term load carrying capability of the material.

Effects of Water on Long-Term Loading: There is no doubt that from the test data shown in Figure 3.23, it will be necessary to protect the material from long periods of running water. It is recommended that both surfaces be sealed. Water of evaporation will have minimal effect. It is only prolonged inundation such as an undetected plumbing leak that would be a problem.

Wear Surface: As in most foam type materials the rice hull foam does not wear well. It must be covered with a wear surface. The minimal acceptable surface would be a tile. However, it would be more preferable to coat the surface with one-quarter inch of magnesium oxychloride cement. This is an elastic type material which does not crack easily and also provides the needed water seal.

Floor Panel Manufacturing Technique: The same techniques as described for the roof panel are applicable for the floor panel. If the casting process is used, the magnesium oxychloride cement surface can be cast ahead of the rice hull foam permitting a one step production. If the extrusion process is used the magnesium oxychloride would have to be cast on the element as a secondary step.

Floor Panel Application and Economics: The primary application for the waste floor panel would be for a floor-ceiling system. The panel could also be used for a floor system but would have less economic advantage. The basic panel produced from elements shown in Figure 3.24 would cost installed $0.728/ft^2. Table 3.32 has details. A ¼" magnesium oxychloride wear surface would add $0.220/ft^2 (see Table 3.33) increasing the total cost to $0.948/ft^2. This compares extremely well with a conventional floor ceiling system itemized in Table 3.34.

There is still a competitive edge for the waste panel as a floor panel when compared with a conventional wood system (see Table 3.35). Their cost compares well with a concrete slab of $1.10/ft^2.

Table 3.32: Cost of Waste Product Floor-Ceiling Panel with Metal Lath Reinforcement

Item	Material Cost	Labor Cost	Total Cost
Rice Hull Foam 10.208 lbs/ft^2 ($0.038/lb)	$0.388	$0.076 *	$0.464
Glass Strands in Cap 0.031 lbs/ft^2 ($0.35/lb)	.011	Included above	.011
Lath Reinforcement 0.5 sq ft ($0.14 sqft)	.007	–	.007
Adhesive 0.5 lb/ft^2 (0.103)	.052	Included above	.052
Assemble on Site: Four Sections (32 sq ft) Put in Place 16 min Apply Adhesive 8 min / 24 min $\frac{11.52/hr}{60}$ 32 sqft		.144 +	.144
Seal and Finish Joints	.020	.030 ‡	.050
Cost/ft^2 #	.478	.250	.728

* Estimate includes factory overhead, depreciation and labor and is based on MSC continuous production technology.

\+ Estimate made from observing demonstration model construction.

‡ Estimate from Current Construction Costs, 1976 – Lee Saylor, Inc.

\# Wear Surface not included.

Source: EPA 600/2-78-111

Table 3.33: Cost of Magnesium Oxychloride Floor Surface

Item	Weight, lbs	Cost/lb	Cost
$MgCl_2 \cdot 6H_2O$	0.72	$0.071	$0.051
MgO	.72	.135	.097
Sand	.72	.010	.072
$Cost/ft^2$			.220

Table 3.34: Cost of Conventional Floor-Ceiling System

Item	Material Cost [*]	Labor Cost [*]	Total Cost [*]
2 x 6 Joists	$0.200	$0.290	$0.490
1/2 inch C-D ext. Plywood	.142	.131	.273
1/2 inch Fire X Sheet Rock	.120	.160	.280
Misc. Hangers and Hardware	.060	-	.060
$Cost/ft^2$ [+]	.522	.581	1.103

[*] Estimates from Current Construction Costs, 1976 - Lee Saylor, Inc.

[+] Wear surface not included.

Table 3.35: Cost of Conventional Wood Floor System

Item	Material Cost [*]	Labor Cost [*]	Total Cost [*]
Same as Table 3.34 Less Sheet Rock	$0.402	$0.421	$0.823
Vapor Seal	.050	.020	.070
$Cost/ft^2$ [+]	.452	.441	.893

[*] Estimates from Current Construction Costs, 1976 - Lee Saylor, Inc.

[+] Wear surface not included.

Source: EPA 600/2-78-111

Recommendation and Conclusions: The system has definite advantages both for economic and fire safety reasons in this application. However, the long-term loading characteristics of the system have not been completely determined and should be evaluated during at least a six month period and preferably during a three year period before using the material for a floor-in application.

Fire Door

Material Selection for Core: The initial work on the fire door core was based on the rice hull foam formulation presented in Table 3.36. This formulation when used to construct the fire door was found to be difficult to work because of (1) rapid setting which made preparation and casting of 2.5 ft^3 of mixture required for a fire door core extremely difficult, (2) a density which was too high and (3) cost somewhat over present materials for fire door cores. When this formulation was used on laboratory size specimens, the rapid set-time could be readily accommodated.

Table 3.36: Rice Hull Foam Formulation

	Grams
Rice Hulls	100
1" Chopped Glass Fiber	15
MSC Additive	40
Gypsum Plaster	60
Casting Plaster	240
Water	225

Source: EPA 600/2-78-111

One other scale-up problem was that a specimen 6" x 6" was readily handleable, even wet, once setting occurred. However, a full-scale door core measures 34.5" x 77" x 1.5". When wet, the cast material will crack on handling because of the high weight (water present prior to drying) and long unsupported distance of cast panel.

It was necessary to reformulate so as to accommodate processing, properties and price requirements. Several approaches were used and these were:

> Reduce density by use of styrofoam beads,
>
> Increase processability by use of beads because of processability and ease of movement to fill the mold, and
>
> Achievement of the above by foaming.

Table 3.37 lists a series of formulations which were made and evaluated in the laboratory. This evaluation was accomplished by exposing each specimen to

Table 3.37: Fire-Door Insulation Material Formulations Based on Rice Hulls

Item	Formulation 1	2	3	4	5	6	7
Water	330	350	330	340	360	350	360
90 min. Casting Plaster	450	450	450	450	450	450	450
MSC Proprietary Binder	60	60	60	60	–	–	–
Styrofoam Beads	5	5	–	–	–	5	–
Rice Hulls	75	75	150	150	150	75	150
$Al_2O_3 \cdot 3H_2O$	–	164	–	–		164	100
$Al_2(SO_4)_3 \cdot 18H_2O$	–	–	50 *	50 *	50	–	50
1/2" Chopped Glass	–	–	–	–	3.5	–	3.5
G-3300 (Surfactant)	–	–	–	–	3.5	3.5	3.5
Density, lbs/ft^3	20.5	26.2	37.3	26.4	27.4	28.6	28.6
Cost, $/ft^3	0.875	1.517	1.712	1.138	1.915	1.208	1.739
Max. Temp, °F after 2 hrs	Failed ‡	300	225	Failed ‡	404	475	235

Formulation	8	9	10	11	12	13	14
Water	360	360	350	425 #	425 #	350	330
90 min. Casting Plaster	450	450	450	450	450	450	450
MSC Proprietary Binder	–	–	–	–	–	–	–
Styrofoam Beads	–	–	–	–	–	–	15
Rice Hulls	150	150	150	12.5	12.5	150	150
$Al_2O_3 \cdot 3H_2O$		–	–	–	38	–	–
$Al_2(SO_4)_3 \cdot 18H_2O$	50	50	50	12.5	12.5	50	50
1/2" Chopped Glass	3.5	–	3.5	3.5	3.5	3.5	3.5
G-3300 (Surfactant)	3.5	3.5	3.5	3.5	3.5	3.5	–
Density, lbs/ft^3	28.5	27.2	33.9	33.0	33.3	33.0	26.8
Cost, $/ft^3	1.038	0.584	0.940	0.796	0.964	0.958	0.919
Max. Temp, °F after 2 hours	340 Failed +	335	155	185	250	300	285

* Added as Solid: All following formulations use 33% solution, thus 150 g sol'n contains 50 g $Al_2(SO_4)_3 \cdot 18H_2O$.

+ Reached 600°F in 28 mins with rapidly increasing rate of heat-up.

‡ Reached 435°F in 20 mins and rising very rapidly.

Water added to make up for that lost because of less amount of $Al_2(SO_4)_3 \cdot 18H_2O$ solution used.

Source: EPA 600/2-78-111

a propane torch kept 3" from the front surface and a thermocouple to the rear face. It must be commented that the propane torch provides a highly erosive action not present in the standard fire test. The use of comparative results and performance of a "standard" material made this test useful for screening.

The data showed that direct replacement of rice hulls by styrofoam beads caused thermal insulation to be unsatisfactory, the most logical reason being the great difference in density from 40.9 lb/ft^3.

Formulation #2 has aluminum hydrate added to provide extra water as a possible way to improve insulative performance. This was very effective without too great an increase in density but large increase in cost. In Formulation 3 and 4, the aluminum hydrate was replaced by an even more efficient source of water, aluminum sulfate. This has 48.6% water as compared to 34.0% for aluminum hydrate and 21.0% for hydrated gypsum.

The incorporation of aluminum hydrate provided improved insulative performance and this was due to the ability of this material to provide water for transpirational cooling. Assuming this to be correct, new addition of a compatible material having a higher water content might give still further improvement. For this purpose, $Al_2(SO_4)_3 \cdot 18H_2O$ was selected.

Addition of this compound to a water-plaster mixture caused setting to occur in about 15 minutes even though 90 minute casting plaster was used. What was unanticipated was a 75% increase in volume due to frothing. It appears as if other additions are needed to prevent cracking or drying of the foam. The glass fibers and/or rice hulls used in the formulations should prevent cracking.

The same frothing and rapid set was obtained when regular wall plaster was used.

Frothing cannot occur between aluminum sulfate and calcium sulfate. The calcium carbonate in the plaster reacts with the acidic aluminum sulfate to generate carbon dioxide, more calcium sulfate and aluminum hydroxide (alumina trihydrate). Therefore use of aluminum sulfate adds water for cooling and forms two other materials which also help in insulation because of water content.

Formulation 5 was adequate for 2-hour use, with a large decrease in cost but with very satisfactory density. Formulations 6 and 7 are too expensive but Formulations 8 through 14 all are acceptable. The amounts of the material in the formulations are in grams. It was decided that further evaluation had to be made on full scale door cores. Initially it was decided to case the core into an upright mold. Modifications to Formulations 5 and 14 from Table 3.37 were used to case five cores. These are presented in Table 3.38.

**Table 3.38: Attempts to Case Full Size Fire Door Core
(34.5" x 77" x 1.5")**

Constituent	Formulation				
	A	B	C	D	E
Rice Hulls	8978	8978	8978	9427	9427
1/2" Glass	209	209	209	219.5	219.5
90 min. Casting Plaster	26933	26933	26933	28280	28280
Water	20948	20948	25436	26708	26708
$Al_2(SO_4)_3 \cdot 18H_2O$ Sol'n	8978	8978	2244	2356	2356
Detergent	80	0	25	26.3	26.3

Source: EPA 600/2-78-111

The panels were not drying on the bottom and were so wet as to cause fracture when moved; support of underside during movement might prevent this. Frothing could also cause weakening, so B formulation was made without detergent. There was now insufficient material to fill the mold. Slight increase in detergent gave better results for formulations C, D, and E but results were still not satisfactory.

It was decided to do further refinement on formulation E with a specimen 24" x 32". This size provided scale up data, permitted E-119 fire test evaluation and used less time and materials.

The processing difficulties from rapid set time were overcome by use of a protein retarder and it became possible to fabricate specimens having a material density of about 28-32 lb/ft^3. An E-119 fire test in which face temperatures were increased (by increment) to 1800°F demonstrated complete protection for a period of 90 minutes as evidenced by failure of cotton linters or Kleenex to ignite when pressed against the back surface during the test.

The maximum recorded back-side temperature was 340°F. After 90 minutes, the test specimen was placed at a 20 foot distance from a fire hose with a 1.5" nozzle and hit with a stream of water at 30 psi for 8 seconds; the door maintained its integrity despite the erosion of material to a depth of about 1.0 inch.

The above evaluation resulted in the selection of the formulation presented in Table 3.39.

Material Selection for Framing Members: The framing material has screw retention requirements as well as fire resistance requirements. The density of this

Table 3.39: Formulation for Fire Door Core*

Item	Percent
Rice hulls	13.7
½" chopped glass fiber	0.6
90 min casting plaster	41.1
MSC binder	3.13
Water	38.0
$Al_2(SO_4)_3 \cdot 18H_2O$	3.4
Detergent	0.04
Retarder	0.03

*Density, 32 lb/ft^3; stabilized moisture content, 10%.

Source: EPA 600/2-78-111

material is no longer critical since the volume of material needed for a frame is small compared to the core.

The first experiments were carried out to compare plaster, magnesium oxychloride and magnesium oxysulfate with phenolic microballoons which impart lower density and helps nail and screw retention. These data indicated the weakness of plaster and superiority of magnesium oxychloride.

The three binder materials were then compared to a fibrous material prepared from Douglas Fir bark, called Silvacon, assuming this would help values using plaster. Use of Silvacon improved the properties of plaster over phenolic microballoons but not sufficiently for application. The magnesium oxychloride again displayed far superior results and adequate properties for framing material.

It was decided to continue formulations with magnesium oxychloride in place of plaster but to investigate other filler materials derived from waste materials. Since Silvacon is produced from a scrap material (Douglas Fir Bark) and is inexpensive, it was included in the study.

A variety of formulations were evaluated with the various waste materials and magnesium oxychloride. Results are summarized in Table 3.40. The properties that resulted from use of Douglas Fir fibers gave excellent results even when the bulk of this material was replaced by waste-derived Silvacon (see Formulation 1). Actually this mixture of fillers gave highest all around strengths. Since the use of Douglas Fir fibers was so successful it was tried with plaster, Formulation 5, and gave poor properties. Formulations 3 and 4 were made with 90 mesh sand added to increase density since nail and screw retention improved with density but with plaster this improvement fell far too short. Magnesium oxychloride and milled rice hulls, Formulation 6, provide nearly an equivalent product to Formulation 1.

Table 3.40:   Use of Various Waste Fillers for Door Framing Using Magnesium Oxychloride

Item	Formulation 1	2	3	4	5	6
$MgCl_2 \cdot 6H_2O$	93.5 g	93.5 g	-	-	-	93.5 g
H_2O	70.5	70.5	175 g	175 g	175 g	70.5
MgO	100.0	100.0	-	-	-	100.0
Regular Rice Hulls	-	35.0	-	-	-	-
=5 Milled Rice Hulls [*]	-	-	-	60 g	-	40.0
Douglas Fir Fibers [+]	25.0	25.0	-	-	50 g	-
Silvacon	50.0	-	60 g	-	-	40.0
Sand	-	-	125 g	125 g	-	-
MSC Binder	-	10.0	-	-	-	-
Casting Plaster	-	-	275 g	275 g	275 g	-
Density, lb/ft^3	74	69.5	74	86	69.5	81.0
Nail Retention lbs	225	200.0	15	65	35.0	-
Screw Retention lbs	455	360.0	100	130	85.0	445.0
Compression, psi	3250	1350.0	500	500	530.0	2400.0

[*] Hammer-milled rice hulls, contains about 33% (wt) of - 20 mesh fines.

[+] From Industrial Paper Company, Longview, Washington. Screened to remove -20 mesh fines.

Source: EPA 600/2-78-111

Mechanical tests were conducted on wood materials used for frames. The 455 pound screw retention capability of inorganic mix #1 and the 445 screw retention capability of inorganic mix #6 are as good as or superior to that of the wood.

One additional problem was noted when 8 ft long sections were fabricated: low flexural strength. To improve this characteristic untwisted sisal strands were incorporated into the mix. This resulted in the selection of the material formulation presented in Table 3.41.

Table 3.41: Formulation for Framing Material

Constituent	Percent
$MgCl_2 \cdot 6H_2O$	26
H_2O	19
MgO	28
MSC Binder	2
Douglas Fir Fibers	6
Silvacon 412	17
Untwisted Sisal	2

Source: EPA 600/2-78-111

Design Selection: The design options on a fire door are limited. The core is limited to one and one-half inches for a 90 minute fire rating. The framing materials are also limited to that of conventional design. A cross-section of the door is shown in Figure 3.25. The primary purpose of the groove in the stiles and rails is to eliminate a direct heat or flame path through the wall.

Mechanical Properties: The mechanical requirements for the core are to be light as possible and capable of being handled. The core when completely dried weighs 32 lb/ft^3. Existing cores weigh between 20 and 35 lb/ft^3 which places the waste core in the higher density classification.

Figure 3.25: Fire Door Design

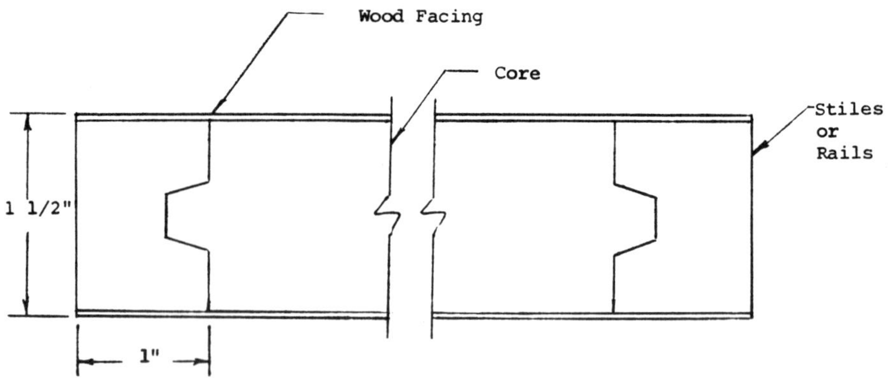

Source: EPA 600/2-78-111

The mechanical requirement of the framing material is screw retention. The screw retention of waste framing material is 400 to 450 pounds. This compares favorably with that of conventional wood framing materials whose retention is from 260 to 495 pounds.

Fire Test: The fire test for the door follows the ASTM E-152 procedure. The difference in procedures is that the door is installed in a wall. The assembly is placed in a furnace for 90 minutes and then removed and sprayed with a 30 psi hose stream for a period of seconds equal to 0.9 times the surface area of the door in square feet.

Preliminary tests were conducted on panels measuring 24" x 32" x 1½", exposed to a furnace programmed to the ASTM time-temperature curve. Temperature on the back side was measured by thermocouple as was the flame temperature. A small wad of cotton and/or tissue was also kept in contact with the back surface.

After 90 minute exposure the backside temperature was insufficient to ignite the tissue. The specimen was moved to where it was exposed to a stream of water at 30 psi from a 1.5 inch nozzle at a distance of 20 feet. After 8 seconds of such exposure, the sample remained intact. Since the cotton failed to ignite and the back panel was in excellent condition and the water did not wash away all of the core, the test was considered to be very successful.

These results were sufficient to encourage a full-scale test. Two sets of cores and framing materials were produced. These elements were shipped to Cal Wood Door for fabrication into a test assembly.

Core Manufacturing Techniques: The core material is cast into a mold and the mold inserted into a matched platen pressure. The mold is closed to its stops and a pressure of one to two pounds per square inch maintained to equalize pressures generated by the foaming action.

Framing Material Manufacturing Techniques: The elements for this study were made in matched molds in a press above. However, the consistency of the compound is such that an extrusion process would be the logical procedure for large quantity production.

Fire Door Product Application and Economics: The application explored here is the 90 minute fire door. Although there are other cores competing for this market, the only framing material is chemically treated wood which is marginal. The economics of the core are presented in Table 3.42. The material cost of the core is $2.038 for a three foot wide, six foot eight inch high door. Labor costs to produce it would be approximately $1.00 per door. Competitive cores are provided the door manufacturer in a price range of $10.00 to $15.00 per unit. When marketing, distribution and waste expenses are added to the waste door, it would appear to be competitive in that market.

The framing material cost in Table 3.43 of $0.0572 per linear foot is commercially competitive. Furthermore, the material is fire resistant and will maintain screw holding power easily for 90 minutes of fire exposure.

Table 3.42: Fire Door Core Economics

Volume	1.896 cubic feet
Dry Weight	60.67 pounds
Wet Weight	79.55 pounds

Item	lbs	Cost/lb	Cost
Rice Hulls	10.9	$0.062 *	$0.676
1/2 inch chopped glass fibers	.5	.40	0.200
Casting Plaster	32.7	.0252	0.824
MSC Binder	2.5	.010	0.025
Water	30.2	–	–
$Al_2(SO_4)_3 \cdot 18H_2O$	2.7	.10	0.270
Detergent	.03	.75	0.023
Retarder	.02	.98	0.020
	79.55		2.038

* Price delivered to factory.

Table 3.43: Framing Material Economics

1 linear foot = 0.78 lbs

Item	Weight, lbs	Cost/lbs	Total Cost
$MgCL_2 \cdot 6H_2O$	0.202	$0.071	$0.0143
H_2O	0.148	–	–
MgO	0.218	0.135	0.0294
MSC Binder	0.016	0.010	0.0002
Douglas Fir Fibers	0.047	0.060	0.0028
Silvacon 412	0.133	0.075	0.0100
Untwisted Sisal	0.016	0.030	0.0005
Cost per linear foot	–	–	0.0572

Source: EPA 600/2-78-111

Production: Calwood Door, a cabinet and door manufacturer, investigated use of these materials in actual production. Calwood assisted during the earlier phases of the development effort by providing performance requirements and realistic full-scale fabrication parameters in laboratory studies.

After the successful preliminary fire test, Calwood agreed to evaluate full-scale production processing. Sample components were fabricated by MSC and incorporated into full-scale doors by Calwood. The manufacturer identified several production problems with the use of the new materials, and MSC developed solutions.

For example, Calwood experienced difficulty in bonding the framing components to the wood facing sheets. Laboratory tests were conducted to find suitable adhesives to eliminate this production problem. Results of tests performed on the two most promising candidate adhesives are presented in Table 3.44.

Table 3.44: Fire Door Adhesive Tests

Borden 07-100 (Casein) Adhesive

Without Veil Mat Failure Load, lb @ R.T.	Type of Failure	With Veil Mat Failure Load, lb @ R.T.	Type of Failure
615	Block Broke	630	Block Broke
495	" "	660	" "
780	" "	635	" "
620	" "	605	" "
525	" "	610	" "
Avg 607		Avg 628	
Tested @ 300°F		Tested @ 300°F	
420	Block Broke	380	Block Broke
515	" "		" "
440	" "	420	" "
520	" "	455	" "
490	" "	430	" "
Avg 477	" "	Avg 436	" "
22% loss in material strength		31% loss in material strength	

Borden RS-125 MD (Resorcinol) Adhesive

Without Veil Mat Failure Load, lb @ R.T.	Type of Failure	With Veil Mat Failure Load, lb @ R.T.	Type of Failure
620	Block Broke	565	Block Broke
630	95% Adhesive Failure	685	" "
750	Block Broke	645	" "
575	" "	705	" "
650	" "	575	" "
Avg 644		Avg 635	
Tested @ 300°F		Tested @ 300°F	
535	Block Broke	415	Block Broke
430	" "	450	" "
520	" "	420	" "
515	" "	460	" "
470	" "	455	" "
Avg 494		Avg 440	
23% loss in material strength		31% loss in material strength	

Source: EPA 600/2-78-111

The test consisted of bonding blocks of the framing material to wood block using the candidate adhesives. The bonded blocks were then tested in tension at room temperature and at 300°F. The use of "veil mat" as a reinforcement of the bond interface was also evaluated in these tests.

From the results of these tests, it was concluded that both of the adhesives would perform satisfactorily. The results also indicated that the use of the veil mat did not increase the strength of the bond. In fact, at elevated temperature, the specimens with veil mat showed lower strength than the ones without it.

Based on these results, the manufacturer repeated his earlier production experiments with the new adhesives and found that they both performed well.

A door fabricated with waste material components developed in this program was fully qualified as a 90-minute rated fire door.

Calwood Door is planning to introduce in next year's product line a new high-performance fire door using components made from waste materials.

DEMONSTRATION UNIT CONSTRUCTED FROM WASTE MATERIALS

Sheets, panels, and test specimens can define a considerable number of properties and evaluate materials and systems to a point. The true and complete evaluation occurs only when these are incorporated into a complete demonstration unit. Only when floors, roofs and walls are used as such can the real applicability be determined. Therefore, a demonstration unit was designed and built using the previously described waste materials.

It was requested that the unit be disassembleable to permit easy transportation to various exhibition sites. The initial site was the Environmental Protection Agency Environmental Research Center in Cincinnati, Ohio. The disassembly requirement created problems with joints and eliminated weather seal capability which requires that the module be exhibited indoors only.

The inorganic panels had to be constructed by hand using the techniques previously outlined. Since this was the first production of any large quantity of these materials considerable information was developed on the use of the waste material in housing units. These details are presented below.

Organic Waste Panels

Effect of Moisture: The organic waste panels, both wood waste and peanut shells, were used as paneling material for both the window and door panels. The construction was accomplished during an extremely humid period. It was determined that the wood waste panels absorbed moisture which caused considerable swelling. This situation was corrected by sealing the surfaces with a urethane coating. The peanut shell material did not demonstrate the same phenomenon.

Applicability: The organic waste panels were workable with conventional tools and could be nailed without difficulty.

Inorganic Waste Panels

Wall Surface Finish: In production it is proposed that the desired surface finish be incorporated into the waste wall panels. However, due to the limited hand-built quantities utilized here it was decided to be more efficient for this unit to apply the surface finish as a secondary step. Conventional dry wall spackling compound was used on the interior surfaces and interacted very well with the waste wall.

Such conventional finishing techniques are completely compatible. On the exterior finish a conventional stucco compound was tried first. Although it appeared to work well on small specimens, it did not adhere well on the surface of the module. This material had to be removed.

Laboratory tests showed that magnesium oxychloride when mixed with sand made an excellent surface coat. It was originally used as a stucco material before the advent of gypsum stucco. Tests showed that the material interacted with the rice hull foam to effect a good bond. However, on small specimens the effect and mechanics of this interaction were not completely displayed. The magnitude was learned only after the exterior of the unit was coated. An outward curvature towards the magnesium oxychloride surface was noted on all walls when the unit was being dismantled for shipment. An upward curvature or crown was noted on the floor panel because the wear surface applied was magnesium oxychloride also.

However, no curvature was detected in the roof panels which did not receive a magnesium oxychloride coat. To verify the effect of magnesium oxychloride on the rice hull foam, an eight foot long section of ½ inch thick rice hull foam was coated with magnesium oxychloride in the same fashion as the unit and observed. The magnesium oxychloride penetrated to a depth of ¼ inch causing an expansion of the rice hull foam which resulted in a curvature towards the coating. Tests indicate no effect on strength. The test specimen indicated that the expansion action ceased after 48 hours. To verify that this action was stabilized, the wall panels were measured over a five day period and no further movement was detected.

Experiments show that if the magnesium oxychloride is cast onto the surface at the time the rice hull foam is cast, no curvature is generated. It also appears that if a very thin film of the solution without sand is applied to the cured surface first a seal is created which eliminates excessive amounts of absorption of the solution by the rice hull foam when the coating is applied. This eliminates the curvature.

Floor Wear Surface: The floor panels were uncoated initially. However, after three weeks of technicians working on the interior of the unit, the foam surface showed signs of considerable wear. It was determined to provide a wear surface of magnesium oxychloride cement. The results of long term studies discussed in previous sections indicated that the floor panel should be reinforced in both surfaces. Therefore, it was decided to apply a reinforced wear surface of magnesium oxychloride cement.

Applicability: The inorganic waste panels were workable with conventional tools and ordinary construction methods were applicable.

Doors

Applicability: The doors required no special consideration and were installed in a similar manner as conventional doors.

REFERENCES

Material Systems Corp. *A Study of the Feasibility of Utilizing Solid Wastes for Building Materials.* Monthly Progress Reports 6023-11 to 14, ERT 94-95, and Phase II Summary, Escondido, CA, 1975.

National Bureau of Standards. *Mat-Formed Wood Particle Board (CS236-66).* U.S. Department of Commerce, U.S. Government Printing Office, Washington, DC, 1966.

USDA Forest Service. *The Outlook for Particle Board Manufactured in the Northern Rocky Mountain Region,* USDA Forest Service General Technical Report INT-21. Intermountain Forest and Range Experiment Station, Ogden, UT, 1975.

Vajda, P. "The Economics of Particle Board Manufacture." Presented at the Particle Board Symposium, Washington State University, 1967.

Vajda, P. "The Economics of Particle Board Manufacture Revisited or an Assessment of the Industry in 1970." Presented at the Particle Board Symposium, Washington State University, 1970.

Vajda, P. "Structural Composition Boards in the Wood Products Picture." Presented at the Particle Board Symposium, Washington State University, March 1974.

Utilization of Fly Ash
and Blast Furnace Slags
in Blended Cements

The information in this chapter is based on *Utilization of Industrial By-Products in Blended Cements* (NTIS PB-259 480) by Paul Wencil Brown, James R. Clifton and Geoffrey Frohnsdorff of the National Bureau of Standards and Richard L. Berger of the University of Illinois at Urbana, Illinois.

Concrete, composed of a hydraulic cement, sand, and aggregate in weight ratios of approximately 1 to 2 to 3, respectively, is the most widely used building material in the world. About 700 million tons (6.5×10^{11} kg) of this material are used annually in the United States alone. The binding ingredient of most concrete used in the U.S. is portland cement and its manufacture uses about 564 trillion Btu (6×10^{17} J) per year (2) or about 2% of the energy consumed in the nation's industrial processes. (Calculation based on concrete placed with an average cement content of 12%)(1).

Although the energy used per unit weight of portland cement is low compared to other building materials (Table 4.1), the energy cost as a percent of value is high (Table 4.2). The large annual domestic production of cement, 85 million tons (7.7×10^{10} kg) in 1974 (3), is the reason for this large energy consumption. The replacement of a portion of portland cement by suitable industrial by-products will not only decrease this requirement, but will also employ these materials in a way which takes full advantage of their reactive properties.

ADVANTAGES

General

For most applications portland cement can be substituted by blended cements.

Blended cements are usually produced by intergrinding fly ash, blast furnace slag, or certain natural pozzolans with portland cement clinker. The use of blended cement often results in a concrete with higher strength and greater durability than that obtained for pure portland cement concrete.

Table 4.1:   Energy Requirements for Manufacture of Some Basic Building Materials (4)

Material	Tons (kg) of Oil/Ton (kg) of Basic Material
Aluminum	5.6
Polystyrene	3.2
PVC	2.0
Paper and board	1.4
Copper	1.2
Steel	1.0
Glass	0.5
Cement*	0.17

*Calculated assuming an energy requirement of 7,400,000 Btu per ton (8.2×10^6 J/kg) of cement produced (1).

Source: PB-259 480

Table 4.2:   Cost of Purchased Energy as a Percentage of Value of Building Materials (5)

Material	Energy Cost as a Percent of Value
Cement	15.6
Blast furnace and basic steel	8.5
Primary nonferrous metals	8.1
Building paper and board	7.6
Structural clay products	7.4
Flat glass	4.3
Plastics	3.1
Concrete and gypsum	2.7

Source: PB-259 480

Advantages which have been observed in the use of fly ash or slag blended cement rather than portland cement are as follows:

    (1) improved workability [fly ash (6)] ;
    (2) lowered heat of hydration [fly ash (7), slag (8)] ;
    (3) increased resistance to attack by sulfates [fly ash (9),
         slag (8)] ;
    (4) decreased expansion due to alkali reactive aggregates
         [fly ash (10)] ;
    (5) higher ultimate strength [fly ash (12), slag (8)] and
    (6) decreased permeability [fly ash (12), slag (1)] .

While the improvement in these properties should be a factor in the expanded utilization of blended cements, it is the potential for substantial energy savings in cement production which will probably provide the major motivating factor.

Pozzolanic Materials

Pozzolanic materials are materials which are not cementitious in themselves but which are capable of reacting with lime in the presence of water at ordinary temperatures to produce cementitious compounds.

The cement manufacturing process may be divided into 3 stages: raw material processing, pyroprocessing, and finish grinding. Table 4.3 lists the approximate percentage of the total energy requirements which goes into each of these.

The introduction of pozzolanic materials into cement manufacture may result in large energy savings. Fly ash, since it is produced by coal burning utilities in virtually every area in the U.S., is a widely available pozzolanic material. It consists of very small particles therefore little initial grinding is required. Because the ash produced from the combustion of coal is usually pozzolanic, pyroprocessing is unnecessary. Thus, fly ash may be added in the finish grinding phase of the cement manufacturing process. This results in an energy savings which is almost directly proportional to the extent of fly ash substitution.

Natural pozzolans, which are usually of volcanic origin, may also be interground with portland cement clinker to make a blended cement. However, because they usually require a greater amount of processing, natural pozzolans offer less opportunity for energy savings.

Table 4.3: Relative Energy Consumptions in the Stages of Portland Cement Manufacture

Process	Approximate Percent of Total Energy (1)
Raw materials processing	
Quarrying and crushing	1.5
Drying	4.3
Initial grinding	3.8–4.3

(continued)

Table 4.3: (continued)

Process	Approximate Percent of Total Energy (1)
Pyroprocessing (kiln fuel)	80
Finish grinding	7

Source: PB-259 480

Blast Furnace Slags

Blast furnace slags may also be used in cement manufacture. Slags, because of their high lime contents, will form cementitious compounds when finely ground and mixed with water, although portland cement or anhydrous $CaSO_4$ are usually added as activators to increase the rate of hydration. Because of their reactivity, many slags, like fly ash, only require final grinding to cement fineness to be useful in blended cements. Slags, however, tend to be somewhat more difficult to grind than portland cement clinker so their use makes finish grinding somewhat more expensive and energy intensive.

PRODUCTION AND UTILIZATION OF BLENDED CEMENTS

Abroad

Although the cement used in the United States is almost exclusively portland cement, many other industrialized countries use large quantities of blended cements. For example, approximately 60% of the cement produced in France is blended cement (13). The Soviet Union produces about 30 million tons of slag portland cement annually accounting for about one-third of its cement production (14). About 20% of the cement produced in South Africa is slag cement with its production limited only by the amount of slag produced. In Japan a similar situation exists with regard to fly ash.

In the United States

In Table 4.4 the amounts of slag and fly ash produced annually are compared with the amounts used in cement and concrete in the U.S.

Considering the level of use and the technology developed on blended cements in Western Europe, the Soviet Union, and Japan, one may wonder why blended cements are not more extensively used in the United States. The reasons are numerous and may include:

> low fuel costs;
> uncertainty as to the availability of fly ash and slag to many cement producers;
> uncertainty as to uniformity and insufficient techniques to assess the quality of fly ash and slag for use in blended cement;

    capital equipment costs required to produce blended
      cement;
    low level of research on blended cements;
    lack of comprehensive specifications and standard
      tests for blended cements; and
    inadequate technical information on specific engineer-
      ing performance of blended cements

Table 4.4: U.S. Production or Utilization of Portland Cements, Fly Ash and Slag

Material	Production or Utilization in tons* x 10^6/yr	Reference
Portland cement types I-V (U.S. production)	85	5
Portland cement (imported)	8	5
Fly ash collected	40	15
Fly ash used in ASTM Type 1P blended cement	0.4	15
ASTM Type 1P blended cement containing fly ash**'***	>1	–
Blast furnace slag produced	25	16
ASTM Type 1S blended cement containing slag***	0.1	–
Slag as aggregate in concrete	2.3	16

   *One ton is equivalent to approximately 907 kg.
  **Fly ash mixed with portland cement at the construction site is not
    considered.
***Estimated output of the cement companies producing this type of

Source: PB-259 480

POTENTIAL FOR BLENDED CEMENTS

As a Portland Cement Substitute

American Society for Testing and Materials (ASTM) specifications currently include 5 main types of portland cement. Table 4.5 lists these types and their characteristics, together with estimates of the amount of each which is used and the possibility of substituting a blended cement containing at least 10% of fly ash or slag for each. As may be seen, blended cements could probably be substituted for every type of portland cement with the exception of Type III high early strength cement. This belief is based largely on successful foreign experience and considerations of cement chemistry. However, there is a need for additional data with regard to certain specific properties or applications before the full potential use of blended cements can be achieved in the U.S.

Table 4.5: Portland Cement Types and Substitution Possibilities

ASTM Type	Purpose or Characteristic*	Amount Used, tons x 10^6/yr	Substitution Possibilities	
			Slag	Fly Ash
I	General purpose	70	yes	yes
II	Moderate sulfate resistance	10	yes	yes
	Moderate heat of hydration	10	yes	yes
III	High early strength	2.9	no	no
IV	Low heat of hydration	nil	yes	yes
V	High sulfate resistance	>1	yes	yes

*Also, because of concern about alkali-aggregate reaction, most portland cement manufactured meets a low alkali requirement.

Source: PB-259 480

Geographic Considerations

Table 4.6 indicates the geographical distribution of the coal burned by utilities in 1965 (17). The amounts of ash produced in each area may be assumed to be about 10% of the weight of coal burned. As this table suggests, ash production is widely distributed suggesting that transportation costs from the utilities to the cement producers would be low. Clearly not all cement producers are in a position to benefit equally from the fly ash produced nor are all utilities in a position to dispose of fly ash in this way. However, many are and the quantity of fly ash blended cement produced could no doubt be substantially increased before serious transportation limitations occurred.

Table 4.6:   Regional Distribution of the Coal Burned in the United States in 1965 (17)

Geographical Area	States	Coal Burned tons* x 10^3
New England	(ME, NH, VT, MA, RI, CT)	8,207
Middle Atlantic	(NY, NJ, PA)	40,553
East North Central	(OH, IN IL, MI, WI)	83,570
West North Central	(MN, IA, MO, KS,NE, SD, ND)	13,749
South Atlantic	(MD, DE, VA, WV, NC, SC, GA, FL)	39,502
East South Central	(MS, AL, TN, KY)	33,902
West South Central	(LA, AR, TX, OK)	10
Mountain	(NM, AZ, NV, CO, UT, WY, MT, ID)	6,644
Pacific	(CA, OR, WA)	None

*One ton is equivalent to approximately 907 kg.

Source: PB-259 480

The number of centers of blast furnace slag production is much smaller than the number for fly ash and the production of slag occurs over a narrower geographic area. Of the 25 million tons (2.3×10^{10} kg) of slag produced in 1972, about 5.3 million (4.8×10^9 kg) were produced in Ohio, 6 million (5.4×10^9 kg) in Pennsylvania, and a total of 5.3 million (4.8×10^9 kg) in Illinois, Indiana and Michigan. The remaining 8.4 million tons (7.6×10^9 kg) were produced in 11 other states (16). Figure 4.1 shows the distributions of cement plants and blast furnaces. With only a few exceptions slag is produced within a relatively short distance (less than 150 miles) from a cement production facility. This seems to indicate that the low utilization of slag by the cement industry is not a result of excessive transportation distances.

Limitations

The temperature at which molten slag is tapped from a blast furnace is generally about $1450°$ to $1500°$C. Variations in the subsequent thermal treatments will result in slags which exhibit substantially different hydraulic activities. Slowly cooled slag, called air cooled slag, solidifies into a dense material with a crystalline structure much like that of natural igneous rock (22).

This material typically has a low reactivity and is of little value as a portland cement substitute. It is, however, widely used as aggregate. If slag is cooled more rapidly in the presence of a controlled amount of water, foamed or expanded slag results. Slag in this form has a high porosity. Because its bulk density is low it is used as lightweight aggregate. Slag which has been very rapidly quenched in a large excess of water solidifies into small glassy granules. This rapid cooling inhibits crystallization and the slag retains sufficient reactivity to form cementitious compounds in the presence of activator and water. Granulated slag, when ground to cement fineness, is the only form of slag suitable for the manufacture of slag blended cement.

Although granulation for use in cement takes full advantage of the potential reactivity of the slag, less than 0.5 million tons (4.54×10^8 kg) of granulated slag are produced for this purpose in the U.S. each year (16). An obstacle to additional manufacture of granulated slag appears to be reluctance on the part of steel producers to invest in granulation plants in the face of increasingly strict environmental standards and an uncertain market.

Specification Limitations: General Restrictions — ASTM specifications for blended cements, specifically those in ASTM C595-74 (18), tend to be restrictive with regard to use of fly ash pozzolans or blast furnace slag. These specifications only allow for the use of 15 to 40% fly ash or 25 to 65% blast furnace slag in a blended cement. Greater or lesser quantities of these materials could be used in the manufacture of cement, with the quantity used depending on the engineering performance desired.

For example, the additions of small amounts, perhaps 5 to 10%, of fly ash or ground slag to portland cement may improve the early strength of concrete for

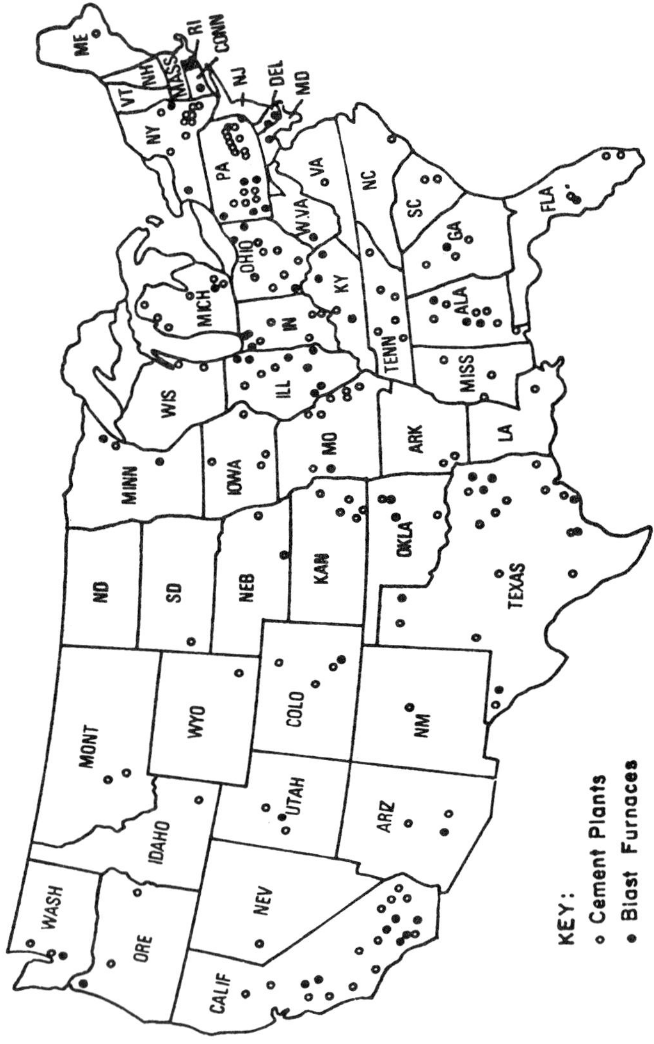

Figure 4.1: Geographic Distribution of Blast Furnaces and Cement Production Facilities (11)

Source: PB-259 480

a given cement content. This is the result of an expanded available space in which the hydration products of cement are precipitated (19) and is called "the finely divided powder effect." Slag or fly ash, because of their reactivity, would also contribute additional strength to the concrete at later stages. However, the present lack of specifications for such cements provides an obstacle to their manufacture and use. While there is movement toward the modification of the ASTM blended cement specifications to include substitution levels outside the presently specified ranges, these possibilities remain to be exploited.

Slag — The suitability of a slag for incorporation into a blended cement depends on its chemical composition and the rate at which it is quenched from the molten state. The rate of quenching influences both the composition and fraction of amorphous or glassy material present. Based on the compressive strengths of slag-portland cement mortars, it appears there may be an optimum composition of slag glass of about 52% CaO, 33% SiO_2 and 15% Al_2O_3 (20). While ASTM Standard C595-74 does not place compositional requirements on slag for use in cement (18), foreign specifications generally contain formulas, such as $(CaO + MgO + Al_2O_3)/SiO_2 \geqslant 1$ (21), by which the suitability of a particular slag may be determined.

While convenient, a specification of this type is more likely to be unnecessarily restrictive than a performance based specification such as the pozzolanic activity index developed for fly ashes. However, current ASTM standards do not provide either type of specification thus leaving a potential user without an accepted method by which the activity may be evaluated.

Fly Ash — The utilization of fly ash is less limited, as it is usually obtained in a form immediately suitable for use with portland cement. There are, however, compositional restrictions on fly ash to be used in cement and concrete. ASTM Standard C595-74 requires that the minimum combined amounts of SiO_2, Al_2O_3, and Fe_2O_3 be at least 70% of the total weight of the ash (18) if a blended cement is to be considered moderately sulfate resistant. This precludes utilization of many fly ashes even though it has not been adequately demonstrated that fly ash which does not conform to this compositional requirement will necessarily result in unsatisfactory blended cements.

This composition requirement will preclude the utilization of many fly ashes from the subbituminous low sulfur coals which are being used in rapidly increasing amounts due to environmental limitations on SO_2 emissions. Ash from these coals is high in CaO with CaO contents sometimes exceeding 30%. While the performance characteristics of blended cements containing these ashes must be shown to be satisfactory before their use is allowed, their use should not be unnecessarily precluded by the 70% composition requirement alone.

While the oxide composition requirement for fly ash pozzolans may be too restrictive, the loss on ignition requirement is vague. ASTM C595-74 (18) requires a maximum ignition loss of 5% for Type IP cement but places no requirement of this type on the ash used. When unburned carbon occurs as an intimate mixture with fly ash, a large or variable consumption of chemical admixtures in blended cement concrete may result. Admixtures, which are usually organic, are used to regulate set times, entrain air, or reduce water requirements.

Apparently, admixtures are adsorbed on the surfaces of the carbon particles present thereby causing a diminution in their effectiveness. From an aesthetic standpoint, high carbon ash may also have an undesirable effect on the color of concrete. Specifying acceptable ignition losses to control the carbon contents would aid in the reduction of these problems. This could be done directly by specifying a maximum ignition loss on the ash or indirectly through the development of appropriate performance criteria for admixture consumption. Specifying a maximum ash ignition loss should not be unduly restrictive since high carbon ash results primarily when a power plant is changing its burning load and provisions can be made for this material to be discarded. Efficiently operating base load generating plants should have little difficulty in producing ash which meets a reasonable ignition loss requirement.

BLENDED CEMENT WORK AT NBS

The Center for Building Technology (CBT) of the National Bureau of Standards, under the auspices of the Energy Research and Development Administration, has initiated a study of blended cements. The objective of this study is to encourage the conservation of energy in construction by facilitating the production and utilization of blended cements.

The immediate approach being taken by CBT emphasizes the development of performance tests and criteria for blended cements which will facilitate comparison of portland cements and blended cements. These tests and criteria should enable the user to better select hydraulic cements for use in concrete construction. As examples, the measurement of the sulfate resistance and soundness of cement and the response to internal frost formation and the reaction with alkali-susceptible aggregates for concretes are areas in which test development or modification is needed. As new test methods are developed, they will be submitted for consideration by voluntary consensus standards organizations, such as ASTM.

SUMMARY AND CONCLUSIONS

While it is possible to conserve raw materials with a substantial savings in energy by the substitution of portland cements by blended cements containing appropriate industrial wastes or by-products, numerous factors have served to keep the production and use of blended cements in the U.S. to a minimum. These factors may include the low cost of fuel and uncertainty as to by-product availability and quality. The lack of a full range of standard tests and specifications is also an important factor in limiting the use of blended cements.

Although certain technical questions remain to be answered prior to further specification development, other concerns regarding blended cement production and by-product utilization can be addressed immediately. This is particularly true with regard to specifications concerning levels of additives. For example, little or no new information needs to be developed to write a specification for a general purpose blended cement which contains 0 to 15% pozzolan.

On the other hand, areas such as the development of tests and specifications for sulfate resistance or the resistance to the alkali-aggregate reaction do require additional research. However, in view of the potential for materials conservation and energy savings, the production and use of blended cements may be expected to increase and technically sound tests and specifications must be made available to help assure their satisfactory performance.

REFERENCES

(1) "Energy Conservation Potential in the Cement Industry," FEA Conservation Paper #26, (1975).

(2) The Conference Board, *Energy Consumption in Manufacturing,* Ballinger Publ. Cambridge, Mass., (1974).

(3) *U.S. Industrial Outlook 1974,* Dept. of Commerce, (1975).

(4) *Plastics and Rubber Weekly,* (Sept. 6, 1974).

(5) *The Costs of Purchased Fuels and Electric Energy by Industry,* Economic Stabilization Program, Cost of Living Council, (Dec. 26, 1973).

(6) Guida, K. *Ash Utilization,* Bu Mines IC 8648, p. 58, (1974).

(7) Elfert, R.J., *Ash Utilization,* Bu Mines IC 8640, p. 88, (1974).

(8) Lea, F.M., *The Chemistry of Cement and Concrete,* Chem. Publ. Co., NY, (1971).

(9) Kalousek, G.L., Porter, L.C., and Benton, E.J., *Cement and Concrete Research* 2, 79 (1972).

(10) "U.S. Army Engineers Waterways Expt. Station Tech. Rept. 6-627," (June 1963).

(11) Grieb, W.E., and Werner, G., *Proc. Highway Resch. Bd.,* 40, 409 (1961).

(12) Abdun-Nur, E.A., *Fly Ash in Concrete,* Chicago Fly Ash Co., (Oct. 1959).

(13) Cembureau, Bull. No. 57, (1974).

(14) Satarin, V.I., Preprint of "Slag Portland Cement," the VIth Intl. Conf. on the Chemistry of Cement, Moscow, (1974).

(15) *Ash Collection and Utilization 1974, Ash at Work,* Vol. 7, #3, (1975).

(16) *Minerals Yearbook 1972,* Dept. of Interior.

(17) Bracket, C.E., *Fly Ash Utilization,* Bu Mines IC 8348, p. 20, (1967).

(18) *Annual Book of ASTM Standards,* Part 14, "Concrete and Mineral Aggregates," ASTM, Philadelphia (1974).

(19) Kokubu, M., *Proc. 5th International Symposium on the Chemistry of Cement,* Tokyo, p. 84, (1968).

(20) Tanaka, T. and Jamani, J., *Zement-Kalk-Gips,* 11, 50 (1968).

(21) German Specification DIN 1164, (1967).

(22) Lee, A.R., *Blast Furnace and Steel Slag,* John Wiley, NY, (1974).

Waste Glass as a Raw Material

The information in the first two sections of this chapter is based on *Waste Glass as a Raw Material for Lightweight Aggregate,* BuMines Report RI 8104, prepared by K.J. Liles and M.E. Tyrrell of the Bureau of Mines (Tuscaloosa Metallurgy Research Laboratory, Tuscaloosa, AL).

The information in the last section is based on *Development of a Glass Polymer Composite Sewer Pipe from Waste Glass,* prepared by M. Steinberg, L.E. Kukacka, J. Fontana, T. Sugama, R. Rayfiel, and B. Galen of the Brookhaven National Laboratory under United States Energy Research and Development Administration Contract EY-76-C-02-0016.

PRODUCTION OF LIGHTWEIGHT AGGREGATE

Research was undertaken by the Bureau of Mines to determine the technical feasibility of producing lightweight aggregate from the waste glass fraction of municipal incinerator residues. Tests conducted to determine the amount and optimum size of glass, the amount of sodium silicate, and the method used to form the material are discussed in this chapter.

Materials

Waste Glass: The glass used in the aggregate tests was a sample of mixed glass, slag, ceramics, and stone reclaimed from incinerator residues at the Bureau's incinerator residue processing plant (5). A chemical analysis of the product is given in Table 5.1.

Table 5.1: Chemical Analysis of Waste Glass Used in Lightweight Aggregate Tests

Constituent	Weight Percent
SiO_2	66.9
Al_2O_3	3.9
Fe_2O_3	0.9
B_2O_3	1.5
Na_2O	11.4
K_2O	1.0
CaO	8.3
MgO	2.1
Sulfur	0.2
Loss on ignition	2.6
Trace elements*	0.5

*Trace elements include Cu, Mn, Pb, and Zn.

Source: BuMines RI 8104

Clay: A coal measure underclay from Walker County, AL was utilized. This clay is a mixture of kaolinite, illite, a small amount of montmorillonite, and about 50% free quartz. Clay was added to the lightweight aggregate mix to provide the following: (1) a plasticizer for the pelletizing process, (2) a stabilizer for the soda content of the waste glass, and (3) a source of added strength for the fired pellets.

Sodium Silicate: Mixtures containing viscous silicates are subject to swelling when exposed to sudden heating (9). The sodium silicate used in the testing program was a dry powder with a $Na_2O:SiO_2$ weight ratio of 1:3.22. Although liquid sodium silicate could be utilized, the powdered form was used in these tests to facilitate ease of handling and accuracy of measurement.

Experimental Work

Grinding: Cellular formation in the lightweight aggregate was evident only when the waste glass was milled to minus 200 mesh. This approximates the standard size of fluxing materials in the ceramics industry. [Previous studies using waste glass as a flux in brick compositions indicated that minus 200 mesh glass was the most effective flux (7).]

A series of tests was conducted to determine the minimum time required to grind the glass to greater than 95% minus 200 mesh. A porcelain mill was used for the test with porcelain balls for the grinding medium. The tests showed that a minimum of 8 hours was required to provide a material containing 95% minus 200 mesh particles.

Aggregate Formulation: A 20% addition of clay was selected for the mix formulation based on tests made to determine dry compressive strength. In these tests, the clay added to the mix ranged from 5 to 25%. The 20% addition showed a high dry compressive strength and was chosen as the most suitable for pellet formation. The results of the dry compressive strength tests are shown in Table 5.2.

Table 5.2: Compressive Strength of Dry Pellets Made with Various Percentages of Clay

Clay Added (%)	Compressive Strength (lb/in^2)
5	29.5
10	58.5
15	147
20	288
25	163

Source: BuMines RI 8104

Testing: Sintering Tests — The results of a series of tests made to determine the optimum sintering time-temperature relationship when using various quantities of sodium silicate are shown in Table 5.3. The pellets used for these tests were made on an 18", variable-speed disk pelletizer.

From the results shown in Table 5.3, the optimum conditions for the most suitable lightweight material appeared to be a mix containing 2% sodium silicate that was fired at 1550°F for 15 minutes. Under these conditions, a pellet with a bulk density of 48 lb/ft^3 with very good pore structure was produced. The objective of the sintering tests was to achieve a structurally sound pellet weighing between 45 and 50 lb/ft^3, and for economic reasons, using as little sodium silicate as necessary.

Table 5.3: Bulk Density of Expanded Glass Aggregate*, pcf

Temperature, °F	......Firing Time, Minutes......			
	5	10	15	20
...............1.0% Sodium Silicate................				
1450	109.2	111.1	113.6	115.4
1500	108.6	108.6	106.1	104.8
1550	84.2	83.0	76.1	72.4
................1.5% Sodium Silicate................				
1450	108.6	103.0	105.5	98.6
1500	104.8	98.6	91.1	87.4
1550	78.6	65.5	65.5	64.3
................2.0% Sodium Silicate................				
1450	97.3	86.7	83.6	78.0
1500	88.6	79.2	68.0	65.5
1550	59.9	51.2	48.0	soft

(continued)

Table 5.3: (continued)

Temperature, °F	. . . . . .Firing Time, Minutes			
	5	10	15	20
. . . . 2.5% Sodium Silicate				
1450	78.6	67.4	62.4	59.3
1500	66.1	56.8	53.0	49.9
1550	46.8	39.3	soft	soft
. . . . .3.0% Sodium Silicate.				
1450	78.6	62.4	48.7	43.1
1500	46.8	38.1	38.1	soft
1550	29.3	soft	soft	soft

*As a function of time, temperature, and sodium silicate content.

Source: BuMines RI 8104

As a result of these preliminary tests, pellets were formed on a 36" diameter, continuous-feed disk pelletizer. These pellets were fired in the box-type laboratory kiln for 15 minutes at 1550°F. A cross-sectional view of one of the expanded pellets is shown in Figure 5.1. As specified by ASTM procedure (2), the loose pour weight of the expanded pellets was 38 lb/ft^3. The loose pour weight is determined by filling a 0.1 ft^3 container to overflowing, leveling the surface of the aggregate with the top edge of the container with a straightedge, and weighing.

Concrete Tests — For use in concrete tests, the glass aggregate produced was crushed by a roll crusher and screened to provide a material that fell within American Society for Testing and Materials (ASTM) grading requirements for ½" to No. 4 coarse aggregate (1). A screen analysis of the crushed glass aggregate compared with ASTM requirements shown in Table 5.4 indicated that the crushed aggregate closely approached the ASTM specifications.

To evaluate the crushed aggregate as a basic ingredient in concrete, 3" diameter by 6" long concrete test cylinders were prepared using the following basic field mix: Type 1 cement, 6 sacks (564 pounds); combined aggregate, 20.0 ft^3 (700 pounds); river sand, 12.5 cu ft (1,256 pounds); and water, 6 gallons per sack of cement (325 pounds).

Table 5.4: Size Analysis of Crushed Glass Aggregate Compared to ASTM Requirements

	. . . . Weight Percent Passing Indicated Screen Size. . . .				
	¾"	½"	⅜"	No. 4	No.8
ASTM C 330	100	90-100	40-80	0-20	0-10
Glass aggregate	100	100	86.2	16.3	6.2

Source: BuMines RI 8104

Figure 5.1: Cross Section of Expanded Glass Aggregate Pellet

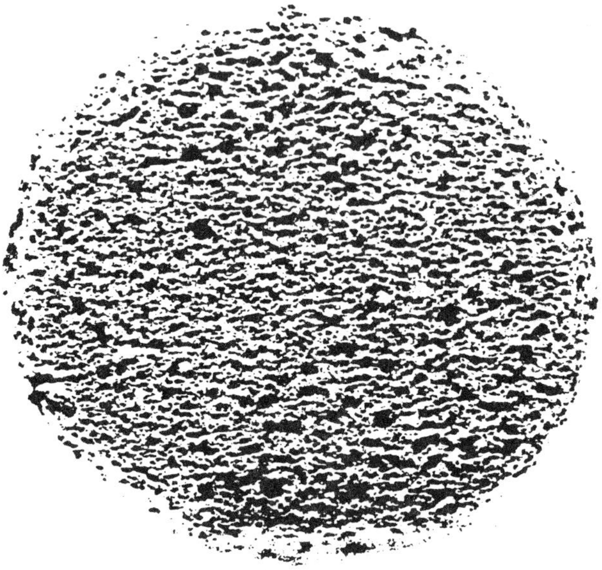

Source: BuMines RI 8104

After steam-curing 28 days, the cylinders were tested for compressive strength and unit weight. Test data from six concrete cylinders are shown in Table 5.5. For comparative purposes the ASTM (1) specifications data are also shown. These data show that the expanded glass aggregate produced lightweight concrete meeting ASTM compressive strength-unit weight specifications. Durability tests were not conducted on the test cylinders during this work.

Table 5.5: Concrete Test Data

Cylinder No.	Unit Weight, lb/ft^3	Crushing Strength, lb/ft^2
1	105	2,700
2	103	2,575
3	102	2,275
4	105	2,425
5	104	2,875
6	105	2,450
Average	104	2,550
ASTM*	105	2,500

*ASTM specification C330-69 after 28 day steam cure.

Source: BuMines 8104

Conclusions

The results of this investigation indicate that lightweight aggregate suitable for use in structural concrete can be produced utilizing waste glass as the principal raw material.

When fired at 1550°F for 15 minutes, a mixture of 78% waste glass, 20% under-clay, and 2% dry sodium silicate produced aggregate having a bulk density of 48 lb/ft^3. Glass aggregate concrete having an average bulk density of 104 lb/ft^3 had an average 28 day compressive strength of 2,550 psi. To meet ASTM specifications C330-69, concrete having a unit weight of 105 lb/ft^3 must have a minimum compressive strength of 2,500 psi.

RELATED WORK AT THE BUREAU OF MINES

The Federal Bureau of Mines has been active in the recovery of by-products from mineral and metallurgical processes for over 60 years (5). Since 1968, the Tuscaloosa (AL) Metallurgy Research Laboratory has conducted waste utilization research concerned with the development of building products from the metal-free glass constituents separated from municipal incinerator residues. The glass fraction obtained from the Bureau's incinerator residue separation process (6) represents about 48 weight percent of the total residue (4). The Federal Bureau of Mines has distributed several publications reporting results of research with waste glass.

The first phase of the research was directed toward producing building brick (7). The second phase of the investigation was concerned with the production of glass wool thermal insulation (3). The third phase was undertaken to determine the fluxing properties of waste glass and how those properties might be utilized to decrease the required firing temperature and/or the firing time of structural clay products made from common clays (8).

DEVELOPMENT OF A GLASS POLYMER COMPOSITE SEWER PIPE

Brookhaven National Laboratory (BNL) has performed preliminary experiments which indicated that glass and paper can be incorporated into composite materials which can be used for construction purposes (10). Glass polymer composite (GPC) sewer pipe containing glass separated from urban waste has been produced and installed for field testing in the Town of Huntington, NY and in Newark, NJ. Other potential applications include building blocks, chemical storage tanks, and insulating panels for use in energy storage systems.

Based upon the above work, a preliminary cost analysis was performed (11) and a technology transfer program was initiated (12). The latter resulted in the establishment of a cooperative program with an industrial company (Teledyne National) to utilize the glass fraction from a large urban waste plant now under construction in Maryland.

Goals

In June 1976 the Office of Conservation of ERDA initiated support of the program. The goals for the program are as follows:

(1) To provide the technical basis for energy conservation by the development, testing, and practical demonstration of products made from industrial waste materials.

(2) Rapid transfer and implementation of the technology in the private sector.

Procedure

The program goals were projected to be achieved in the following tasks:

(1) Determination properties of GPC sewer pipe to a degree that they are statistically acceptable with respect to relevant ASTM methods and standards.

(2) Perform field testing of prototype and full-scale specimens.

(3) Prepare energy budgets and cost analyses.

(4) Involve the solid waste utilization industry in all phases of the program in order to provide a technical basis for the rapid implementation of the technology.

Accomplishments during the period July-September 1976 are reported here.

GPC Property Measurements: Work has been started to determine the minimum wall thickness of 8" i.d. GPC sewer pipe required to meet the ASTM standard C–76.

7,000 pounds of glass, separated from municipal waste at the Bureau of Mines, College Park, Maryland facility, was received for use in the test series. The glass has been ground and blended to give the desired particle size distribution. All required chemical materials have also been obtained.

The design and construction of a series of pipe molds has been completed. 12" sections of 8" inside diameter pipe with wall thicknesses of 0.625, 1.0, and 1.5" will be fabricated. The GPC pipe was fabricated and sites selected for installation, field testing and periodic inspection.

Field Testing and Inspection: Monitoring of the performance of GPC pipe in test in Huntington, NY and Newark, NJ was continued. At Huntington, a total of 35 ft of 8" diameter pipe was installed during October 1972. Two pieces of pipe contained methyl methacrylate and 8 contained polyester-styrene. To date no problems with the pipe have been reported.

In November 1975 about 12' of 12" diameter pipe was installed in a sewer line in Newark, NJ. The pipe is in an industrial part of the city and is exposed to acid-type waste from several chemical plants. Prior to installation the pipe was shown to conform to the ASTM strength and hydrostatic test specifications. The leakage rate at the joints was also measured as well below that specified by the City of Newark. A T.V. inspection of the pipe was made on September 17, 1976 after about 10 months in service. No signs of deterioration were apparent.

REFERENCES

(1) American Society for Testing and Materials. "Standard Specifications for Lightweight Aggregates for Structural Concrete." C330-69 in *1974 Annual Book of ASTM Standards: Part 14, Concrete and Mineral Aggregates; Manual of Concrete Testing.* Philadelphia, Pa., 1974, pp 229-232.

(2) American Society for Testing and Materials. "Standard Method of Test for Unit Weight of Aggregate." C29-71 in *1974 Annual Book of ASTM Standards: Part 14, Concrete and Mineral Aggregates; Manual of Concrete Testing.* Philadelphia, Pa., 1974, pp 4-5.

(3) Goode, A.H., Tyrrell, M.E., and Feld, I.L. *Glass Wool From Waste Glass.* BuMines RI 7708, 1972.

(4) Johnson, P.W. and Barclay, J.A.. *Economic Studies of Uses of the Glass Fractions From Municipal-Incinerator Residues.* BuMines IC 8567, 1973.

(5) Kenahan, C.B., Kaplan, R.S., Dunham, J.T., and Linnehan, D.G. *Bureau of Mines Research Programs on Recycling and Disposal of Mineral-, Metal-, and Energy-Based Solid Wastes.* BuMines IC 8595, 1973.

(6) Sullivan, P.M., and Stanczyk, M.H. *Economics of Recycling Metals and Minerals from Urban Refuse.* BuMines TPR 33, 1971.

(7) Tyrrell, M.E., Feld, I.L., and Barclay, J.A. *Fabrication and Cost Evaluation of Experimental Building Brick From Waste Glass.* BuMines RI 7605, 1972.

(8) Tyrrell, M.E., and Goode, A.H. *Waste Glass as a Flux for Brick Clays.* BuMines RI 7701, 1972.

(9) Vail, J.G. *Soluble Silicates in Industry.* Am. Chem. Soc. Mono. Series, No. 46, The Chemical Catalog Co., Inc., New York, 1928, pp 185-186.

(10) Beller, M. and Steinberg, M., *Glass Polymer Composites,* BNL 17555, Jan. 1973.

(11) Lindstrom, R.S. and Milgrom, J., *Glass Polymer Composite Sewer Pipe, An Initial Evaluation of Its Commercial Potential,* Arthur D. Little, Inc., C-74228, 1972.

(12) Steinberg, M., et al, *Promoting the Utilization of Solid Waste Glass Polymer Composite Technology in the Public and Private Sector,* BNL 19394, October 1974.

Coal Mine Refuse

The information in this chapter is based on *Feasibility Study of Utilization of Coal Mine Refuse, Estill County, Kentucky,* ARC Report 74-217-KY-3685 prepared by the University of Kentucky Research Foundation for the Appalachian Regional Commission, Washington, D.C. Other contributors were the Bluegrass Area Development District, the South-East Coal Company and the U.S. Bureau of Mines Tuscaloosa Metallurgy Research Laboratory.

INTRODUCTION

Economic development is the result of using available material resources to provide for the needs of people. These resources come in many forms; some are natural and renewable, some are natural and nonrenewable, some are formed by a process in a system, and in certain cases resources may result in ingenious application of seemingly useless matter. The formation of large concentrations of coal mine refuse may conform to the latter designation as a resource.

The cleaning of coal in varying degrees has been practiced since the advent of coal as a major industrial energy source. The cleaning consists of removing undesirable materials from the coal as mined. The undesirable materials consist of dirt, rock, shale, clay, sulfur compounds and other impurities.

The main objectives of cleaning are to improve the quality of the coal, but, beyond that, current air pollution regulations and the cost of transport dictate to a large degree the cleaning measures used and the extent of refinement achieved. There are many and varied methods of cleaning coal and the selection for a given operation is based on the character of the coal mined, the ultimate products desired, local costs of cleaning operations and many other factors.

In any case where coal is cleaned in large quantities there is a large amount of reject material to be dealt with, usually in the range of 10 to 30 percent of the raw coal.

Since the cost of transport for the undesirable material is equal to that of product transport, the coal is either cleaned at or near points of production or otherwise at locations accessible to economical transport facilities.

Historically, the high volatile matter, high heat value coals from Eastern Kentucky seams have been cleaned to provide product coals for their markets throughout the world. This has resulted in the generation of many large accumulations of coal mine refuse throughout the mining area. One of the largest single accumulations of refuse is located at the South-East Coal Company cleaning facility at Irvine, Kentucky. This particular refuse accumulation has resulted primarily from the cleaning of coals from Knott and Letcher Counties over a period of many years. The transport of raw coal in this case was accomplished by main-line haul of the Louisville and Nashville Railroad which essentially passes through the plant grounds.

Demand for coal is expected to increase substantially in the near future. With higher coal production will come a corresponding increase in the associated waste material.

In spring 1975 a project was undertaken to determine the economic feasibility of utilizing coal refuse for construction purposes. Specifically, the refuse studied was that produced at the South-East Coal Company preparation plant in Estill County at Irvine, Kentucky. The project involved refuse sampling, laboratory testing, product testing, market analysis of potential commercial products and overall commercialization cost estimates. Each category will be treated in detail. References appear at the end of the chapter.

REFUSE PRODUCED AT SOUTH-EAST COAL COMPANY'S PREPARATION PLANT IN ESTILL COUNTY, KY

In order to dispose of coal refuse in an economical and safe manner, the physical properties and engineering characteristics must be known. The composition and behavior of coal refuse is variable and differs significantly from soils and other conventional embankment and foundation materials. Many factors contribute to this variability.

Geology of the coal seam being mined, methods used for mining the coal, cleaning and preparation processes used, and disposal techniques all have an effect on refuse. Also, the refuse is highly sensitive to both chemical and physical weathering processes when placed in a waste pile. All these factors combine to make coal refuse a rather unusual material to analyze and work with.

Location

The coal preparation plant and coal refuse disposal facilities of the South-East Coal Company are located in Estill County, Kentucky, along the Kentucky River approximately 2.5 miles northwest of Irvine, the county seat. To reach the plant and disposal facilities, Kentucky Highway 89 is followed to the northwest out of Irvine. Figures 6.1 and 6.2 are maps of Kentucky counties showing project refuse site and coal origin and locations of other major refuse storage sites in the general area.

Coal cleaned and processed at the plant is mined in Knott and Letcher Counties, about 100 miles east-southeast of Estill County. The coal is transported by rail from the mines to the preparation facilities.

Estill County is situated at the boundary between the Blue Grass and Eastern Coal Field physiographic regions of Kentucky. The area is referred to as the Knobs Region because of the conical hills which dominate the landscape. The Pottsville Escarpment which passes through Estill County is the boundary between the regions. It is a prominent physiographic feature extending from Greenup County on the Ohio River to Wayne County on the Tennessee border. The escarpment is characterized by an abrupt rise in elevation averaging between 300 and 600 feet. The South-East Coal Company facilities are located just to the west of the escarpment in the Knobs.

Topography in the immediate area of the coal washing facilities is a combination of the narrow flood plain of the Kentucky River and the moderate to steep slopes associated with the Knobs. Relief in the immediate area is on the order of 200 feet with elevations ranging from 590 to 820 feet. A few miles further to the east elevations exceed 1,200 feet. The area adjacent to the facilities can be described as hilly.

Knott and Letcher Counties are located in the eastern section of the Eastern Coal Field region. This region is also referred to as the Cumberland Plateau. It is a mountainous region which has been formed by the erosion of an ancient peneplain. The region is characterized by narrow stream valleys and steep hillsides. Relief between stream valleys and hilltops is as high as 1,000 feet in some areas. This mountainous terrain, with its associated construction and refuse disposal problems, no doubt influenced locating the cleaning and preparation facilities in Estill County.

Preparation and Disposal Facilities

Techniques and facilities for coal refuse disposal used by the South-East Coal Company are similar to others currently used elsewhere. In the preparation plant all refuse is combined and then transported hydraulically by pumping to the refuse embankment. When discharged onto the embankment the particles separate and segregate according to size. The finer particles remain in suspension longest and sedimentation lagoons are required. Coarser materials are rehandled and used

Figure 6.1: Coal Mine Refuse Storage and Coal Origin Locations in Kentucky

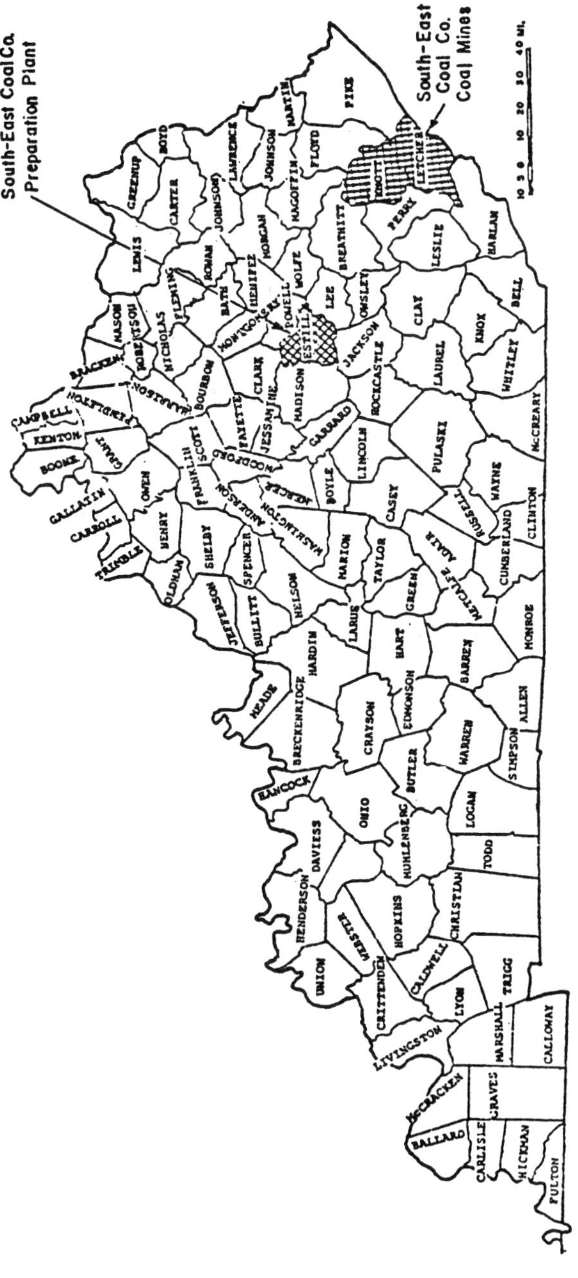

Figure 6.2: Location of Major Coal Mine Refuse Disposal Sites

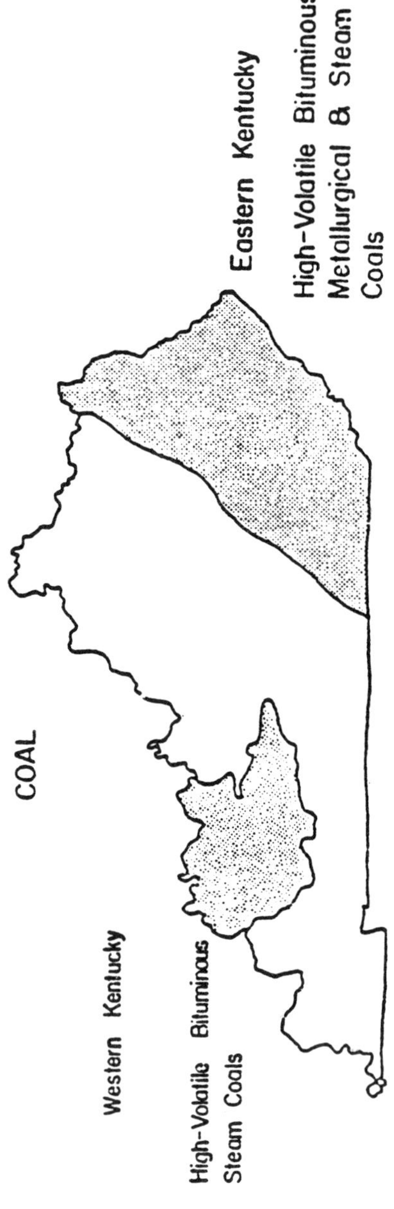

Source: ARC 74-217-KY-3685

to construct the embankments around the sedimentation lagoons. The refuse embankments presently contain an estimated three million tons of material. Capacity of the disposal facilities is estimated to be 25 million tons. These figures indicate that the embankments contain only 12 percent of their estimated capacity.

Two separate disposal embankments have been put into use at Irvine. The larger and older of the two is located to the north of the preparation plant. It consists of a heap type of embankment with dikes along the sides to impound lagoons. Along the west end, adjacent to the Kentucky River, the embankment reaches a height in excess of 50 feet. The embankment is situated in a "meander" bend of the river. Foundation soils under a major portion of the embankment are alluvial deposits of sand and silt. Thickness of these soils may be as much as 80 feet.

The second refuse embankment is located east of the preparation plant and is approximately half the size of the other embankment. It is a cross valley fill type of embankment. Being located further from the river and higher in elevation, the embankment is underlain by rocks of the Crab Orchard Formation. The rock type is principally shale of Silurian age. Some dolomite is present in the shale, but thickness of beds is five feet or less. In natural outcrops, the Crab Orchard Formation weathers to a plastic clay.

Coal cleaning and preparation is accomplished by a two-circuit process in the preparation plant. Coarse coal is separated from refuse materials by a Jeffrey Air Jig. This is a hydraulic process where particles are stratified in the unit according to their density. The less dense coal floats while the heavier refuse materials sink. Fine coal processing is handled by Deister tables and froth cells. In the frothing process, a flotation reagent is added to the water containing suspended fine coal. The reagent tends to coat particles and increase surface tension which aids in separation of the coal. Thermal dryers and vacuum filters are used to dewater the coal.

Refuse materials from each of the preparation processes are taken to one central point in the plant. There they are passed through a crusher which reduces all particles to a size of one inch or less. The refuse is then combined with water and pumped through a 12-inch pipe to one of the refuse embankments.

The refuse discharge point consists of a pipe approximately 100 feet long with holes cut into the bottom at 10-foot intervals. This allows continuous discharge for a several-day period. As materials build up under one hole and block it, the flow will continue to the next. This method of placement results in separation and stratification of particle sizes within the embankment. Coarse particles segregate near the discharge point and the silt and clay-size particles remain in suspension requiring lagoons for settlement.

The refuse discharge can continue for several days at either embankment. When one point is completely filled and covered by refuse, the flow is shifted to the other embankment.

Self-loading pan scrapers are then used to remove the materials that are immediately adjacent to the discharge point. These materials are then used to raise the embankments around the lagoons. Compaction of these materials into the embankment is accomplished by a scraper moving over them. The compacted refuse materials form the perimeter of the refuse embankments and dikes dividing the lagoons.

Refuse disposal techniques utilized by the South-East Coal Company have resulted in embankments which consist of both compacted and normally consolidated to under-consolidated materials. Segregation and stratification of particle sizes exist within the lagoons. The segregation consists of gradation from coarse to fine as the distance from the discharge point increases. The two refuse embankments at Irvine are typical of those which exist throughout the coal regions.

Geological Aspects

Coal processed at the preparation plant is from the Hazard No. 4 and Elkhorn No. 3 seams, as mined in Knott and Letcher Counties in eastern Kentucky. Percentages of coal being mined presently from each seam are 66 percent from the Elkhorn and 33 percent from the Hazard. In the past Hazard No. 7 and No. 9 have made up a large percentage of production. These deposits correspond in age with the well-known Coal Measures in Great Britain and with others around the world. In the United States the Carboniferous has been divided into two periods, Mississippian and Pennsylvanian. The Pennsylvanian units are the coal-bearing rocks in Kentucky.

Rock types encountered in Pennsylvanian units are conglomerates, sandstone, shale, siltstone, thin beds of limestone or dolomite, and coal. Underlying many coal seams is a bed of fire clay which may range from a few inches to more than a foot in thickness. The interbedded sandstone and shale is the most common rock sequence encountered. Coal beds of varying thickness occur throughout the Pennsylvanian rock sequences.

Rocks associated with coal seams comprise the bulk of coal refuse. Shale makes up the largest portion of the discard, with sandstone, siltstone and fire clay being present in various percentages. Impurities such as pyrite and low-grade coal are present in many seams and are mined along with the rest of a seam.

Thin beds of shale and clay may be present in the middle of a seam. Occasionally a coal seam will divide into two thin seams with a layer of shale or clay filling the space between. With mechanized equipment it is easier and cheaper to extract the entire thickness with the unwanted impurities than to mine only the pure coal.

In underground mining it is sometimes necessary to extract part of the roof or floor rock for various reasons. In doing this, shale, fire clay and possibly sandstone are being taken as part of the raw coal. The impurities and unwanted rock constitute the refuse pile.

Coal refuse materials are extremely susceptible to weathering processes. The component materials which make up refuse have been through at least one previous cycle of weathering, transportation, and deposition. Rock materials making up refuse can be divided into two categories: detrital and nondetrital.

Detrital material consists of broken and abraded fragments and particles of a preexisting rock. These particles are the aggregate of which the rock materials in the refuse are composed. Nondetrital material consists principally of cementing materials which hold the particles together. Rocks associated with coal seams are usually weakly cemented, which adds to their susceptibility to weathering processes. Both physical and chemical processes attack refuse.

Clay minerals in the detrital portion of the shale take up water and swell, causing the shale to break along laminations and bedding planes. Laminations are planes of weakness associated with depositional processes; they also provide a route for water to enter the rock. Kaolinite, illite, and montmorillonite, the common clay minerals, are found in varying amounts in all refuse.

Pyrite is the principal nondetrital material, with other sulfur compounds and some carbonate materials being present. Pyrite oxidizes at low temperatures which contributes to the breakup of the shale as well as forming sulfate compounds and sulfuric acid, which are the principal stream pollutants.

The major effect of the weathering process is to reduce the sizes of the particles which make up the refuse. This results in an increase in the silt and clay size particles in the refuse. Effects of the weathering processes are pronounced at first and will continue to some degree indefinitely. Unlike conventional embankment materials, the physical character of refuse will change with age (1)(2).

SAMPLING AND TESTING

Sampling Methodology

Objectives of sampling were to obtain representative samples of the coal refuse materials in the waste embankments. For this purpose, materials which had been produced in the past as well as material presently being produced were sampled. Also, both the embankment and lagoon deposits were sampled.

Locations of the drill holes to obtain the needed samples were determined with the help of the plant foreman who was familiar with the history of the disposal facilities. Four drill hole locations were chosen such that the most recent and some of the oldest refuse would be encountered. The approximate age of the refuse taken from each hole was as follows:

Hole	Years
1	0–3
2	0–3
3	2–5
4	5–10

The holes were positioned such that embankment materials would be encountered near the surface and then the hole would continue into lagoon deposits. Thus the age of the materials increased from the top down.

Samples were obtained using the University of Kentucky's CME Model 55 truck-mounted drill rig. Six-inch hollow stem augers were used to obtain disturbed samples. The procedures used to obtain these samples were very simple. A five-foot section of augers was attached to the drill and advanced into the refuse pile. When the auger was fully into the pile, it was allowed to continue rotating, thus feeding refuse out of the hole. This continued until no material was being fed out of the hole.

The disturbed sample was then taken. It consisted of a five-gallon bucket (0.67 cubic feet) filled with the refuse which had been fed out of the hole. Also, a small moisture content sample was taken and sealed in a jar for later testing. In preparation for sampling the next five-foot interval, the area around the auger was cleared of loose refuse materials with a shovel. Then another five-foot section of auger was attached and the hole advanced. Samples were taken for each five-foot interval up to 50 feet or until natural ground was encountered. All sample holes were logged at the time of drilling.

Present production samples were obtained over a five-day interval during which the plant was operating on a typical schedule. A 50-pound portion of each size was taken each day for a combined 250-pound sample of each size. Two coarse sizes were obtained from the jig washer and a fine size was obtained from the Deister table.

Samples for testing were taken at five-foot intervals in all the auger holes. A visual comparison of all the samples from each hole indicated that for each hole, two or possibly three characteristic refuse materials were encountered. The top embankment material was a relatively dry clay loam material with numerous gravel-sized particles present. In the bottom of each hole was a wet sandy loam material which was associated with the lagoon deposits. A possible third material was found in the transition zone between the two.

Based on these observations, it was decided to take samples for testing in two different manners. The materials in holes 1 and 3 were tested at ten-foot intervals. Materials in holes 2 and 4 were tested based on visual determination for the intervals. The testing of holes 1 and 3 was completed before that of 2 and 4 in order to substantiate and provide a basis for the visually determined intervals.

Physical Properties (Soil)

For the purpose of evaluating coal refuse as an engineering material for use in embankment and foundations, the typical soil mechanics classification tests as well as moisture-density relationship, bearing ratio, triaxial and permeability tests were conducted. Coal analyses and mineralogical studies were also performed in order to determine composition of the coal refuse and further characterize it for product potential.

All testing was performed according to applicable ASTM specifications or otherwise noted. Samples for soil testing were prepared according to ASTM-D421, "Dry Preparation of Soil Samples for Particle-Size Analysis and Determination of Soil Constituents." Samples for other tests were prepared accordingly. All test samples were prepared by splitting from a larger sample.

Tables 6.1 through 6.4 contain the results for the basic soil mechanics tests (gradation, Atterberg Limits, specific gravity and classifications) and they summarize the bulk of the testing performed with regard to engineering properties of coal refuse.

Table 6.1: Summary of Test Results, Auger Hole 1

Sample	Depth, feet				
	0–10	10–20	20–30	30–40	40–50
Composition, %					
Gravel	18.0	17.0	15.0	19.5	17.0
Coarse sand	34.5	31.0	30.0	31.5	21.0
Fine sand	9.5	11.0	13.0	8.0	9.0
Silt	14.5	13.5	14.0	15.5	15.0
Clay	10.5	10.0	10.0	9.5	14.0
Colloids	13.0	17.5	18.0	16.0	24.0
Liquid limit	28	25	28	26	30
Plastic limit	19	15	17	18	22
Plasticity index	9	10	11	8	8
Specific gravity	2.24	2.42	2.43	2.28	2.16
Classification					
Textural	clay loam	clay loam	clay loam	clay loam	clay
AASHO	A-4(1)	A-4(1)	A-6(1)	A-4(1)	A-4(3)
Unified	SC	SC	SC	SC	CL
Dry density, pcf	114.4	114.4	114.5	97.4	97.4
Moisture, %*	9.6	9.6	8.8	14.5	14.5
California bearing ratio	6.8	6.8	6.8	8.7	8.7

*Optimum

Source: ARC-74-217-KY-3685

Table 6.2: Summary of Test Results, Auger Hole 2

Sample	Depth, feet		
	0–25	25–35	35–45
Composition, %			
Gravel	25.0	18.0	8.5
Coarse sand	34.0	28.0	28.5

(continued)

Table 6.2: (continued)

Sample	Depth, feet		
	0–25	25–35	35–45
Fine sand	9.0	15.0	23.0
Silt	9.5	17.0	19.0
Clay	11.5	10.5	13.0
Colloids	11.0	11.5	8.0
Liquid limit	29	28	28
Plastic limit	20	23	26
Plasticity index	9	5	2
Specific gravity	2.52	1.92	1.85
Classification			
Textural	sandy clay	sandy clay loam	sandy clay loam
AASHO	A-2-4(0)	A-4(1)	A-4(1)
Unified	SC	SM	SM
Dry density, pcf	111.5	89.8	80.8
Optimum moisture, %	11.0	12.8	13.5
California bearing ratio	9	14.8	14.8

Table 6.3: Summary of Test Results, Auger Hole 3

	Depth, feet				
	0–10	10–20	20–30	30–40	40–50
Composition, %					
Gravel	21.0	17.0	19.0	15.5	20.0
Coarse sand	31.5	32.0	36.0	29.5	32.5
Fine sand	9.5	12.0	8.5	9.5	8.5
Silt	15.0	12.0	12.5	8.5	10.5
Clay	10.0	13.0	11.0	16.0	16.0
Colloids	13.0	14.0	13.0	21.0	12.5
Liquid limit	26	26	31	35	35
Plastic limit	18	16	22	23	22
Plasticity index	8	10	9	12	13
Specific gravity	2.31	2.37	2.38	2.35	2.19
Classification					
Textural	clay loam	clay loam	sandy clay	clay	clay
AASHO	A-4(0)	A-4(1)	A-4(0)	A-6(3)	A-6(3)
Unified	SC	SC	SC	SC	SC
Dry density, pcf	114.3	114.3	107.8	96.7	96.7
Moisture, %*	7.5	7.5	10.2	13.5	13.5
California bearing ratio	6.5	6.5	—	5.7	5.7

*Optimum

Source: ARC-74-217-KY-3685

Table 6.4: Summary of Test Results, Auger Hole 4

| | . . . . Depth, feet . . . . | | |
Sample	0–25	25–40	40–50
Composition, %			
Gravel	25.0	10.0	9.0
Coarse sand	36.0	31.0	30.5
Fine sand	7.0	18.5	16.5
Silt	10.0	18.5	16.0
Clay	10.5	13.0	13.0
Colloids	11.5	9.0	15.0
Liquid limit	30	28	32
Plastic limit	21	24	23
Plasticity index	9	4	9
Specific gravity	2.36	1.83	2.01
Classification			
Textural	clay loam	sandy clay loam	sandy clay loam
AASHO	A-2-4(0)	A-4(1)	A-4(2)
Unified	SC	SM	SC
Dry density, pcf	107.9	81.4	86.2
Optimum moisture, %	10.5	12.4	13.7
California bearing ratio	9.9	13.3	13.3

Source: ARC-74-217-KY-3685

Grain Size: Grain size analyses were performed to determine the relative proportions of the different grain sizes which make up a particular material. It is not possible to determine individual particle sizes; the test only brackets the particles within various size ranges. The grain size analysis test is universally used in engineering classifications of soils. Information obtained can be used to predict the behavior of various materials.

The grain size analyses were performed according to ASTM D42263, "Standard Method for Particle-Size Analysis of Soils." Both the mechanical and hydrometer procedures were utilized. In order to speed the testing procedure a second 100-gram sample of material passing the No. 10 sieve was taken at the same time as the hydrometer sample. This second sample was washed over a No. 200 sieve, dried, and then sieved to determine the gradation of the sand sizes. This was the only modification of the prescribed testing procedure.

Results — Results of the grain size analyses performed on the coal refuse samples indicate a particle size range from 19.05 mm to less than 0.001mm. Tables 6.1 through 6.4 contain results for each particle size range comprising a sample. Average percentage by weight for each particle size range is as follows: gravel 17%, sand 43%, silt 14% and clay 26%. The refuse materials seem to be well graded. A few of the samples tend to be gap graded because of smaller percentages of fine sand and silt size particles.

The numerical analyses indicate that the median particle size generally decreased with hole depth, but there were exceptions. The median particle size was in the medium-to-fine sand size range (2.00 to 0.074 mm), with the average for all samples being 0.441 mm. The effective size for all samples except one was 0.001 mm. Effective size relates the maximum diameter of the smallest 10% particle size. In most cases the 10% size was smaller than 0.001 mm, but the value is reported as 0.001 mm due to limitations in testing sizes of small particles (3).

Values for the coefficient of uniformity (CU), which relates the size range of particles, also tended to decrease with hole depth, but exceptions to this trend exist. Values range from 2,300 to 172. Lower values indicate smaller percentages of coarser particles of uniform size within a narrow size range are present.

All samples contained appreciable amounts of fine sand, silt, and clay-size particles. Variations in the amount of gravel and coarse sand was the controlling factor with respect to gradations. If these were not present in large percentages, the fine sand and silt size percentages increased.

Numerical analysis results tend to correspond well with what is expected for a coal refuse material, considering its origin and history. Large values of CU indicate that a large range of particle sizes is present. These values are significantly higher than what might be expected for natural soils. The general trend of decreasing particle size with hole depth and the exceptions to this trend relate well with the methods of refuse placement used. Results of the analysis agree well with the fact that the gradation has been somewhat artificially created by crushing to one inch during preparation and hydraulic placement on the refuse embankment.

Accuracy of the grain size distributions for the fine particle sizes is questionable. The chemical and mechanical treatments given fine grain soils prior to the performance of the hydrometer test could affect the results. The assumptions and theory upon which the hydrometer test is based, spherical particles of equal specific gravities, obviously have limitations. When testing coal refuse the inadequacies of the test are compounded. Coal refuse is known to contain particles with a wide range of specific gravities. Particle shapes will also vary depending on coal preparation equipment, minerals comprising refuse, and the age of the refuse. Based on these factors, the gradation curve for the fine coal refuse particles can only be regarded as approximate (3)(4).

Specific Gravity: The specific gravity of bituminous coal is about 1.4 whereas common soil minerals have specific gravities in the range of 2.6 to 2.8. Therefore, it can be expected that the specific gravity of coal refuse would lie somewhere between 1.4 and 2.6 depending on the coal content.

To determine specific gravity the procedures given in ASTM-D-854, "Standard Method of Testing for Specific Gravity of Soils," was used. Only the material passing the No. 4 sieve was tested. The material retained on the No. 4 amounted to an average of 15% or less of the sample and consisted of shale. Two or three tests were run on each sample to check the repeatability of the results. It was found that the results were not consistently repeatable, varying by as much as ±0.4 and averaging ±0.03. The specific gravities of the coal refuse materials were found to vary over the range of 1.83 to 2.52. This data is included in Tables 6.1 through 6.4.

Results — Coal refuse is known to contain particles with a wide range of specific gravities. Carbonaceous materials have values which range from 1.3 to 1.6, whereas common soil and rock minerals have values from 2.6 to 2.8. The combination of these materials has resulted in the specific gravity of coal refuse materials varying over a wide range. Published values for samples previously tested range from 1.45 to 2.63, with average values in the range of 1.9 to 2.2 (1)(5)(8). Values for the Irvine refuse show a similar range and the average values correspond to those published.

Test results reported by Busch (6), where the + No. 4 size and – No. 4 size materials were tested separately according to ASTM procedures, showed a slight difference in specific gravity between the two size ranges. It was reported that the + No. 4 materials had an average specific gravity of 2.00 while the – No. 4 average was 1.91. Considering the variability in coal refuse materials and the lack of reproducibility in test results experienced with the Irvine samples, the results of tests on the – No. 4 materials are a reasonable approximation for the entire sample.

The lack of reproducibility in test results could be attributed to several factors. Absorption of water by the individual particles could be one source. Rock types associated with coal refuse have granular textures. They, therefore, have internal void spaces which would have to fill with water to obtain the true specific gravity. The effective permeability of the granular particle structure would determine if and how fast the voids would fill. Clay minerals present in refuse would also tend to attract and absorb water. The time allotted to deair the sample may or may not be adequate for saturation of voids in the individual particles. The time for deairing is not specified in the test procedure and is therefore a variable with each test. Bryenton and Rose (9) reported similar problems in determining the specific gravity of coal refuse materials using prescribed ASTM test procedures for concrete aggregates.

Testing procedures presently used give an approximation of the specific gravity of coal preparation plant refuse. Modifications in these procedures may be necessary to obtain precise results. Possible modifications to the existing procedures would be prescribing time periods for deairing and possibly providing for agitation during deairing. A reasonably accurate determination of specific gravity is essential since many tests and parameter calculations depend on it.

Atterberg Limits: The Atterberg Limits tests have been devised to determine the moisture content of a soil when it changes from one physical condition to another, thus relating moisture content to physical behavior. The liquid limit (LL) is the moisture content at which a soil passes from a plastic to a liquid state.

Plastic limit (PL) is the moisture content at which a soil changes from a semi-solid to a plastic state. The plasticity index (PI) is defined as the numerical difference between the liquid limit and the plastic limit. It therefore represents the range of moisture contents at which the soil will behave as a plastic material.

Typical values for LL of soils are 20 or less for sandy soils and between 40 and 60 for most clays in the U.S. The plastic limit of soils is governed by the clay content. It is therefore possible for soils which have large amounts of sand-size particles to not possess a plastic limit. These soils are classified as nonplastic (NP). The tests to determine LL and PL were conducted in accordance with ASTM D-423 and D-424, "Standard Method of Testing for Liquid Limit of Soils" and "Standard Method of Testing for Plastic Limit and Plasticity Index of Soils."

Results — Results of tests on the coal refuse samples from Irvine indicate ranges of values for the Atterberg limits tests are as follows: liquid limit, 25 to 35 with an average of 29; plastic limit, 15 to 26 with an average of 20.5; and plasticity indexes of 2 to 13 with an average of 8.5. Results for each sample tested are contained in Tables 6.1 through 6.4.

Results of these tests correspond reasonably well with other published test results. The *Engineering and Design Manual for Coal Refuse Disposal Facilities* (8), reports the range of values for the fine portion of coarse refuse materials to be between 25 and 35, and the values for PI to be less than 12. Lagoon deposits are reported to have LLs in the range of 30 to 40 and PIs of less than 15. Other published values correspond well to those given above (10).

Since the values for the Atterberg limits of a material are affected by both the amount and kind of clay minerals present, these test results can be used as a guide to the clay mineralogy. Activity of a clay is defined as the plastic index divided by the percentage 0.002 mm clay content. Values of activity have been correlated with clay mineral types. Correlations of activity and clay mineral type are given below (3)(4).

	Activity
Montmorillonite	1–8
Illite	0.3–1
Kaolinite	0.1–0.4

Values of activity for the coal refuse samples tested ranged from 0.17 to 0.70 with an average value of 0.46. From these values it can be concluded that the dominant clay mineral is illite, with some kaolinite being present.

Little experience has been gained at the present time with regard to the applicability of Atterberg limits to coal refuse material. The principal drawback to application may be in the moisture content determination. Coal refuse is known to contain carbonaceous and organic materials which are volatile. These substances may be driven off along with the water when the samples are heated for water content determinations. This aspect of application of a basic soil mechanics technique to coal refuse needs further investigation.

Soil Classification: In order to relate the characteristics and properties of coal refuse to those of soil, the coal refuse must be identified using criteria for soil classification. The primary purpose of a soil classification system is to identify a material in sufficient detail to permit an engineer to recognize it and thus relate characteristics and properties based on the classification.

The coal refuse materials were classified using three soil classification systems. These were the U.S. Department of Agriculture Textural Classification System, the AASHO Classification System, and the Unified Soil Classification System. All of these systems base classifications on gradation and Atterberg Limits. Results of the classifications of the coal refuse materials are contained in Tables 6.1 through 6.4.

There have been no published reports where soil classification systems have been applied to a large number of coal refuse materials. A need exists to correlate classifications for refuse to observed behavior and laboratory test results. The only published work of this type is presented in a paper by Anderson (5), but this was for only a limited number of samples which were principally composed of sand and gravel-size materials. Soil classification systems may or may not be applicable to coal refuse materials due to its unnatural and changing gradations, low specific gravities, and the unusual nature of the materials composing it.

Moisture-Density Relationship: The density of a soil is measured in terms of weight/volume, and is usually expressed as pounds of wet or dry soil per cubic foot. These measurements are designated as wet density and dry density respectively. Several factors influence the value of density for a soil. Of primary importance are: (1) moisture content; (2) gradation and physical properties; and (3) the type and amount of compactive effort. Moisture content and density play a major role in determining the behavior of a soil when a load is applied to it. Artificially densifying a soil by compaction will improve many soil properties.

Compaction of coal refuse is very important to the long-term safety of a refuse embankment. The increase in shear strength along with the decrease in permeability are two important aspects. Another is the decrease in air voids which lessens the combustion potential associated with carbonaceous materials. These factors point to the definite need for adequate compaction of refuse.

The purpose of a laboratory compaction test is to determine the water content for compaction which will result in the maximum density. Procedures for running the test are given in ASTM D-698, "Standard Methods of Tests for Moisture-Density Relations of Soils Using 5.5-lb Rammer and 12-in Drop." Twelve tests were run using the prescribed procedures. Samples to be tested were determined based on classifications of materials and specific gravity.

Results for all the tests are tabulated in Tables 6.1 through 6.4. The range of values for maximum density of the refuse material was 80.8 to 114.5 pounds per cubic foot with the range of optimum moisture contents being 14.5 to 7.5 percent.

Permeability: Permeability is dependent on the size and number of continuous pores in the soil. The permeability varies with such factors as void ratio, grain size and distribution, particle structure, degree of cementation and degree of saturation. It will also vary with the degree of compaction, since this influences the size and number of pore spaces within the soil mass. The permeability of compacted coal refuse is a very important parameter when analyzing the long-term stability of a refuse embankment.

The coefficient of permeability is a constant proportionality relating to the ease with which a fluid passes through a porous medium. Two laboratory test procedures are available for determining the coefficient of permeability, the constant-head method and the falling-head method. The first is usually used with sandy soils and the second with clay soils. For the purpose of testing compacted refuse samples, the constant-head method was chosen. It was felt that the compacted refuse would be very nearly impermeable and the falling-head method would not respond to the small volumes of water which might or might not flow through the sample.

Test specimens were prepared by compacting the refuse samples into special permeameters. The permeameter was very similar to a compaction mold having a diameter of 6 inches and a height of 7 inches. Refuse materials were compacted at optimum moisture and using the equivalent amount of compaction energy based on volume of material as was used in the moisture density test procedure ASTM D-698. All samples which were tested were compacted to 97% or greater of their maximum dry density. The only exception was the sample for Hole 3, depth 0–20 feet, for which the density was 93.5% of maximum.

Table 6.5 summarizes the results of these tests. Based on the testing procedure used and the results obtained, it can be concluded that the compacted refuse samples were impermeable.

Table 6.5: Refuse Permeability Data

Hole	Depth, ft	Classification	Permeability, ft/min
1	0–30	SC, clay loam	1.01×10^{-7}
2	0–25	SC, sandy clay	6.13×10^{-7}
2	25–50	SM, sandy clay loam	2.42×10^{-7}
3	0–25	SC, clay loam	2.07×10^{-6}
3	30–50	SC, clay	8.99×10^{-8}
4	25–50	SC, sandy clay loam	9.15×10^{-6}

Source: ARC 74-217-KY-3685

Shear Strength: Shear strength parameters are the most important soil engineering properties for evaluating soils and other materials for embankment fill or foundation uses. These parameters represent the controlling factors in all stability or bearing capacity analyses.

Results for the triaxial tests performed on the coal refuse materials from Irvine are contained in Table 6.6 along with other significant soil properties. Values for angle of internal friction and cohesion given in the table are effective stress parameters determined by a consolidated undrained test with pore pressure measurements.

Several reports have been published where limited triaxial test data have been presented. The range of values for the effective stress strength parameters given in these reports is $\overline{\phi}$ = 25 to 41 for both compacted laboratory samples and undisturbed field samples. Values for cohesion range from C = 0 to 12.6 psi, with average values of 1 or 2 psi (5)(8)(10). Results for the coal refuse samples from Irvine fall within this range.

Table 6.6: Triaxial Test Results

Hole No.	Depth (ft)	Specific Gravity	Maximum Dry Density	. . Classification. . .		Shear . Strength .	
				Unified	AASHO	$\overline{\phi}$	C
1	0–30	2.36	114.4	SC	A-4	29.7	0.0
3	30–50	2.27	102.3	SC	A-6	29.4	0.0
4	25–50	1.92	83.8	SM	A-4	34.1	0.0

Source: ARC 74-217-KY-3685

Direct shear testing performed by Busch (6) gave similar results to those obtained by triaxial testing. Values for $\overline{\phi}$ tended to be only slightly higher. The only published total stress parameters appear in the report prepared by M.B. Baker, Jr., Inc. (7). The range of values for $\overline{\phi}$ were plotted to the left of the 10% air void line. The percentage air voids for this sample would be on the order of 12 to 14% at maximum dry density. Results somewhat similar to these were reported (7). The range of values for $\overline{\phi}$ was 18 to 30, with C ranging from 9 to 16 psi. Most shear strength testing in the U.S. is performed with effective confining stresses of less than 100 psi.

National Coal Board data on British tests indicate that failure envelopes tend to flatten at high effective confining stresses. In an extreme case the effective angle of friction decreased from 38.25 to 20 when an effective confining stress of 200 psi was used (8). Shear strength characteristics of coal refuse materials are not yet well established.

The stress-strain behavior for the Irvine refuse samples was plotted. All samples tested behaved as normally consolidated material with no incurred peak stress. Specimens tested at effective confining pressures of 10 and 20 psi did show similar values for stress and strain. This indicates that overconsolidation in the range of 10 to 20 psi was experienced during construction or testing. Strength parameters for these samples are not peak strengths but are residual values which would be expected considering the unnatural origin and stress history of the materials.

The coal refuse materials from Irvine classify as SM, SC and CL soils. Typical values for the effective shear strength parameters of soils of the same classifications are given below. These values are taken from Reference 11.

Classification	$\bar{\phi}$	C, psi
SM	34	3.0
SC	31	1.6
CL	28	1.9

The values for SM soils correspond directly with the results for the coal refuse samples. SC soil has a higher value for friction angle than the coal refuse. Variability of refuse may prevent any correlation of test results between soil classifications and strength parameters.

In reviewing Table 6.6 it should be noted that Hole 1 is an embankment material and Holes 3 and 4 represent lagoon deposits. Also, the age of the materials tests increases with the hole-numbering scheme. Specific gravity and density appear to be inversely related to strength, but insufficient data are available for a generalization to be made. Results for the tests performed represent what might be expected for the range of materials encountered in the refuse embankments at Irvine, Kentucky.

California Bearing Ratio (CBR): The CBR test measures the shearing resistance of a soil under controlled moisture and density conditions. It yields a bearing ratio number which is the ratio of the unit load required to effect a certain depth penetration of the piston into a compacted specimen, to the standard unit load required to obtain the same depth of penetration on a standard sample of crushed stone. The CBR number is commonly used to rate the performance of soils for use as bases and subgrades beneath pavements for roads and airfields.

Often two molds of soil are compacted for each sample, one for immediate penetration testing for CBR value and one for later testing after soaking in water for a prescribed period. Swell readings are taken on the specimen while it is soaking. The testing of two samples, one soaked and the other unsoaked, gives two important pieces of information. It gives information concerning expected soil expansion in the field when it becomes saturated and secondly it gives an indication of strength loss from saturation.

For the purposes of coal refuse evaluation two molds were compacted and tested for each sample. Sample preparation and testing were conducted according to procedures described in ASTM D-1883, "Standard Method of Test for Bearing Ratio of Laboratory-Compacted Soils." Results of the tests are summarized in Tables 6.1 through 6.4. The range of values for unsoaked samples was 10.8 to 40.4 and soaked samples 5.7 to 14.8. These results indicate that these coal refuse materials could be used for subgrades and subbase in situations where proper considerations were taken.

CBR values for compacted soil samples of the same classifications (from Reference 11) are: 5–20 for SC; 10–40 for SM; and 15 for CL. The CBR values for the coal refuse materials fall within the range of values given for soils. These tests indicate that it may be possible to correlate CBR results to triaxial test results.

There have been few CBR test results published for coal refuse materials. The report in Reference 7 contains data on mine tests. The range of values was 4.3 to 32.5. These samples were tested under a 30-pound surcharge, and only 3 samples were tested. Each sample was divided into three parts and each was compacted with a different amount of energy input.

A gradation was conducted on each test specimen following the CBR test, which indicated that the particle sizes in each sample were reduced with increasing compaction energy. Gradations were not performed after testing of the Irvine samples, but the CBR values correspond reasonably well to those published.

Conclusions: Coal refuse is an unusual material with which engineers have only a moderate amount of experience. Its characteristics and properties differ somewhat from soils and rocks which comprise most embankments and foundations. With an understanding of these differences and appropriate considerations taken in design, coal refuse can be used in place of, or along with, the conventional materials.

Results of the laboratory testing program indicate that the engineering properties of the coal refuse are only slightly lower than would be expected for typical soils. Shear strength is lower than in soils with the same classification. The effective angles of internal friction are on the order of 3 less. Density of compacted samples was also less; this corresponded directly with lower specific gravities and does not mean that the refuse cannot be adequately compacted. High air voids percentages do indicate that additional compactive effort may be needed.

CBR values for the compacted samples averaged 9, which would classify the refuse as a fair subgrade or subbase material for roadway construction. Since greater than 10% of the material is smaller than 0.02 mm, frost heave might represent a problem with roadway pavements in cool climates. Based on the testing results, there are no adverse engineering properties associated with the coal refuse which would prevent its use as a construction material.

Permeability of compacted coal refuse samples was very low, with some samples being impermeable. This characteristic would allow the refuse to be put to other uses related to retention or infiltration prevention. In situations where infiltration of water is undesirable the refuse could be used as an impervious blanket.

The coal refuse materials from the South-East Coal Company in Estill County, Kentucky can be used for many construction purposes. They do have limitations, but with their characteristics and engineering properties known, proper design considerations can be taken.

Typical Coal Refuse Analyses

Testing operations were conducted in the College of Engineering Coal Testing Laboratory. Heating value, percent ash, and percent sulfur were determined on the refuse samples using standard ASTM procedures (12). A Parr adiabatic calorimeter was used for heating value determinations. One-gram samples were ashed at 760°C in a muffle furnace. The bomb-wash method with alternate Eschka procedure was used for sulfur determinations.

The analyses were conducted on both the raw refuse samples, as taken in an unaltered condition from the plant and pile, and on processed refuse. The processed refuse represented the sink portion after the +30 mesh size refuse had been sink-floated in a 1.7 specific gravity liquid (perchloroethylene) and after the –30 size refuse had been froth-flotated using MIBC (methylisobutyl carbinol). The raw refuse samples contained various coal-type and other lightweight contaminates, whereas the processed refuse had lower percentages of contaminates. Ash contents of raw refuse samples averaged about 65 to 70%, sulfur contents about 1% and heating values about 4,000 Btu/lb.

Test data for both the sink and float portions of the processed refuse are given in Tables 6.7a through 6.7d. About 15% of the processed samples was float material and the remaining 85% was sink material. The sink portions had higher ash and lower Btu contents than the raw refuse. Better separations were obtained for the coarser (+30 mesh size) materials.

For comparisons, typical Eastern Kentucky metallurgical coals have sulfur contents between 0.6 and 1.5%, ash contents between 6 and 8%, and Btu/lb heating values of 13,500 to 14,000. Eastern Kentucky seam coal will generally have higher ash content and a lower Btu value. Typical Western Kentucky seam coals have sulfur contents between 3 and 4%, ash contents between 10 and 18%, and Btu/lb heating values of 11,000 to 12,500.

Table 6.7a: Typical Coal Analyses (Raw Refuse Samples, Past and Present Production)

Production	Location	Depth (ft)	Ash	Sulfur	Heating Value (Btu/lb)
			.....(%).....		
Past	Hole 1	0–30	78.26	1.31	1,895
Past	Hole 1	30–50	55.83	1.02	5,863
Past	Hole 2	0–25	77.58	1.36	2,160
Past	Hole 2	25–50	45.16	1.33	7,436
Past	Hole 3	0–30	75.18	1.51	2,337
Past	Hole 3	30–50	65.83	1.41	3,958
Past	Hole 4	0–10	80.20	1.82	2,172
Past	Hole 4	10–25	63.13	1.70	3,835
Past	Hole 4	25–50	41.20	0.96	10,417
Average		—	64.71	1.38	4,452

(continued)

Table 6.7a: (continued)

Production	Location	Depth (ft)	Ash	Sulfur	Heating Value (Btu/lb)
			..... (%)		
Present	Draw 1*	—	77.13	0.91	2,444
Present	Table*	—	64.41	1.12	4,899
Present	Draw 2*	—	67.57	0.70	3,541
Average		—	69.70	0.91	3,628

Note: Draws 1 and 2 obtained from the jig washer;
Table samples obtained from the Deister table.

*Average.

Table 6.7b: Typical Coal Analyses (Processed Refuse Samples*, Past Production, Float Portion)

Mesh Size	Ash	Sulfur	Heating Value (Btu/lb)	Raw Sample (% by wt)
	..... (%)			
+30	21.57	1.46	11,292	14.5
-30	58.24	0.88	5,596	2.7

*Average of four holes.

Table 6.7c: Typical Coal Analyses (Processed Refuse Samples*, Past Production, Sink Portion)

Mesh Size	Ash	Sulfur	Heating Value (Btu/lb)	Raw Sample (% by wt)
	..... (%)			
+30	74.77	1.57	2,420	49.5
-30	68.44	0.77	3,609	33.3

*Average of four holes.

Source: ARC 74-217-KY-3685

Table 6.7d: Typical Coal Analyses (Processed Refuse Samples, Present Production, Sink and Float Portions)

	Mesh Size	Ash	Sulfur	Heating Value (Btu/lb)	Raw Sample (% by wt)
		..... (%)			
Sink					
Draw 1*	+30	84.18	0.69	640	85.6
Draw 1*	-30	71.88	1.62	2,721	8.8

(continued)

Table 6.7d: (continued)

	Mesh Size	Ash	Sulfur	Heating Value	Raw Sample
		. . . . .(%).		(Btu/lb)	(% by wt)
Draw 2**	+30	86.71	1.38	720	72.1
Draw 2**	-30	64.45	1.69	4,310	13.5
Table***	+30	71.97	1.50	2,660	64.5
Table***	-30	75.94	1.47	1,928	9.0
Average	+30	80.95	1.19	1,340	74.1
Average	-30	70.76	1.59	2,986	10.4
Float					
Draw 1*	+30	12.16	1.98	12,967	4.8
Draw 1*	-30	34.10	1.70	9,273	0.8
Draw 2**	+30	11.90	1.95	13,110	13.2
Draw 2**	-30	49.51	0.97	6,938	1.2
Table***	+30	29.52	2.85	10,030	26.2
Table***	-30	73.26	2.72	2,145	0.3
Average	+30	17.86	2.26	12,035	14.7
Average	-30	52.39	1.80	6,119	0.8

  *Coarse
 **Medium
***Fine

Source: ARC 74-217-KY-3685

PRODUCT CHARACTERIZATION, DEVELOPMENT AND POTENTIAL

Chemical and Mineralogical Characterization

Analytical Technique: Refuse samples ranged in size and consistency from slurry to coarse material containing pieces up to two inches in size. The slurry material was oven-dried and disaggregated to a powder. Larger samples were crushed in a jaw crusher to approximately a half-inch size. Samples were mixed with shovels and then spread out on a clean floor to a depth of two to three inches. Two to ten pounds (depending on size fraction) were withdrawn for elemental analysis. This fraction was dried at 90°C for 24 to 48 hours. All samples were recrushed to approximately $\frac{1}{16}$-inch in a jaw crusher and about 20 grams split off in a ten-division sediment splitter. This fraction was pulverized in a Spex Industries Shatterbox for 90 seconds. This was ashed, and sulfur and heating values were obtained. The ash was subsequently split into fractions for elemental analysis.

X-ray fluorescence was used to determine SiO_2, K_2O, CaO and TiO_2. Oxide concentrations were obtained for these elements from working curves constructed with international rock, clay and mineral standards (13).

For atomic absorption analysis, the samples were put into solution by hydrofluoric acid in a closed Oak Ridge type centrifuge tube submerged in a water bath set at 90°C. The solutions were then stabilized with boric acid. Again, working curves were constructed using international rock, clay and mineral standards. The concentration of P_2O_5 was determined colorimetrically using techniques outlined by Shapiro and Brannock (14).

The calculation of normative mineralogy was an extension and modification of that of Augenstein and Sun (15). The normative calculation began with the computation of molar fractions of the analyzed oxides. The mol fraction of illite was determined first. An illite of the composition

$$1.5K_2O \cdot 4Al_2O_3 \cdot 5Fe_2O_3 \cdot MgO \cdot 14SiO_2$$

was chosen. This is similar in composition to that determined by Weaver (16), but the hydroxyl groups have been discarded and balanced by oxygen for the sake of simple stoichiometry. The weight percent of the K_2O in this illite was 9.61%, somewhat more potassium rich than that chosen by Augenstein and Sun, which was 8.93% (15). The molar fraction of illite was calculated as 66% of the total molar K_2O. Molar fractions in the proportions dictated by the above formula were subtracted from the appropriate oxides.

Kaolinite ($Al_2O_3 \cdot 2SiO_2 \cdot 2H_2O$) was calculated as the molar fraction of the remaining Al_2O_3 and SiO_2 was then adjusted. The mol fraction of normative quartz (SiO_2) was calculated as being equal to the remaining SiO_2. Normative pyrite (FeS_2) was calculated from sulfur analysis of the bulk material (sulfur is oxidized during ashing and driven off as a gas). The mineral fraction sulfur was determined by dividing the bulk sample sulfur value by the ash fraction of the sample. Fe_2O_3 was then adjusted by the subtraction of half of this mol fraction. In a few cases the molar values of sulfur exceeded that of Fe_2O_3. In these cases pyrite was set equal to total Fe_2O_3 and the sulfur mol fraction adjusted, leaving a residual-free sulfur content.

Small amounts of free sulfur were observed most frequently in past production samples and may possibly be accounted for by the fact that much of the sulfur in these somewhat weathered samples was present as a sulfate and not as a sulfide. In addition, high excess sulfur was found in a few of the samples with very low ash content. This may have been due to the amount of nonpyritic or organic sulfur in the coal fraction of the sample. Two samples were deleted from the normative averages for this reason.

Apatite [$Ca_5(PO_4)_3F$] was calculated next from the P_2O_5 analysis and calcium readjusted. The remaining molar CaO and MgO were set equal to their carbonates, calcite ($CaCO_3$) and magnesite ($MgCO_3$). The remaining MgO was probably contained in the mineral dolomite [$CaMg(CO_3)_2$]; magnesite was used for the sake of simplicity. Rutile (TiO_2) was also calculated but not reported in the normative mineralogy tables because it is commonly found only in this simple oxide phase and its mineralogic weight percent will be equal to the TiO_2 weight percent in the oxide tables. The normative mineralogic weight percent was calculated from the molar fractions as determined above.

The simple mineralogy chosen is in agreement with other investigators (15)(17). Feldspar, chlorite and solid montmorillonite were considered to be minor or not present due to the low concentrations of Na_2O found in all samples. Pyrophyllite $(Al_2O_3 \cdot 4SiO_2 \cdot H_2O)$ was found in a few samples from the Pennsylvanian anthracite fields (15), but this metamorphic mineral is not thought to be of importance due to the lower rank of Kentucky coals.

Discussion: Tables 6.8a and 6.8b present the major element chemistry for the present and past production samples, respectively. The normative mineralogy calculations for these samples are presented in Tables 6.8c and 6.8d. To give some idea of how the refuse compares in composition with other shales in the Appalachian region, an analysis of the shale APSC is also given in Table 6.8a. APSC is a composite sample of all the Paleozoic shales which outcrop along the Pennsylvania Turnpike and is weighted on the basis of unit thickness. The gross chemistry of the refuse from the Irvine plant is similar to APSC but the refuse is considerably enriched in Al_2O_3 and depleted in CaO.

Table 6.8a: Elemental Analyses—Present Production Samples

| | . . . . Location . . . . | | | | |
Sample	Draw 1*	Table*	Draw 2* . . . . (percent)	Overall*	APSC
SiO_2	54.11	53.51	54.48	54.07	56.61
TiO_2	1.28	1.53	1.25	1.35	0.85
Al_2O_3	28.12	27.18	27.66	27.65	14.11
Fe_2O_3	6.00	8.44	6.09	6.54	8.60
MnO	0.03	0.02	0.03	0.03	0.08
MgO	1.58	1.22	1.60	1.47	2.80
CaO	0.35	0.77	0.49	0.54	7.04
K_2O	3.81	3.36	3.81	3.66	3.62
Na_2O	0.44	0.39	0.46	0.43	0.50
P_2O_5	0.11	0.11	0.09	0.10	0.23

*Average

Source: ARC 74-217-KY-3685

Table 6.8b: Elemental Analyses*—Past Production Samples

Sample	Percent
SiO_2	54.86
TiO_2	1.29
Al_2O_3	27.03
Fe_2O_3	7.37
MnO	0.04
MgO	1.56

(continued)

Table 6.8b: (continued)

Sample	Percent
CaO	0.53
K_2O	3.85
Na_2O	0.39
P_2O_5	0.10

*Average of holes 1 through 4 (depth
  0–50 feet below surface).

Source: ARC 74-217-KY-3685

Table 6.8c: Normative Mineralogic Calculation—Present Production Samples

| | . . . . .Location . . . . | | | |
| Sample | Draw 1* | Table* | Draw 2* | Overall* |
	. . . .(percent)			
Illite	39.78	34.66	39.53	37.99
Kaolinite	42.28	43.11	41.18	42.19
Quartz	11.28	12.73	12.23	12.08
Pyrite	1.95	3.66	1.79	2.47
Hematite	1.25	1.60	1.55	1.47
Calcite	0.36	1.10	0.71	0.72
Magnesite	1.03	0.55	1.08	0.59
Apatite	0.32	0.31	0.25	0.29

*Average

Source: ARC 74-217-KY-3685

Table 6.8d: Normative Mineralogic Calculation*—Past Production Samples

Sample	Percent
Illite	39.84
Kaolinite	39.77
Quartz	13.00
Pyrite	3.35
Hematite	0.01
Calcite	0.73
Magnesite	0.95
Apatite	0.28

*Average of holes 1 through 4 (depth
  0–50 feet below surface).

Source: ARC 74-217-KY-3685

An important factor in the determination of the chemical character of the refuse appears to be the method used to separate it from the coal. The strongest difference observed at the Irvine plant is between the refuse collected from the Deister table and that of the two draws. The refuse produced by the Deister table is higher in Fe_2O_3, CaO, TiO_2 and lower in MnO. This is also reflected in the normative mineralogy with the table refuse having higher normative calcite and pyrite than the rest of the plant refuse. These differences are probably due to the table's greater relative efficiency in removing the pyrite and calcite fraction of the refuse as opposed to the clay and quartz fractions of the refuse.

In summary, the chemistry of the refuse material is similar to most other Paleozoic shales except that it is enriched in Al_2O_3 and depleted in CaO. The major factor controlling the variation in the chemistry of the refuse is what seam it is associated with. The chemistry of the past production refuse is consistent with observations made for present production refuse. The method of separation of the refuse from the coal is of some interest, especially with regard to its Fe_2O_3 and CaO content.

Electric Furnace Firing Tests

Firing tests and subsequent evaluations were made at the U.S. Bureau of Mines, Tuscaloosa Metallurgy Research Laboratory at the University of Alabama. Raw samples, containing inherent amounts of coal, and processed samples, from which the majority of the coal has been removed, were evaluated for possible commercial utilization. The appraisals are preliminary in nature, but are considered valuable since they indicate the use for which the material is best suited, determine whether additional testing is warranted, and direct the course of specific testing that is required to make a complete evaluation. Samples were evaluated by both the slow and quick-firing methods.

General discussions of the test procedures and criteria used for evaluating the refuse materials for possible commercial uses are contained in the following sections. Specific details are described by Klinefelter and Hamlin in a previous Bureau of Mines publication (18).

Slow-Fire: Data obtained from slow-fire electric furnace tests were used for preliminary evaluation of material for potential use in the manufacture of structural clay products, refractory products, whiteware materials, and pottery. Emphasis was placed on evaluating refuse for structural clay products or possibly refractory products. Fired-color requirements precluded its use for whiteware and for pottery.

Structural clay products can be made from a wide range of clays. Workability (plasticity) is the most important property of the raw material, particularly if stiff mud extrusion (the most common method) is used for processing. Overly plastic clays tend to laminate when extruded, while nonplastic clays will not extrude in a smooth column. Clays that fall between these limits are more desirable.

The raw clay must dry uniformly at a reasonable rate without warping and crack-ing. The raw material must have sufficient binder to develop adequate green strength so that the product can be handled in the unfired wet and dry condi-tions. The fired product should mature at a temperature of about 2100°F and provide a very hard product with low absorption and shrinkage. Color is not too important since mineral pigments can be added. Blending two or more clays of differing properties to produce structural products has become fairly common practice.

A two-pound representative sample was dried at 110°C and ground so that 100% would pass a No. 20 sieve. One hundred grams of the dried material was mixed with sufficient (measured) water to form a plastic mass. The working properties of the plastic material were noted and small test specimens (approximately 1.5 x 2.5 x 0.25 inches) were made using a steel mold. The test specimens were marked for shrinkage determinations, dried at 65°C for 12 hours, and at 110°C for an ad-ditional 12 hours. Six of the dried specimens were placed in the laboratory fur-nace and the temperature was increased slowly to prevent disintegration as the mechanical and chemically combined water was released. Approximately 3 hours were required for the furnace to reach 1800°F. Test specimens were removed from the furnace at 1800°F, 1900°F, 2000°F, 2100°F, 2200°F, and 2300°F after a 15-minute soak at each temperature. About 4 hours were required to cover the 1800° to 2300°F range. These temperatures cover the range used in most ceramic firing and are considered adequate for general appraisals.

The laboratory procedure used for making the test specimens is essentially the soft mud process and, in comparing it with the stiff mud process normally used in commercial production, the amount of water used for achieving plasticity is higher. Firing shrinkages are also higher since the clay is not deaired and the forming pressure is much less.

From the slow-fire tests, the following data were obtained: workability, plastic-ity, pH and soluble salt determinations, water of plasticity, drying and firing shrinkages, color (fired and unfired), percent absorption, drying characteristics (warping or cracking), apparent specific gravity (fired), and hardness. These data provide the necessary information for evaluating usefulness as a raw material in the manufacture of structural clay products.

Twelve raw refuse samples were evaluated. Four samples were classified as satis-factory and one as marginal; all were from weathered refuse taken from upper portions of the test holes. The majority of the samples contained insufficient clay binder to hold the mass together and to provide the necessary degree of hardness. This was partially due to voids being created due to carbon (coal) burn-out during firing.

Twenty-four processed refuse samples were evaluated. None were noted as satis-factory or marginal in quality. As with the raw samples, lack of sufficient binder was judged the main reason for the majority of the samples not meeting the cri-teria. Removal of the majority of the coal from the refuse prior to firing did not appear to significantly improve brick-making possibilities for most of the samples.

A literature search was conducted to identify processes for the manufacture of brick. This study was conducted parallel to the above effort by the U.S. Bureau of Mines to produce samples of brick from the coal mine refuse using bench apparatus. No commercial processes could be identified in the U.S. for the manufacture of brick from coal mine refuse. It is recommended that this area remain open for further investigation. Brick has been manufactured from shales associated with coal on a commercial scale in both England and France (19).

Quick-Fire: Data obtained from laboratory quick-fire electric furnace tests were used for preliminary evaluation of material for potential use in the manufacture of lightweight aggregate by the rotary kiln method. Expansion (bloating) of clays and shales was determined within the range of commercial working temperatures, starting just under the bloating temperature and increasing the temperature until over-bloating or sticking occurred.

Lightweight aggregate is produced commercially by either the rotary kiln or sintering grate method. The properties of the raw material determine which method of processing can and should be used. The fired product must have a density less than 70 lb/ft^3 but generally no less than 40 lb/ft^3, depending on the size and the gradation.

For the rotary kiln process, the raw material should dry readily without undue disintegration and must be of proper size when crushed for kiln feed with a minimum of fine-sized (–8 mesh) material. It should expand (bloat) well when heated rapidly below 2300°F. Expansion or bloating of discrete particles must occur with a gradual weight decrease through the bloating range. Chemical composition of the material must be such that gases generated by decomposition of various compounds on the interior will be entrapped within the particles during the bloating process, thus providing lightweight effects.

With the sintering grate process, unfired drying, strength, and crushing characteristics are not critical (except if particles tend to be thin and platy), since the material is finely crushed and mixed with water and coal, and pelletized or nodulized prior to firing. The raw material should vitrify at 2300°F or lower with slight expansion, and the particles should have a slightly glazed exterior. Lightweight effects are produced by agglomeration during vitrification which entraps air pockets between particles and by voids produced by solid fuel (carbon) burnout during the firing process.

For the laboratory evaluations, five pounds of the raw material was dried overnight at 110°F and the larger particles were crushed to ½- inch maximum size. Twenty grams (about 7 pieces of –½ to + ¼-inch size) were placed on a refractory slab (boat), inserted into a preheated (1800°F) electric furnace for 15 to 30 minutes, and then removed. The process was repeated with the furnace temperature raised in 100°F steps until 2300°F was reached or until the material was overfired and became sticky or began to melt.

The bloating test results indicated that none of the raw or processed refuse samples was satisfactory for use in the manufacture of lightweight aggregate by the rotary kiln method. As with the slow-fire tests, 12 raw samples and 24 processed samples were evaluated.

Sintering into Lightweight Aggregate

Preliminary Bench Scale Tests: Preliminary batch sintering tests on coal mine refuse were performed in order to obtain an indication of product quality with respect to its use as lightweight aggregate.

Raw Material Samples — Four drums of coal mine refuse, each containing approximately 500 pounds, were received at the Dwight-Lloyd Research Laboratories on October 3, 1975, for this sinter test program. These drums were identified as "Kentucky Coal Refuse." Two of the drums consisted of material from Hole 3 and the other two consisted of material from Hole 4.

The average percentage moistures of the samples from Holes 3 and 4 were 8.0 and 6.9, respectively. The "as received" coal mine refuse contained material which appeared too coarse for adequate sintering, hence the first unit operation consisted of hammermilling the material to –½ inch. This was followed by other unit operations and processes.

Test Procedures — Sintering tests were conducted on the refuse from Hole 3. The bench scale apparatus for simulating conditions on the pilot plant circuit consisted of a 39-inch diameter balling disc and a sinter test pot. The pot has a cross-sectional area of one square foot and is provided with standard grates at the bottom. A torch consisting of a natural gas-air premixed burner can be swung into position directly above the pot. Material to be processed is charged into the pot above the grates and a draft can be induced through the bed by means of a fan-duct arrangement connected to the windbox below the grates. This pot simulates conditions on the D-L sintering machine which is standard for conversion of various raw materials into sinter cake product. Temperature of the blast and draft within the bed are measured by thermocouples located above and within the bed, respectively. Manometers indicate the windbox vacuum and pressure drop across an orifice giving a measure of the draft flow through the bed.

The first test consisted of using the hammermilled refuse alone, whereas in the subsequent tests returns material (–¼ inch) obtained from previous tests was blended with the hammermilled refuse in specific ratios. This blending operation simulated transfer of materials from bins to conveyors. The material was nodulized in the balling disc and charged into the sinter pot to a bed depth of 6 inches. The torch was lighted, swung into position and the bed ignited for 90 seconds while maintaining a constant vacuum of 20 inches of water column. After ignition, ambient air was induced through the bed for a certain period of time maintaining the same vacuum so that the heat zone reached the bottom of the bed to complete the sintering cycle and then to cool the bed.

Temperature readings of the blast, the bed, the windbox, and the gases near the orifices were recorded every minute. Also, readings of windbox vacuum and pressure drop across the orifice were periodically recorded. Visual observations of the exhaust stack during the run were also noted.

Since the exhaust gases contained considerable smoke-sulfur emissions (as particulates of carbon and condensable hydrocarbons), tests simulating the Improved Sintering Process were also made. Briefly, the Improved Sintering Process involves recycling relatively cold draft from the initial windboxes of sintering to the terminal windboxes of the operation. The recycled draft is warm, slightly humid, and slightly depleted of oxygen. The primary stage of cooling is carried out with recycled draft from the terminal sintering stages which is high in humidity and slightly preheated to provide annealing during the terminal sintering-primary cooling stages.

Final cooling is carried out with cool draft from the discharge-crushing end operation wherein the dust for final cooling is recycled to the initial phase of sintering. Herein the dust is arrested to a considerable extent by the hot semifused sintering bed and lower moist layers of nodular sinter burden. Exhaust from sintering-cooling is directed to the stack through a final particulate treatment stage if warranted.

Bench scale apparatus for simulating this process is conventional except for the burner-hood arrangement. This consists of a natural gas-air burner wherein the temperature of the blast is controlled by controlling the amount of natural gas input.

Two tests were performed using this technique. These consisted of first lighting the burner and bringing the temperature of the combustion gases to approximately 2000°F. Next, the sinter test pot charged with nodules (in the same manner as for the previous tests) was swung into position directly under the burner-hood, simultaneously inducing a downdraft through the bed with the blower. The general thermal cycle used was:

Time (min)	Temperature (°F)	Pressure Drop Across Bed (in H_2O)
0–1.5	2000	20
1.5–10	400–500	20
10–20	200–300	20
20–30	300–400	20
30–35	ambient	20

Pertinent data were collected during and after the tests as described for the previous tests. After completion of the sintering and cooling cycle, material from the pot was discharged and individual weights on the +¼-inch and –¼-inch products recorded. Also, material which trickled through the grates was collected and its weight was recorded.

Block mix structure lightweight aggregate samples were prepared by stage crushing the sintered product in the laboratory jaw crusher and this was screened to ASTM size specifications. Bulk density was obtained by carefully filling a one-eighth cubic foot box with the sized sample and weighing the contents. Also, bulk density of sintered product, jaw-crushed to –1 inch, was determined by filling a one-half cubic foot box with the materials.

Test Results — Bulk density measurement of the sintered product based on the ASTM size specifications for fine aggregate was determined to be 48.6 lb/ft^3. ASTM high-limit designation for this aggregate is 70 lb/ft^3, hence the product appeared to fulfill the bulk density requirements for lightweight aggregate. The –1-inch sintered product had a bulk density of 40.1 lb/ft^3. Though strength measurements were not determined, the physical effort required for manually crushing the product indicated it to be of exceptionally high strength.

Aggregate Evaluation: Procedures — Approximately 70 pounds (2 cubic feet) of sintered aggregate was obtained from the preliminary batch sintering tests described above.

Aggregate Tests: Various aggregate tests were conducted to determine if the aggregate met the following American Society for Testing and Materials specifications: ASTM C-330, "Standard Specification for Lightweight Aggregates for Structural Concrete" and ASTM C-331, "Standard Specification for Lightweight Aggregates for Concrete Masonry Units."

Concrete Mixes: In addition, tests to determine concrete-making properties were conducted as specified in the above references. Two concrete mixes were made in the laboratory with the following mix designs:

	Mix 1*	Mix 2
Cement factors, bags/yd^3	7.0	7.0
Coarse aggregate	60% by volume 1 in–No. 4 size sintered refuse	74% by volume 1 in–No. 0 size sintered refuse
Fine aggregate	40% by volume natural river sand	26% by volume natural river sand
Air content, %	5	2
Slump, inch	3	5
Unit weight, lb/ft^3	114.6	110.5
Workability	good	poor

*Mix 1 appeared to be the better mix. Mix 2 had poor workability and insufficient air content.

Test Results — General Characteristics: General characteristics of aggregate include grading, unit weight (loose), presence and amounts of deleterious substance and absorption. Grading was determined by ASTM C-136 and results appear in the following table. It should be kept in mind that any number of specified gradings are possible since the sinter cake must be crushed, thereby providing any desired size, depending on the type of crushing.

| | . . . . Percent Passing . . . . | | | |
Size	1 in–No. 4*	1 in –0**	⅜-in–0***	No. 4–0†
1 inch	100.0	100.0	—	—
¾ inch	63.2	78.2	—	—
½ inch	38.4	63.5	—	—
⅜ inch	24.3	55.4	100.0	—
No. 4	0.0	40.8	93.5	100.0
No. 8	—	26.8	72.7	65.7
No. 16	—	18.0	57.7	44.1
No. 30	—	12.3	33.4	30.1
No. 50	—	6.5	19.6	15.9
No. 100	—	3.0	12.9	7.3

*Meets ASTM requirements for Coarse Aggregate in Structural Concrete.

**Grading as received.

***Meets ASTM requirements for Combined Coarse and Fine Aggregate in Structural Concrete and Masonry Units.

†Meets ASTM requirements for Fine Aggregate in Structural Concrete and Masonry units.

Unit weights (loose), determined by ASTM C-29 are tabulated below:

Size	Unit Weight (lb/ft^3)	ASTM Specifications (maximum)
1 inch-No. 4	30.4	55
1 inch-0	36.8	65
⅜ inch-0	45.3	65
No. 4-0	45.0	70

Deleterious substances are identified by tests for organic impurities, staining, clay lumps and loss on ignition. No organic impurities (ASTM C-142) were found and visually no clay lumps were observed. Insufficient amount of material was available to conduct the ASTM C-641 staining test; however, under normal curing conditions no staining was evident. The following loss on ignition was observed (ASTM C-114): 1 inch-No. 4 size, 2.84%; No. 4-0 size, 2.89% (ASTM maximum is 5% loss).

Absorption-time curves were developed for the 1 inch-No. 4 and 1 inch-0 gradings. Absorption values were comparable with generally used lightweight aggregates and are listed in the following table.

Time	. . . . . Absorption, percent	
	1 Inch-No. 4	1 Inch-0
5 min	2.1	2.1
10 min	3.3	2.7
30 min	4.0	3.5
60 min	4.0	3.8
100 min	5.2	4.3
12 hr	7.3	6.2
24 hr	9.3	7.8

Concrete-Making Properties: Two mixes, using the 1 inch-No. 4 and 1 inch-0 material, were made in the laboratory according to the mix design specified earlier. Natural river sand was added to both mixes. Specimens, as noted below, were made for testing after prescribed curing times. Sufficient amount of aggregate was not available to make the required number of specimens in some cases.

Compressive strength was determined by ASTM C-39. Two test cylinders were made for each mix. These were tested at 28 days cure. Strength requirements only apply to structural concrete. Compressive strengths, in psi, were as follows.

	Mix 1	Mix 2
Cylinder 1	4,230	3,150
Cylinder 2	3,960	3,450
Average	4,095	3,300

Unit weight (ASTM C-567) was 114.57 pcf (wet), 109.95 pcf (dry) for Mix 1 and 110.46 pcf (wet) for Mix 2. ASTM maximum is 115 pcf (dry).

To determine drying shrinkage by ASTM C-157 one specimen was made for each mix and tested at 35 days cure. Mix 1 showed shrinkage of 0.624%; and Mix 2 showed shrinkage of 0.831%.

There was an insufficient amount of material to conduct testing for popouts, as specified by ASTM C-151; however, after five hours of boiling in water no popouts or staining was noticeable.

Durability was determined by ASTM C-666. Two freeze-thaw specimens were made for each mix. After 14 days of moist cure, these were subjected to 300 freezing and thawing cycles. Mix 1, containing 5% entrained air, withstood the freeze-thaw durability tests and showed no degradation after 300 cycles. Mix 2 failed after 7 freeze-thaw cycles; however, this was due to lack of sufficient air entrainment.

Modulus of elasticity values, ASTM C-469, were as follows:

Mix 1 (average of 2)	2.32×10^6 psi
Mix 2 (average of 2)	2.18×10^6 psi

Bituminous Mix Properties: Mixes of two different asphalt contents were made in the laboratory using the sintered material less than the No. 4 sieve and No. 8 limestone aggregate. To meet specifications of Type 1-Class A bituminous concrete, a gradation of 85% by weight of sintered aggregate and 15% No. 8 limestone aggregate was determined to be optimum. It was decided that an asphalt content of 15.5% by weight would be near the optimum, but proved to be too dry when the mix was prepared. The asphalt content was then increased to 17%. Due to an extremely limited supply of the sintered aggregate, mixes with these two asphalt contents were the only ones produced. The mixes produced appeared typical of a lightweight asphalt concrete and the results of testing proved to be typical also.

The asphalt concrete mixes were prepared and tested by the Marshall Method as outlined in ASTM D-1559, with the exception that only two specimens at each asphalt content were made due to the material shortage. The test results were as follows:

Asphalt content, %	15.5	17.0
Bulk specific gravity (mix)	1.314	1.333
Maximum specific gravity (mix)	1.504	1.499
Air voids, %	12.63	11.10
Unit weight, pcf	81.99	83.15
Adjusted stability, lb	787	727
Flow, 0.01 in	11	15

Estimated Costs: Two potential continuous processes were identified for the production of lightweight aggregate from coal mine refuse. The first of these processes, which produces a rotary kiln aggregate, was abandoned after laboratory bench tests were conducted on the Estill County coal mine refuse. The second process, which produces a sintered aggregate, appears to be superior (from results of laboratory tests) to the kiln process for treatment of coal mine refuse. Requirements of a continuous sintering process for the coal mine refuse have not yet been determined. Therefore, operating costs and fixed capital costs of the study estimate type (20) cannot be generated. The reliability of the study estimate type is generally placed at ±30% (20). The necessary components for a study estimate type (generally made for established processes) are the following: site location, rough sketches of process flow sheet, preliminary sizing of equipment, approximate sizes of building and structures, rough estimates of utility requirements (water, electricity, etc.), preliminary piping flow sheet and specifications, and a preliminary motor list.

The cost and capital estimates made herein are the "order of magnitude" type which are not intented to be within the ±30% accuracy of the study estimate type. The purpose of cost analysis at this stage of the process testing is only to determine an order of magnitude product selling price (fob refuse process plant). If this price is in line with other lightweight aggregate fob plant prices, testing in a continuous pilot process should be considered.

The installed capital costs of a lightweight aggregate plant (1,000 tpd) with a flow sheet as shown in Figure 6.3 have been updated from 1961 to 1976 using the Chemical Plant Cost Index published in *Chemical Engineering* April 28, 1975. The index for 1961 (time of installation of the lightweight aggregate plant depicted in the flow sheet) is 101.5 and the estimated 1975 index is 182. These indexes yield a multiplier of approximately 1.8 to the 1961 plant cost. The cost of the plant in 1961 is stated to have been slightly over $2 million (21). The cost of the same plant in 1975 would have been $3.6 million.

Figure 6.3: Flow Diagram for Sintered Lightweight Aggregate

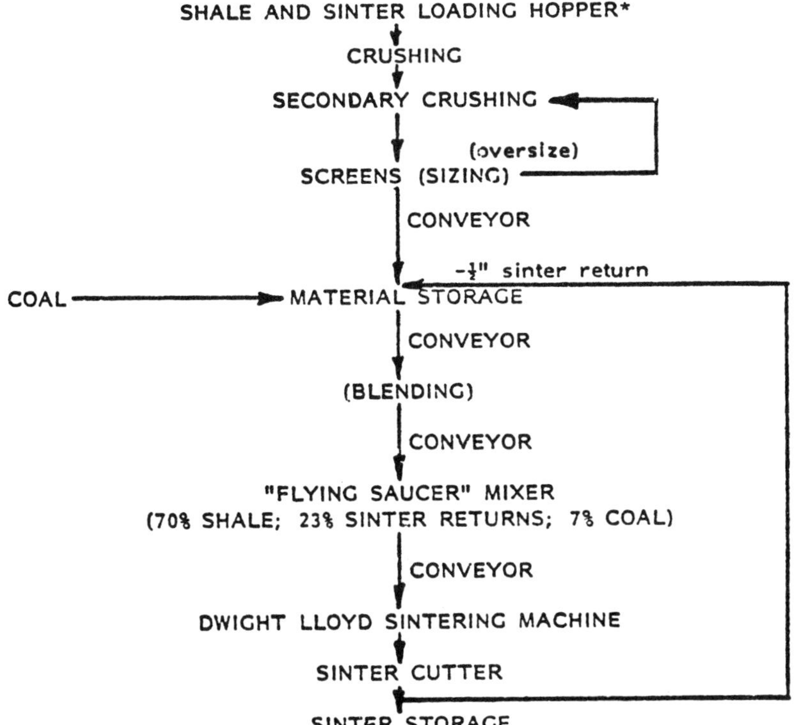

*Common crushing section for both raw and sintered material
which are crushed at different times.

Source: ARC 74-217-KY-3685

With the inflationary spiral, the costs can be expected to rise. The plant was redesigned in 1972 to lower costs and meet pollution control standards (22). Capital costs of the changes were not reported. The plant capacity of 1,000 tons per day (tpd) was not changed. A plant size of 1,000 tpd is indicated by McDowell-Wellman personnel to be the minimum possible to justify modern pollution control equipment. As reported by Stearn (1972) the New England plant "operates three shifts per day with a total of 16 employees, including quarry personnel." Drilling and blasting in the quarry is subcontracted, indicating that company personnel are involved only in loading and haulage to the plant.

The operating costs presented herein are based on a 5-day-per-week plant operation, 52 weeks per year, or 260-day operating year. Considered in direct costs are raw materials (zero cost for refuse at the coal preparation plant and no additives in the processing), utilities, labor, maintenance, payroll, overhead, and operating and maintenance supplies. Indirect costs include plant overhead, quality control, safety, etc.

It is anticipated that quality control facilities of the type incorporated in the New England plant would be adequate for the processing of coal mine refuse. Consumption of fuel (No. 2 fuel oil) for ignition of the raw refuse is reported by Bergstrom (21) to be 3 gallons per ton of product. Although more efficient ignition may be possible with present-day furnaces, the above value should represent a conservative order of magnitude estimate for the determination of a rough market price. Fuel oil is estimated at 40 cents per gallon or a total of $1.20 per ton of product.

Water, other than potable and wash water which are included in the indirect costs, may be necessary in the milling, mixing and dust-control operations. The cost of water for dust control should be insignificant in the analysis. It is probable that the water for milling could be recycled from settling ponds. From a 1971 study estimate made by the U.S. Bureau of Mines for processing an urban refuse for metals (1,000 tpd plant, with screening, heavy media, float-sink, and magnetic separators) the water and electric energy costs totaled 8 cents per ton processed (23). These costs are increased to 30 cents per ton of product from the coal refuse plant to reflect increased unit costs since 1971 and heavy crushing facilities required for the breakup of the sintered product. The estimated total utilities cost including fuel oil, electric power and water is $1.50 per ton of product.

Product selling prices are calculated using after-tax rates of return on invested capital of 12 and 15%. The discounted cash flow revenue requirement method is utilized. Working capital would be recovered at the end of the 20-year life, but is disregarded in this order of magnitude estimate. The income tax rate is assumed to be 50%. Depreciation is based on the straight-line method using the initial plant cost with a 20-year life and zero salvage value.

The year-end cash flow convention is used throughout. Capital is assumed to be invested as a lump sum to facilitate calculations. Positive cash flows are assumed to begin at the end-of-year after capital investment. If all components, including the selling price, respond equally to inflation, the rate of return on invested capital would be only slightly affected due to the nonresponsive nature of depreciation for income tax purposes. Depreciation is the only nonresponsive deduction for computation of tax liability included in this order of magnitude estimate. Estimates of manning requirements, production costs and capital requirements are shown in Tables 6.9 and 6.10.

Development of Selling Price Equation:

PSP $=$ Product selling price.

GR $=$ Gross annual revenues from product sales $=$ PSP x 168,000.

AE $=$ Annual expenses (not including depreciation) $=$ \$859,586.

BTCF $=$ Annual before tax cash flow $=$ GR $-$ AE $=$ (PSP x 168,000) $-$ 859,586.

D $=$ Annual depreciation $=$ \$200,000.

TI $=$ Taxable income $=$ BTCF $-$ D $=$ (PSP x 168,000) $-$ 1,059,586.

t $=$ Income tax rate (combined effective rate is assumed to be 50%).

AT $=$ Annual taxes $=$ TI x t $=$ (PSP x 84,000) $-$ 529,793

ATCF $=$ Annual after tax cash flow (amount available for capital recovery and return on remaining investment) $=$ BTCF $-$ AT $=$ (PSP x 84,000) $-$ 329,793.

CRF $=$ Capital recovery factor $= [i(1+i)^n]/[(1+i)^n-1]$, where $i =$ rate of return and $n =$ number of years.
CRF, 20 years, 12% $=$ 0.13388.
CRF, 20 years, 15% $=$ 0.17102.

C $=$ Initial capital investment $=$ \$4,214,897.

The requirement for capital recovery and return on remaining investment is:

$$C \cdot CRF = ATCF \text{ or } C \cdot CRF = (PSP \times 84{,}000) - 329{,}793.$$

Solving for PSP, the result is:

$$PSP = (50.177 \times CRF) + 3.926.$$

Results — Product selling price (fob plant) for capital recovery and 12% rate of return on remaining capital is \$10.64 per ton. Product selling price (fob plant) for capital recovery and 15% rate of return on remaining capital is \$12.51 per ton. The above minimum selling prices are order of magnitude estimates only. The error involved could be greater than ±30% because no information is available concerning the response of coal mine refuse to the continuous sintering process. Also, because this response is unknown, costs and capital requirements of smaller and larger plants are not considered at this time.

Table 6.9: Manning Table, Labor and Supervision Cost

Personnel	Total Man-Hours (per day)	Assumed Wage Rate per Man-Hour	Daily Cost (dollars)	Annual Cost (260 days per year)
Raw material haulage				
Equipment operators (3, 1 shift per day)	24	6.00	144	37,440
Plant				
Plant operator (foreman-supervisor) (3, 1 per shift), salary	—	—	—	45,000
Utility man (equipment operator) (3, 1 per shift)	24	6.00	144	37,440
Maintenance (electrical-mechanical) (3, 1 per shift)	24	7.00	168	43,680
Office, Purchasing, Sales				
Manager, salary	—	—	—	25,000
Quality control supervisor, salary	—	—	—	15,000
Laboratory assistants (2, 1 per shift)	16	5.00	80	20,800
Secretary	8	4.00	32	8,320
Purchasing, sales accounting (3), salary	—	—	—	36,000
Total personnel (20)	—	—	—	268,680
Payroll overhead (30% of annual labor/supervision)	—	—	—	80,604

Note: Yearly product production (assuming 30% weight loss on throughput and 240 production days per year)
700 tons per day x 240 days per year = 168,000 tons per year; total labor/supervision cost = $1.60 per ton of product;
total labor/supervision cost including payroll = $2.08 per ton of product.

Source: ARC 74-217-KY-3685

Table 6.10: Estimated Annual Production Costs and Costs per Ton of Product (Dollar Base, 1976)

	Annual Cost	Cost per Ton of Product
	. . . .(dollars)	
Direct Costs		
Raw materials	0	0
Total labor	147,680	0.88
Supervision and Managerial	121,000	0.72
Operating and Maintenance supplies (3% of first cost)	120,000	0.71
Utilities (fuel oil, water, electric power)	252,000	1.50
Payroll overhead (30% of total labor and supervision)	80,604	0.48
Total	721,284	4.29
Indirect Costs		
15% of total labor and supplies = 0.15 (1.60 + 0.71)	58,302	0.35
Fixed Costs		
Taxes (other than income taxes) and insurance (2% of plant cost)	80,000	0.48
Depreciation (20-year life)	200,000	1.19
TOTAL	1,059,586	6.31

Source: ARC 74-217-KY-3685

Conclusions: The limited test results indicate that the sintered aggregate meets ASTM grading, unit weight, and deleterious substances specifications for lightweight aggregate. Absorption values were comparable with those normally obtained with specification lightweight aggregates. Although strength tests were not conducted on the discrete aggregate particles (there is no accepted test method for this), the manual effort required to break the large particles apart indicated a very high strength material. High strength was also apparent by visual observation since the particles appeared well melted and fused together.

The sintered aggregate appears satisfactory for use in structural grade portland cement concrete. A 28-day compressive strength in excess of 4,000 psi was obtained, with a unit weight less than the ASTM maximum of 115 pcf. Freeze-thaw durability is satisfactory since the air-entrained mix showed no degradation after 300 freeze-thaw cycles. The bituminous concrete test specimens made with the sintered aggregate proved to be typical of similar asphalt mixes made with lightweight aggregate.

An order-of-magnitude type estimate of the selling price (fob plant) for lightweight aggregate from coal mine refuse indicates that the selling price of aggregate produced from coal mine refuse could be of the same order of magnitude as aggregate produced by the sintering process from non-coal-refuse shales.

MARKET ANALYSIS

General Review

This study originally envisioned that there might be several potentially marketable products developed from engineering tests, each of which would require extensive market survey and development work. Included in this initial list of potential products were: lightweight aggregate for use both as highway fill and in the production of cinder or cement block; brick; and filler for certain rubber and/or plastic products.

As the laboratory and engineering tests progressed, the market research and survey efforts maintained close coordination with the testing results. This process led to the elimination of several of the anticipated derived products from further marketing considerations due to the inconclusiveness of the bench-type analysis, the inappropriateness of coal refuse for a given use, or the nonfeasibility of actual production from coal refuse given the present state of the art. The laboratory and engineering tests then narrowed the scope of the marketing surveys to a few basic feasible products. These were lightweight aggregate uses, certain other fill uses, and soilless growing medium. A concentrated program of market research was undertaken to obtain as much useful marketing information as possible on these potential utilizations.

Lightweight Aggregate: Lightweight aggregate is in the general industrial category of expanded rock products. As part of the marketing survey an analysis was conducted as to types of industries which use, or might use, lightweight aggregates. Following is a general list of these types of industries and their SIC code numbers.

Product	SIC
Brick and structural clay tile	3251
Ceramic walls and floor tile	3253
Viterous plumbing fixtures	3261
Concrete block and brick	3271
Concrete products exterior block and brick	3271
Ready-mixed concrete	3273

Research and market surveys were conducted in each of these product areas to identify specific companies which could be potential users in the primary market area. Selection was confined to what was felt to be the primary market area because it was felt that this area might be looked at to supply the main financial and economic support of any production of lightweight aggregate at an Estill County site.

Other Uses: Highway Fill — Initial engineering and lab tests indicated that the physical properties of the coal refuse were such that they could be useful as highway fill.

Highway Nonskid Surfacing — New Federal Highway regulations will require all new or resurfaced U.S. Highways and Interstates to have a nonskid surfacing. In Kentucky nearly all highway surfacing is done with an asphalt mix with limestone base. Studies have proven limestone to be unsatisfactory as a nonskid surface since it has a high tendency to "polish" under use. The Kentucky Department of Transportation, Division of Highways has expressed a great deal of interest in utilizing an asphalt-lightweight aggregate mix for the purpose of meeting the nonskid surfacing requirements. The only other viable option for the Division of Highways appears to be to work with crushed granite, which must be imported from outside the state.

Coal mine refuse converted by sintering process into lightweight aggregate should be very competitive for this purpose. The University of Kentucky and the Division of Highways have agreed to perform initial "mix" tests which will lead to the laying of test road strips and other wearability tests.

Landfill — Analysis revealed that coal refuse, used properly, could serve as landfill. Inquiries into industrial site needs and values were conducted in the immediate area of the Estill County coal refuse site. The demand for landfill for industrial sites in the area is contingent on future activities in industrial development in the area. This use may proceed apace as the immediate area develops its industrial potential in the near term future. Exact demand is difficult to determine at this juncture.

Survey Approach

After assembling this initial data, various market research approaches were considered leading to the formulation of a personal interview approach with individuals in the various companies who have primary responsibility for purchase of raw materials such as lightweight aggregates. A market survey questionnaire was developed and evaluated by a psychological consultant for possible biased results and leading questions. After this evaluation and planning as to approaches to be taken during interviews, the interview and questionnaire were pretested in the immediate area of Lexington, Kentucky. The results of these test interviews were evaluated and appropriate changes were made in interview approach. After interviewing several concerns it was determined that another major force exists as to selection and use of building materials, namely engineering and architectural firms.

Several samples of the lightweight aggregate in different consistencies, and sample bench-manufactured blocks were taken on the interviews to obtain the most accurate reaction to the product possible. It should be pointed out that the actual completion of the interview forms was only part of the interview process. It was felt that one-on-one conversations that ventured beyond the questions on the form would result in more meaningful information. All interviews were conducted personally by a Certified Public Accountant with no telephone or mail canvassing attempted. In all cases, an attempt was made to interview the highest level personnel possible that was appropriate in the circumstances.

Primary Market Area Background: The manufacture of lightweight aggregate essentially is dominated in the primary market area by one company. This company's facilities are located west of the primary market area and freight costs into the primary market area are a major factor. The major competitor for lightweight aggregate derived from coal refuse in the primary market area then is regular aggregate. There are several reasons for this situation; the primary one is the high cost of lightweight aggregate now available compared with regular aggregate delivered in the primary market area.

It is essential when making such comparisons, however, to remember two important factors. First, the dominant lightweight aggregate firm in the area must both mine the native clays used in its process and pay for fuels, such as coke breeze and fly ash, with which to operate the sintering process. These factors tend to markedly increase the cost of the final output. Coal mine refuse-lightweight aggregate would have neither of these problems. Second, when comparing lightweight aggregate with regular aggregate, it must be remembered that lightweight aggregate produces about twice the volume of final product for the same weight as regular aggregate. Thus, to make the same volume of end product only costs $8.25 versus $3.50 for regular aggregate. Finally, regular aggregate costs have been rising at least as fast as lightweight aggregate production expenses using noncoal refuse raw materials.

Market Interviews: Concrete Products — Interviews with concrete and block-manufacturing concerns revealed they tend to manufacture what is demanded by design people. All those interviewed were shown samples of the product and none voiced concern over their equipment being able to use it in their process if the demand existed. Therefore, the demand is largely in the hands of design concerns.

The interviewing process revealed a general consensus that at a lower cost than presently available, lightweight aggregate made from coal refuse would be utilized at minimum on a spot-type market basis. A few of the larger manufacturers of block voiced a considerable interest in manufacturing lightweight block from the product on a speculative basis and inventorying the block. The impression of these larger concerns was that with a lower price of coal refuse aggregate the lighter weight would make it a highly marketable product. Efforts to determine how important this spot-type market might be from a quantitative standpoint proved futile, as the concerns were unwilling or unable to estimate potential usages which were accurate enough to be given much weight.

Design Concerns — Interviews with design concerns revealed an interest in two main properties of the product. First, the insulation properties, as fuel usage for heating and cooling purposes has become a critical factor in building design. Second, the potential saving from these insulation properties when coupled with the lower cost of coal refuse derived aggregate made the design concerns enthusiastic about the possibilities provided by this product. However, some wait-and-see attitude was apparent. It was felt that the University of Kentucky Engineering Faculty could pay a major role in softening this wait-and-see attitude due to the rapport enjoyed between the faculty and the practicing design people.

Brick, Clay and Ceramic Products — As stated earlier, engineering and laboratory tests indicated that the coal refuse would not produce a marketable product for these industries given the present state of the art in production known in this country. Some brick is being produced from coal refuse in England. However, details of the economic success of this venture were not obtainable nor was complete information on the production process utilized. Further investigation into this market area is felt to be warranted based on the limited success of lab tests performed so far. It is felt that the general market for such a product has at least as broad a potential as the lightweight aggregate concrete products should the production problems be overcome.

Structural Concrete — As marketing work progressed, it became apparent that two characteristics of concrete products produced with lightweight coal refuse aggregate were real marketing advantages. First, both block and structural concrete made with lightweight coal refuse aggregate had superior insulation qualities as compared with standard mixes. Secondly, the end products were lighter in weight, leading to potential savings in construction labor and other material costs.

Precast and structural concrete products, therefore, represent another market with major potential. Here, as elsewhere however, it became very difficult to get an accurate reading as to the potential level of usage. With no ability to produce actual test samples of structural or precast forms estimates of usage both from a production and marketing standpoint were difficult to achieve. Some small tests on a laboratory basis were done with various potential mixes. Further investigation is definitely warranted by the results.

Concrete Block-Mine Usage — While working with the coal mining industry on material sources, discussions were held on the coal industry use of concrete block for underground ventilation purposes. Estimates from several major coal producers indicate that about 12 tons of underground coal are mined for every block used in building underground ventilation walls. Therefore, a fair estimate of potential use in Eastern Kentucky can be made from the table on the following page. Assuming Eastern Kentucky will continue to mine approximately 37 to 40 million tons per year that would create a demand for some 3.1 to 3.3 million blocks for this use per year. Estimating a mix of 20 pounds of aggregate per block, that would create a demand for between 31,000 and 33,000 tons of aggregate per year for this purpose.

If a single 900 block-per-hour block machine were to be installed along with a sintering grate, this machine would produce approximately 1.8 million blocks per year, or about 56% of the demand for block in Eastern Kentucky mines. This utilization would require about 7 to 9% of the lightweight aggregate plant output per year (1,000 ton-per-day plant) for this one block use alone.

Underground Coal Tonnage Mined in Kentucky

Year	Total	Eastern	Western
	. . . . (millions of tons)		
1960	44.9	*	*
1961	41.4	*	*
1962	43.6	*	*
1963	48.1	35.2	12.8
1964	50.2	*	*
1965	51.1	37.6	13.5
1966	56.4	*	*
1967	59.0	*	*
1968	61.2	*	*
1969	63.8	*	*
1970	63.5	43.9	19.4
1971	52.7	36.7	15.8
1972	56.5	37.9	18.5
1973	63.4	42.3	21.1
1974	64.0	41.2	22.8

*Breakdown not available for these years.

Results

The marketing work accomplished on this study revealed that there are potential markets for at least some of the products which were originally envisioned as being producible from coal refuse.

Lightweight Aggregate-Cement Products: From a marketing point of view, the processing of coal refuse and the manufacture of lightweight aggregate and/or concrete blocks presents some unique challenges and opportunities. In order to develop a framework for considering these challenges, a number of facts must be kept in mind:

> Present production of lightweight aggregate made from native clay suffers cost disadvantages in the primary market area due to the transportation expenses from outside the area and due to the costs of production.

> There are distinct advantages from an architectural and engineering point of view in using lightweight aggregate in construction.

These advantages are reflected in original cost. However, the main cost-saving efficiencies are of a less measurable nature, e.g., insulation and density mass which show up after construction (mining industry being the exception).

The construction industry is extremely cost conscious and tends to relate to basic costs as opposed to extended benefits.

In the potential primary market area, weight has not been a critical factor for normal building to this time, mainly due to the infrequency of high-level construction. However, the potential labor savings should be realized from lighter weight. Also, weight is a significant factor in underground mine utilization.

Transportation of certain of the contemplated finished products is limited due to weight; rarely is material of this nature transported more than 100 miles from point of manufacture.

Building Industry — Since cost is a major consideration within the construction industry, affecting the continued costs of both construction labor and maintenance, the benefits of using materials from the proposed Estill County facility must be "sold" aggressively to architects. Sale literature and trade advertising as well as one-to-one promotional activities could be effectively employed to produce a better educated consumer for these materials. The basic point that must be communicated is that initial cost is not the only cost; ease on handling, and therefore less construction time and insulation costs saving have to be considered.

Coal Industry Utilization — A major and highly promising user of construction materials produced from lightweight aggregate is the coal mining industry itself. Several coal mining companies, including South-East Coal Company, have expressed a desire to try the block in underground mine ventilation functions. Again, this could be a major user just based on Eastern Kentucky operations.

Other Uses: Lightweight Aggregate—Soilless Growing Medium — This potential product was brought to the attention of the research team by producers of regular aggregates. Every indication points to a potentially profitable, if relatively small (in terms of physical quantity), market for such a product in the primary and secondary marketing areas.

Lightweight Aggregate—Highway Utilization — Of all the major uses which appear feasible at this juncture the highway nonskid surfacing seems the most promising in terms of physical amounts. Roughly 50 to 60% of an aggregate plant's output could be expected to be required to fulfill this requirement. It is in fact conceivable that this use could expand to serve a much broader area than the original estimate since the only competitive product is crushed granite from Georgia. Conceivably a larger aggregate plant may be needed.

Fill Materials — The research on markets for fill materials resulted in the determination that potential markets do exist for use of coal refuse as highway fill, sanitary landfill and landfill.

ENVIRONMENTAL ASPECTS

Storage

Coal mine refuse of two general size classifications is usually conveyed to storage piles as slurried fines by pumping and as dry coarse material by truck or conveyor. The storage piles are usually left uncovered due to their size and the need for continuous accessibility. Fugitive dust may, at various points in these processes, become an emission problem and this may require treatment of the stored material. The extent of the problem is a function of the geometry of the pile, the size consist of the surface of the pile, the wetness of the storage, the ambient air characteristics and other factors. There is also the possibility of spontaneous combustion within the refuse storage.

Such matters as these present formidable challenges to personnel responsible for the refuse. The overall situation must be continually monitored and appropriate state-of-the-art measures taken to maintain acceptable environmental conditions.

Sintering

Among the product tests made on the Estill County coal mine refuse, sintering of the refuse for production of lightweight aggregate seemed to have considerable merit. Here, after sizing, agglomerating and other treatment, the refuse was fired on a laboratory grate and oxidized to form a cake of low density mineral and metal oxides.

In the transition from the raw state to the oxidized or inert state the coal mine refuse is subjected to chemical and mechanical changes whereby particulate matter and sulfur oxides form a part of the combustion gases.

The particulate matter can be precipitated from the gas stream by conventional and fairly inexpensive methods. The difficulty in the extraction of sulfur oxides as dictated by environmental regulations may present a challenge to the facility designer in providing acceptable gaseous emissions. In the work to date on the Estill County coal mine refuse sulfur levels of the samples have been in the range of 1.0 to 2.0% by weight of the refuse.

In a conventional sintering process the gas flow is in the range of 7 to 10 pounds of gas per pound of product and is an open process. This results in release of a large amount of generated SO_2 to the atmosphere. The process proposed in the continuation of this project is a closed one with combustion gas recirculation wherein about 2 pounds of gas is exhausted per pound of product. Here the recirculation is designed to reduce the SO_2 levels in the gas streams by retention in the sintered material.

Critical analysis of emissions during continued research and development will provide further control guidelines. Data obtained during sintering of refuse in a pilot operation will serve to establish environmental control levels on the basis of the material flow and the emission levels experienced.

SUMMARY AND CONCLUSIONS

Laboratory studies of coal mine refuse stored in Estill County have provided a preliminary insight into the technical and economical potentials of the refuse. Bench test work at the research laboratories of the University of Kentucky; Bureau of Mines, Tuscaloosa, Alabama; and McDowell-Wellman Engineering Company, Cleveland, Ohio has provided information for use in further product development and marketing studies. Certain results realized in the production of a lightweight aggregate for various masonry construction needs and results indicating physical acceptability of the raw refuse as a fill material are considered favorable at this time. Efforts continue toward elimination of problems related to providing a competitive face brick.

Markets for lightweight aggregate within economic transport limits remain contingent on competitive pricing of the product and on designer education and orientation. The priorities are not totally clear at this time in light of many related factors.

The economic aspects of commercialization of coal mine refuse-derived products are in a formative stage. Since the production of lightweight aggregate from coal mine refuse has little history from both technical and economic considerations, projects in this regard are difficult. However, material flow diagrams have been drawn and production cost estimates made for a plant of approximately 1,000 tons per day of raw refuse flow. Production costs as derived in this work compare favorably with costs of a similar product (from other raw materials) marketed to a limited extent in a geographical area.

The great need for a more environmentally acceptable disposal method for coal mine refuse is being met as an objective of this project. The possibility of significant economic development in Estill County through research on coal mine refuse is substantiated by the work reported.

REFERENCES

(1) Lawrence, J.A., "Some Properties of South Wales Colliery Discards," *Colliery Guardian* (June 1972).

(2) Taylor, R.K. and Spears, D.A., "Breakdown of British Coal Measure Rocks," *International Journal of Rock Mechanics and Mining Science,* Vol. 7, No. 5 (1970).

(3) Spangler, M.G. and Handy, R.L., *Soil Engineering,* Third Edition, Intext Educational Publishers, NY (1973).

(4) Lambe, T.W. and Whitman, R.V., *Soil Mechanics,* John Wiley and Sons, Inc., NY (1969).

(5) Anderson, D.A. et al, "Coal Mine Refuse, an Engineering Material," Proceedings, First Symposium on Mine and Preparation Plant Refuse Disposal, sponsored by National Coal Association, Louisville, KY (October 1974).

(6) Busch, R.A. et al, "Physical Property Data on Coal Waste Embankment Materials," U.S. Bureau of Mines Report of Investigations 7964 (1974).

(7) *Investigation of Mining-Related Pollution Reduction Activities and Economic Incentives in the Monongahela River Basin,* prepared by Michael Baker, Jr., Inc., for the Appalachian Regional Commission (April 1975).

(8) *Engineering and Design Manual, Coal Refuse Disposal Facilities,* prepared by E. D'Applonia Consulting Engineers, Inc., for U.S. Department of the Interior Mining Enforcement and Safety Administration, U.S. Government Printing Office (1975).

(9) Bryenton, D.L. and Rose, J.G., "Utilization of Coal Refuse as a Concrete Aggregate (Coal-Crete)," Proceedings, Fifth Mineral Waste Utilization Symposium, U.S. Bureau of Mines and IIT Research Institute, Chicago, IL (April 1976).

(10) Buttler, P.E., "Utilization of Coal Mine Refuse in the Construction of Highway Embankments, " Proceedings, First Symposium on Mine and Preparation Plant Refuse Disposal, sponsored by National Coal Association, Louisville, KY (October 1974).

(11) *Design Manual, Soil Mechanics and Earth Structures,* Navfac DM-7, Naval Facilities Engineering Command, Department of the Navy, Washington, DC (March 1971).

(12) "Gaseous Fuels; Coal and Coke; Atmospheric Analysis," *1975 Annual Book of ASTM Standards,* Part 26, American Society for Testing and Materials (1975).

(13) Flanagan, F.J., "1972 Values for Internation Geochemical Reference Standards," *Geochemica et Cosmochimica Acta,* Vol. 37 (1973).

(14) Shapiro, L. and W.W. Brannock, *Rapid Analysis of Silicate, Carbonate and Phosphate Rocks,* United States Geologic Survey Bulletin 1144-A (1962).

(15) Augenstein, D. and Sun, S.C., *Methodology for the Characterization of Anthracite Refuse,* Special Report SR-86, Coal Research Section, The Pennsylvania State University (1971).

(16) Weaver, C.E., "The Significance of Clay Minerals in Sediments," in Nagy, B. and Columbo, U., *Fundamental Aspects of Petroleum Geochemistry,* NY, Elsevier, p 37-71 (1967).

(17) Rao, C.P. and Gluskoter, H.J., *Occurrence and Distribution of Minerals in Illinois Coals,* Illinois Geologic Survey Circular 476 (1973).

(18) Klinefelter, T.A. and Hamlin, H.P., *Syllabus of Clay Testing,* Bulletin 565, U.S. Bureau of Mines (1957).

(19) Gilbert, H., "Brick Making in France," *Brick and Clay Record,* Vol. 141, No. 2, p 42-44 (August 1962).

(20) Weaner, V.B. and Bauman, H.C., "Cost and Profitability Estimation," Section 25 in *Chemical Engineers' Handbook,* Perry, R.H. and Chilton, C.H., ed., McGraw-Hill Book Company, Fifth Ed. (1973).

(21) Bergstrom, J.H., "Lightweight Launched in New England," *Rock Products* (October 1962).

(22) Stearn, E.W., "Open House Unveils Revitalized Shale Plant," *Rock Products* (December 1972).

(23) Sullivan, P.M. and Stanczyk, M.H., "Economics of Recycling Metals and Minerals from Urban Refuse," Bureau of Mines Solid Waste Research Program, Technical Progress Report-33 (April 1971).

Sources Utilized

The following reports were used in the preparation of this book.

ARC 74-217-KY-3685

Feasibility Study of Utilization of Coal Mine Refuse, Estill County,KY prepared by the Kentucky University Research Foundation for the Appalachian Regional Commission, Washington DC under contract 74-217 (August 1976).

BNL 50577

Development of a Glass Polymer Composite Sewer Pipe from Waste Glass (Progress Report No. 1) prepared by M. Steinberg, L.E. Kukacka, J. Fontana, T. Sugama, R. Rayfiel and B. Galen of the Brookhaven National Laboratory for the United States Energy Research and Development Administration under contract EY-76-C-02-0016 (1976).

BuMines RI 8104

Waste Glass as a Raw Material for Lightweight Aggregate prepared by K.J. Liles and M.E. Tyrrell of the Bureau of Mines, Tuscaloosa Metallurgy Research Laboratory (January 1976).

EPA 600/8-77-006

The Feasibility of Utilizing Solid Wastes for Building Materials, Executive Summary prepared by G. Jackson and S. Ware of Ebon Research Systems for the U.S. Environmental Protection Agency Office of Research and Development, Municipal Environmental Research Laboratory, Cincinnati, OH under contracts 68-03-2460-1 and 68-03-2056 (June 1977).

EPA 600/2-78-091

A Study of the Feasibility of Utilizing Solid Wastes for Building Materials, Phase I Summary Report prepared by B.L. Duft, H. Levine and A. McLeod of the Material Systems Corporation for the U.S. Environmental Protection Agency Office of Research and Development, Municipal Environmental Research Laboratory, Cincinnati, OH under contract 68-03-2056 (April 1978).

EPA 600/2-78-092

A Study of the Feasibility of Utilizing Solid Wastes for Building Materials, Phase II Summary Report prepared by B.L. Duft, H. Levine, A. McLeod and Y. Tsur of the Material Systems Corporation for the U.S. Environmental Protection Agency Office of Research and Development, Municipal Environmental Research Laboratory, Cincinnati, OH under contract 68-03-2056 (April 1978).

EPA 600/2-78-111

A Study of the Feasibility of Utilizing Solid Wastes for Building Materials, Phase III and Phase IV Summary Reports prepared by Material Systems Corporation for the U.S. Environmental Protection Agency Office of Research and Development, Municipal Environmental Research Laboratory, Cincinnati, OH under contract 68-03-2056 (May 1978).

NBSIR 77-1244

Survey of Uses of Waste Materials in Construction in the United States prepared by J.R. Clifton, P.W. Brown, and G. Frohndorff for the National Bureau of Standards (July 1977).

PB-259 480

The Utilization of Industrial By-Products in Blended Cements prepared by P.W. Brown, J.R. Clifton, G. Frohnsdorff and R.L. Berger of the National Bureau of Standards for the Energy Research Development Administration (1976).

ENERGY FROM SOLID WASTE 1979
RECENT DEVELOPMENTS

Edited by Francis A. Domino

Energy Technology Review No. 42
Pollution Technology Review No. 56

The emphasis in the field of solid waste has shifted from disposal to utilization. Vast stores of energy are waiting to be tapped through competent technology.

When we consider that every day each resident of the United States generates about four pounds of waste from products of great diversity, it is apparent that solid waste may someday serve as a sizeable source of energy. But first technical and environmental aspects, as well as social, legal and economic factors, will have to be examined in depth. This book reviews the many phases of waste disposal and energy recovery, discussing recently tested technology. It describes plants presently producing power from refuse while also salvaging material. Technological difficulties are also discussed. It also presents a proposed waste utilization system for the city of New York, as an example that could be applied to other cities.

The final chapter offers greatly detailed recommendations for municipal officials on waste processing and energy recovery plants.

Examples of some important subtitles are found along with chapter headings in the partial, condensed table of contents given below:

1. OVERVIEW OF ENERGY RECOVERY
Preprocessing Techniques
Incineration
Pyrolysis
Biodegradation—Composting, Methane
  Production, Biochemical Processes

2. NASHVILLE THERMAL TRANSFER CORPORATION PLANT
Components of Plant—Refuse Handling,
  Grates, Residue Removal
Major Problems—Emission, Corrosion

3. ST. LOUIS DEMONSTRATION PLANT
Equipment Evaluation
Characteristics and Costs
Environmental Evaluations
Electrostatic Precipitator Performance

4. COMBUSTION POWER UNIT (CPU-400) PILOT PLANT, CALIFORNIA
Vertical Combustor & Support Equipment
Hot Gas System—Particle Collection,
  Residue Removal
Controls, Instruments, Gas Analysis

5. COLUMBIA PLAN, NEW YORK, N.Y.
Recommendations

Cost Benefit Analyses
Markets for Energy Products
Solid Waste Receiving and Processing
Reclaiming Matter in Metal Recovery
Economics of Purox Gas Utilization

6. TECHNICAL EVALUATION OF PYROLYSIS SYSTEMS
Vertical Furnace—Occidental "Flash"
  Pyrolysis
Rotary Kiln—Monsanto "Landgard"
  Process
Vertical Shaft Furnace—Union Carbide
  "Purox" Process
Vertical Shaft Furnace—Hamilton
  Standard "Refu-Cycler" Process

7. FUEL AND ENERGY FROM WASTE BY BIOCONVERSION
Major Waste Streams—Agricultural,
  Animal, Forestry, Municipal, Industrial
Nonproteinaceous Bioconversion of
  Cellulosic Wastes
Hydrolysis of Cellulose
Anaerobic Digestion
Biophotolysis
Economic Analysis
Comparison to Other Energy Recovery

8. ENVIRONMENTAL ASPECTS
Federal and State Air Pollution Curbs
Emissions from Waste-Energy Processes
Waterwall Incineration
Refuse-Derived Solid Fuel Processing
Pyrolysis Gas Processing and Use
Emission Control and Costs
Water Pollution Considerations
Solid Residue Disposal
Noise and Other Occupational Health Data

9. MUNICIPAL SCALE THERMAL PROCESSING OF SOLID WASTE
Incineration and Pyrolysis
Costs
Site Layout and Plant Design
Public Acceptance
Utilities—Electric, Water, Communication
Precombustion of Solid Waste
Incinerator Furnace Design
Instrumentation
Control of Liquid and Solid Effluents
Air Pollution Control
Special Solid Wastes—Plastics,
  Obnoxious Wastes, Sewage Sludge

ISBN 0-8155-0750-X

321 pages

INSULATION GUIDE FOR BUILDINGS AND INDUSTRIAL PROCESSES 1979

Edited by L.Y. Hess

Energy Technology Review No. 43

The question today is not whether to insulate but "How?" and "How much?" This definitive guide provides the answers. It assesses thermal insulation materials and systems for residential and industrial building applications, appraising building insulation as used for different purposes in Part A.

Recent rapid rises in fuel prices have confirmed the economic value of insulating as a fuel conserving practice. At the same time that maximum insulation of buildings effects considerable savings in costs, it confers the added benefit of increasing the availability of fuel, thus providing industry with more fuel to be used for productive purposes.

Part B of this book explores the use by industrial plants and utilities of thermal insulation to conserve energy, protect personnel and maintain process temperatures. It considers the effective temperature range and optimum thickness of insulating materials, their applicability in industrial processes, and the resultant economic rewards, noting the high rate of return on investment from insulating. It also evaluates sources of information on heat transmission.

The following condensed table of contents with chapter headings lists examples of **some important subtitles.**

ISBN 0-8155-0752-6

200 pages

TA
403.6
B83   Building materials
       from solid wastes

DATE			